ADVANCE PF

"Like a Japanese fable, *The Connection Quotient* provides the reader with a long line of shimmering input, encouraging and even requesting the reader's complete attention. Buschman acts like a shaman, ending each chapter with assignments and numerous questions for reflection which the reader can use to connect with themselves, their network and their organization."

Erik Korsvik Østergaard, Author, *Teal Dots in an Orange World*, and leadership advisor (Søborg, Capital Region, Denmark)

"*The Connection Quotient* challenges you to 'see with new eyes' how you connect with yourself, others, your team, your organization and the world by weaving a compelling narrative through evocative stories, insightful observations and supporting wisdom. This is a timely book on what makes us truly human – the power of connection."

Prasad Deshpande MCC, CEO, Empowered Learning (Pune, India)

"Marco's work on *The Connection Quotient* is a deeply personal account demonstrating the importance of human connection; starting with yourself, others, the people you work with and society at large. A beautiful systemic perspective offering practical and easy-to-use guides to deepen your own CQ as well as nurturing and managing your connections. The future of humanity lies in our collective capability and connectedness, making this a must read."

Inge Simons, Partner, 42virtual Schweiz AG & Kaleidos BVBA (Zürich, Switzerland)

"Marco Buschman has written a powerful field guide to connection as a life and leadership endeavour. This very personal and practical book draws the reader in to explore the many ways connection is expressed and provides a mirror for personal discovery. In a world where effective work and meaningful life is so relationship-based, *The Connection Quotient* provides a unique lens for reflection."

Phillip Sandahl, Co-author, *Teams Unleashed: How to Release the Power and Human Potential of Work Teams*, and co-author of worldwide bestseller, *Co-Active Coaching: The Proven Framework for Transformative Conversations at Work and in Life* (Sausalito, California, USA)

"*The Connection Quotient* demonstrates that the essence of leadership is about creating powerful connections with yourself, others, your team, your organization and the world around you. Who are you as a function and who are you as an individual? Marco discusses these themes with a youthful business-like élan, rendering them tangible."

Dr. Boris Blumberg, Academic MBA Director and Senior Lecturer, Maastricht University (Maastricht, The Netherlands)

"In the 21st century, connection is of key importance: connected people, ideas, corporations and countries make it possible to run the world as globalized as it is today. Connection is fundamental for successful innovations and competitive nations since our world becomes more and more complex and the stakeholders are increasingly interdependent. For me, Geofusion is destiny and connectivity. Connectivity on a personal level is yet another factor of success to be aware of. This book clearly depicts how vital it is that we are connected to each other. Highly recommended!"

Norbert Csizmadia, Author, *Geofusion: The Power of Geography and the Mapping of the 21st Century* (Hungary)

"Making a genuine connection with others while at the same maintaining your own autonomy is definitely possible. The basis for this is mutual trust, allowing each other space, and thinking and acting consistently based on the belief that 1+1 is at least 3. Marco has integrated this principle into his own life, applying it on a daily basis, and expanding on it in *The Connection Quotient*. For me, this practical book is a superb example of the simplicity, subtlety and power of this principle."

Ingrid Eras-Magdalena, SVP Global HR, Belmond – Hotels, Trains & Cruises (London, United Kingdom)

"Connection occurs when an employee or manager is able to add meaning to relationships in the broadest sense of the word. Essentially, this is all about intention, communication and genuine contact. In my opinion, this primarily means listening, approaching others in a respectful way and giving the other person space. These themes are superbly covered in this book."

Arco Solkesz, Brigadier General, Joint Support and Enabling Command (JSEC) Director, NATO (Ulm, Germany)

"Marco was able to articulate a remarkable 'no nonsense' and pragmatic guide to becoming a better person, a better friend and a better leader! *The Connection Quotient* makes you reflect deeply on yourself and your connections. It provides a powerful balance of individual stories underlined with the latest research in leadership development. It embarks you on a journey of consciously building personal and professional connections (starting with yourself), so that you surround yourself with high energy and fulfilling relationships. You can expect a stunning impact on your personal life and your business environment!"

Régis Chasse, Dean, The Leadership Institute, Majid Al Futtaim (Dubai, UAE)

"*The Connection Quotient* shows the importance of individual and collective connections in mastering the current and future challenges we are facing on our planet. The book explains the how power and quality of human relations in our organizations and societies make these connections happen. Marco does a marvellous job of demonstrating what leaders and teams need to work on."

Curt Blattner, Author, *The Heartbeat of Excellence* (Lausanne, Switzerland)

"I decided to read this as a reference book and to select chapters that were relevant for myself. However, once I started reading I became so captivated by the story that I couldn't wait for the next chapter to start, and the next, and the next... The personal reflections, practical theory and challenging assignments contained within ensure that *The Connection Quotient* is more than just another book about leadership. It is a unique and holistic experience that compels you to rethink your vision on business and on life."

Barbara van der Heijden, Global Talent Director, Capgemini Invent (London, United Kingdom)

"The power of *The Connection Quotient* lies in the divergency of topics that Marco Buschman has succeeded in covering in one book. These topics are not only bundled in various circles (in connection with yourself, others, your team, your organization and the rest of the world), but are also subdivided into the functional versus the personal. This makes *The Connection Quotient* a valuable reference for every professional today to use to their advantage."

Bart Terlunen, HR Director, ENGIE
(Den Bosch, The Netherlands)

Published by
LID Publishing Limited
The Record Hall, Studio 304,
16-16a Baldwins Gardens,
London EC1N 7RJ, UK

info@lidpublishing.com
www.lidpublishing.com

A member of:

businesspublishersroundtable.com

© Marco Buschman, 2020
© LID Publishing Limited, 2020

Printed in Latvia by Jelgavas Tipogrāfija
ISBN: 978-1-912555-79-6

Cover and page design: Matthew Renaudin
Figures made by Scribent.nl

HOW A **CULTURE OF UNDERSTANDING** TRANSFORMS TEAMS AND ORGANIZATIONS

THE **CONNECTION QUOTIENT**

MARCO BUSCHMAN

MADRID | MEXICO CITY | LONDON
NEW YORK | BUENOS AIRES
BOGOTA | SHANGHAI | NEW DELHI

This book is dedicated to Laura, Frank and Erin.
You are my mirrors of happiness and vulnerability.

CONTENTS

FOREWORD

OUR WORLD'S TRANSFORMATION PACE IS INCREASING

As today's world is ever accelerating its shifts, we are more exposed to the impacts. We now find ourselves in a relationship environment that is open, transparent and immediate for which the 'continuous evolution' is an important driver. Continuous feedback, continuous conversation, continuous information, continuous learning, continuous new technology options, continuous adaptation, etc. One could also read 'instantaneous': if we like instantaneous feedback, we expect instantaneous answers, which is more demanding for others. The counterpart of this real-time and on-demand approach is the speed of obsolescence: our organizations, our products and services and even our people can quickly be out of relevance, and maybe the market if we don't skill up and adapt actively, continuously... All these developments are, amongst others, increasing the pressure on the performance conditions and requirements, the adaptation to evolving work conditions and the pressure on all employees' contributions and interactions.

THE NEW GENERATION(S)

Not seldom I hear youngsters say they want to go through multiple different job experiences in ten years. Their focus on 'here and now' means less vision on 'there and then.' Their need for speed may take away the attention from the need to reflect. Since their main driver is focused on obtaining things instantaneously, they are not bothered too much with a long-term strategic vision nor investment efforts. The open and real-time access to any kind of information makes youngsters appear not to value experience like their elders used to, and creates the problem that the new generation sometimes has the impression that they know more than their forebearers... And to a certain extent it is true. They are indeed multi-purpose, multi-channel and multi-curious, upskilling at unprecedented pace and eager to 'consume' knowledge, at the risk of missing how professionalism or expertise are built.

THE MANAGERS' CONDITIONS ARE HENCE CHANGING

In this environment of instantaneous demands, constant pressure, need for adaption and dealing with the new generation's expectations, the managers' conditions are naturally changing as well. It seems only a few years ago that I established my own legitimacy as a manager mainly on my quality of performance; and this based on knowledge and the drive to ensure that things were done as expected, from the client's need, the rationale and ultimately the benefits expected. But nowadays, this rationale approach is becoming less valid, less helpful – and I would even debate that this traditional approach is becoming more and more irrelevant. We don't need managers who are solely focusing on result and rationality anymore. Teams now need managers to focus on the internal and external connections, their quality, their impacts and their relevance. By facilitating others to connect and be successful, they create the pre-conditions to be adaptive and successful as an organization in this ever-changing world, so we can build the new collective performance conditions. That has impact on the way the managers must develop, act, adapt and behave in their role and position and on how we identify, educate, train and foster them.

TOWARDS A NEW PROFILE... THE CONNECTED MANAGER

The added value of a manager in the 21st century is not 'knowing better' anymore; it is much more about showing better, sharing better, experimenting better and connecting better. Trying to describe this new role, I sometimes use the phrase "the manager-coach", although I am aware that the roles of manager and coach cannot be integrated on all levels, because their purposes are not the same. Yet, the double assignment that is at the core of this new manager profile is as follows: you need to take accountability and responsibility to recognize the assets and skills available, articulate this continuous flow of contributions and facilitate others in getting results while at the same time needing to elevate and bind – all – the people around you. Not *your* team anymore, but *the* teams, composed of all players contributing to the end goal. And this is where this book, *The Connection Quotient*,

comes into account. The author Marco Buschman addresses the manager's new role and new ways of playing to focus both on:
a) functionality, rationality and getting results; of course,
b) leveraging the human being, capabilities, emotions and relationships to create the best team possible.

And although we need to focus on both, I believe the paradox is that focusing on the relationship and therefore on the connection is now more important and required to build performance. This book comes as an example to show best practices on how a manager in this new era can evolve his/her practices in these two connection capacities.

One of the Development programs at Capgemini – *The Connected Manager* – is based upon this new logic. These new management practices and behaviours require the combination of different contributions and contributors, to integrate a variety of experiences, horizons and perspectives. And, like this book's structure, the arenas of connections can be subdivided into: the connection with yourself, the connection with other individuals, the connection with the collective (*the collective not necessarily being your own team*), the connection with the network and, ultimately, the connection with a network of networks. So, it starts with the question, 'who am I?' and ends with the question, 'what is our relation, our responsibility and our liaison towards the rest of the world?'

The manager today can only sustain their legitimacy – and their value to the organization and the people composing it – through the quality, the relevance and the focus on the connections they can make on all these levels both from a functional and a personal perspective.

GROWING YOUR CONNECTION QUOTIENT (CQ)

This new capability – *the power of connection* – is the fundament of new management and is at the core of being a good or bad manager in today's environment. This book can help you to work and reflect upon growing your own CQ, and gives you a lot of how tos regarding your position and potential towards the other, your team and your organization. *The Connection Quotient* can help you learn to integrate new people-driven ways of working, thus helping people to grow around you. And "people growing around you" is by no means the equivalent of "growing *your team*." People are no longer in the manager's 'possession.' Our influence and responsibility are not bound by our position on the organogram nor the role we play. It's still is our responsibility to develop people, and now independently of their functional relationship towards us.

THREE EXTRA POINTS OF ATTENTION

I would like to emphasize in this foreword three beliefs on the question how you can make *The Connection Quotient* work for you and for your organization.

1. *The Connection Quotient* is by no means limited to the 'soft skills' aspect. It is not only about building proximity and perspective based on elements like empathy, trust and shaping courageous conversations. It is first about performance and therefore about building high performance environments where people can thrive, and the collective can succeed. Therefore, one still needs to develop the functional/technical aspects of work. Traditionally, management, leadership and effective work have been based on rational facts (Intelligence Quotient) while trying to introduce the soft side of things with various behavioural methods (Emotional Quotient) as it was needed. *The Connection Quotient* seeks to base a new work effectiveness on the Emotional Quotient (EQ). Combining and integrating IQ and EQ is what CQ is all about.

2. You can apply all the key success factors or recipes, without practice, they are useless. The ways you are going to apply these learnings are the recipes for success... Your Connection journey starts while reading the book to reflect on your own thoughts, feelings, behaviours and impact and applying the concepts through the offered exercises as well as creating your own experiments in your day-to-day business. Practice makes perfect!

3. Working on your CQ is all about behavioural change, which requires time. Building trust, for example, is an effort producing effects in the long term, so is developing an openness towards others – especially if

you are not naturally inclined to it. Only over longer periods of time will you be able to really see, feel and make the difference. So taking time to focus on growing your CQ, defining your first steps and consciously spending time on it each day, is now essential in becoming a (more) relevant manager. It takes commitment and resolve, are you up for it?

A FINAL THOUGHT

Ultimately, Marco Buschman describes in *The Connection Quotient* a "mind shift." I agree it almost describes a philosophy of behaviours, applicable to all aspects of one's life. It is about developing the connection with yourself and with others. Whether it is your family, your community, your sports club… your role and contribution to society or whether it is about you doing your job in an organizational context: all of these are relevant terrains to practice your CQ.

I want to congratulate Marco on the experience-sharing and pedagogy efforts put in his book, and I hope it will be an inspiration to all readers to recognize, acknowledge and enhance their CQ and by doing so improve impact and results.

Stephan Paolini
Chief Talent and Learning Officer,
Capgemini Group

GENERAL INTRODUCTION

THE FRAMEWORK OF THE CONNECTION QUOTIENT

I believe in a connected world. A world that starts small, by connecting with yourself. Then, by making connections externally, you build bridges between yourself and the other, both professionally and personally. It's only when things flow smoothly between people that things can flow smoothly in business.

The Connection Quotient (CQ) is about more than just maintaining your business network. It's an ability to understand other people's positions and expand your own capacity to discuss differences. A connection enables you to stand up for yourself *and* continue to see the other for who he or she is, despite any differences between you. A connection makes it possible to play 'hard on the ball, and soft on the individual.'

'Connection' as a term has a soft quality and it is also the hardest prerequisite for creating fruitful and long-term business deals. After all, *no contact, no contract.* Your CQ is a prerequisite for doing business successfully. It is a rock-solid requirement for getting things done. On top of that, it's a mirror that reflects your own functioning and learning.

But this connected world doesn't come free. You will need to do something in order to tap into its promise and potential.

To create this world, the first thing you need to do is connect with your whole self. If – based on this strong connection with yourself – you then engage with others, you create a deep and respectful connection with the other, as prime representative of the outside world. If you can make contact with the other, you open up their horizon, because from that point on you are building a foundation for a future collaboration. From then on, the sky's the limit. First with the other, then with a team, and after that with the organization, and on to the rest of the world, however large and extensive you make that rest of the world, or however close to home.

So, the Connection Quotient contributes to creating a respectful world. This is what I believe in and this is what I want to help us all achieve. This is my life purpose.

THE CONNECTION QUOTIENT IN RELATION TO LEADERSHIP
Today's literature on leadership

A lot of managers (as well as a lot of management books) define their starting points for leadership as leading others and managing an organization. In other words: someone's leadership begins as soon as they are appointed as manager of a team, of a number of teams, of a department or of a whole organization. If they bear responsibility for an entire organization, this then marks the limit of their leadership. In terms of the Connection Quotient, however, this line of reasoning does not apply.

Through the lens of the Connection Quotient, leadership embraces all forms of connection: from connection with yourself right through to connection with the rest of the world. That is the all-embracing power of connection. So, the Connection Quotient is simultaneously about:

- Connecting with yourself
- Connecting with the other
- Connecting with your team and your organization
- Connecting with the rest of the world

First extension to leadership: in connection with yourself

Many attempts to transform leadership do so by providing another idea of leadership. But it's not so much the idea of leadership that needs to change; what's needed is rather a change within each leader.

Your leadership does not begin with leading and connecting with teams or whole organizations. But this is what leadership in the classical sense focuses on or starts with. Your leadership should start by being in contact with yourself. Leadership begins by leading yourself and connecting with yourself. If you can't lead yourself, ultimately, you'll be unable to lead others. In Part I of this book, we will start with this important connection: the connection with yourself as an integral element of your leadership.

Developing this part of the Connection Quotient is typically compared to personal effectiveness rather than leadership development. That leads to this part being shaped by notions such as: mindfulness, meditation, career anchors (what do I actually want?), personality tests, coping with stress, dealing with aggression, time management, your own driving forces, etc. See the left side of **Figure 1** on the next page.

The Connection Quotient as the whole domain of leadership			
New leadership	In connection with yourself	In connection with the other	In connection with the team and the organization	In connection with the rest of the world
Classic leadership	Domain of personal effectiveness	Classic domain of leadership		Economic and charitable domain

Figure 1: The Connection Quotient as new leadership versus the classical boundaries of leadership

Second extension to leadership: in connection with the rest of the world

The Connection Quotient doesn't stop at the boundaries of your own organization. With classic leadership, the rest of the world is viewed predominantly from an economic perspective: as a labour market, a selling market, a domain of partners to collaborate with, a domain of competitors that you want to beat or a charitable domain. The connection with the rest of the world was primarily made based on the economic paradigm: leaders viewed the world as a market full of prospects in which competing organizations hunt simultaneously. Or, as an environment where suppliers or new employees can be found. Leaders viewed this as being separated from their own leadership. It fell outside their domain and consisted of essentially another work field: one that was part of marketing, sales or account management, and was associated with supply chain management or stakeholder management, or it was defined by recruitment and selection in the functions of HR managers, recruiters and headhunters. And doing good for the world was dismissed as a charitable occupation and often viewed in the negative light of marketing and greenwashing. For the rest, if you wanted to work for a better world, you had to do that on your own time.

When employing the Connection Quotient, however, the leader makes genuine contact with the rest of the world. This means more than contact with your nearest and dearest, and goes further than connecting with the people in your own organization. Anyone who works with their CQ not only makes explicit connection with themselves, but also the connection with the rest of the world. A completely new domain of social entrepreneurship – with growing numbers of people working in the sharing economy, facilitating the rise of the connection economy and contributing to a circular economy – is currently unfolding and allowing *people*, *planet*, *profit* and *purpose* to flourish.

The intimate role of the leader (connection with yourself), including the corresponding path inwards, as well as the impact on the world (connection with the rest of the world) with an eye towards the bigger picture are an integral part of the framework through which I view leaders of the future.

THE FRAMEWORK OF THE CONNECTION QUOTIENT

When you make a connection based on the whole of your person, you are not locking yourself up in your own organization but continue to be in contact with the outside world. Take Uber or Airbnb, for example. Both these organizations connect people with a demand to people with a supply. The physical elements with which they generate their turnover (in this case, cars or houses) are located outside the boundaries of their own organization. The core business of these companies is creating connections.

When you learn to look through the lens of the Connection Quotient, you will almost automatically practice leadership differently and see the world full of fellow human beings rather than market potential. This kind of leadership is not 'soft.' On the contrary, it ensures that people start to realize what their leadership really encompasses. The question concerning what responsibility leaders have towards themselves, towards the organization *and* towards the rest of the world is a logical one to ask. But also, we must ask what business opportunities suddenly present themselves as a result of looking beyond the boundaries of your own organization to the world as a place where fellow human beings live and work.

The ever-expanding circles of the Connection Quotient

Although I talk about connecting in every phase, I have chosen – for the sake of the book – to split up the Connection Quotient in various forms of connecting. Can you feel – as you read this – that this division is at its core a contradiction of the essence of the Connection Quotient?

In connection
with yourself

In connection
with the other

In connection
with your team and
your organization

In connection
with the rest of
the world

Figure 2: The ever-expanding circles of the Connection Quotient

With the paradoxical feeling of connecting and dividing in mind, four ever-expanding circles are created with which the leader is able to embrace larger parts of the reality. The sharp-eyed reader will discover the form of a shell in **Figure 2** in which the connection with yourself is the pearl.

1. **In connection with yourself**. All leadership starts with self-leadership. In terms of your CQ, this is about connecting with yourself. 'Lead yourself' means to make a connection with yourself. What do I see? What do I feel? What do I think? What are my values? What are my beliefs? What are my deepest desires and fears? First you need to establish who you are as a human being and only then can you ask yourself what type of leader you are or want to become – essentially, who you are as a human doing.

2. **In connection with the other**. In the first circle radiating out from the pearl, your CQ serves to build a one-on-one relationship with the other in the outside world. The circle of connection with yourself suddenly transforms into an infinity symbol. Can you include the other without excluding yourself? Does the connection have a suffocating effect (an unhealthy connection)? Does it remain a fragmented whole (too loose of a connection) or is there a dynamic balance in the relationship between the other and yourself (a powerful connection)?

3. **In connection with your team and your organization**. To be successful as a team and an organization and to achieve powerful results, differences will increasingly need to be bridged. By using your CQ, you're building

a connection between different teams, between hierarchical layers and between internal stakeholders. The leader plays a key role here, without necessarily needing all communication to flow through them. Is it possible to continue to listen to all the different perspectives? How do you ensure that everyone acts based on the same core values? Are the stories you tell about the organization and its goals attractive and inspiring? The key lies in expressing and accepting the emotional side next to the rational side. Do you have the guts to do that?

4. **In connection with the rest of the world.** The rest of the world is the selling market and labour market for your own organization. Leadership doesn't stop at the boundaries of the organization and the economic connection with the outside world. The moment leaders realize that they themselves are part of the greater whole, they can consciously decide to use their CQ to also make a contribution to society and the world and leave a footprint for the next generation.

The Connection Quotient works in such a way that the leader is primarily concerned with connecting the different circles with each other.

The Connection Quotient of the leader as a role and as a person

The Connection Quotient starts on a different level: the human level. It's not just about being a visionary, making strategic, tactical and operational choices, and stakeholder management. The leader of the future is above all a person: a human being who also has a role (human doing). If you want to be a successful leader, it is important to give both elements the attention they deserve.

The connection therefore always takes place based on the leader as a person *and* on the leader as a role. **Figure 3** on the next page expresses this duality by means of a horizontal dotted line. This specifies that a leader is continually making a connection in all phases.

In connection
with yourself

In connection
with the other

In connection
with your team and
your organization

In connection
with the rest of
the world

The leader as a role – function-to-function connection

Figure 3: The framework of the Connection Quotient

Should you leave your emotions at home or do you prefer to bring yourself as a whole human being to your work and to your leadership? This book is about how as a leader you need to build on your strengths and show your vulnerability, while also acknowledging your dark side and learning to embrace it. You may find it difficult to reveal this personal side of yourself, but if you demonstrate your sincerity at work you will likely be rewarded with understanding.

HOW TO READ THIS BOOK

AN ENRICHING PERSPECTIVE ON LEADERSHIP

The Connection Quotient does not have to compete with other insights in the field of leadership. It is not a battle for truth. It's about offering an enriching perspective. It is an extra pair of glasses enabling you, among other things, to learn to look at teams and yourself. The Connection Quotient covers many of the concepts that have already been described concerning leadership and can be found at many different levels.

LEADING AND READING WITH THE CONNECTION QUOTIENT

Once you realize that I'm interested in enriching the existing literature by adding the Connection Quotient, you're already *engaging* in the Connection Quotient. If I were to introduce this concept as a competing perspective (better, new, an alternative) I wouldn't be engaging in the Connection Quotient.

In this context, I was moved by the statement: "The conversation isn't about the relationship, but the conversation *is* the relationship." For instance, if you talk at the content level about trust or about guts, but you express distrust and fear in the conversation, then you mustn't make the mistake of confusing the content with the truth. The Connection Quotient works in the same way. You can talk about it as a concept, but it's much more important just to start using your CQ for connecting consciously from now on.

You can always apply the Connection Quotient to yourself as reader. If you see this book as being about the concept of the Connection Quotient, you aren't making a connection. It's only when you open up while reading the book that you'll be engaged in the Connection Quotient and develop your own CQ. If you go into it with all your heart, you will immediately notice a shift in yourself. But if you view this primarily as a concept, then you will be making very little use of your potential. You will be cutting off your cognition from the rest of your existence. By doing so, you will be making very limited use of the potential of your CQ.

There's no need to wait until a specific moment. You can apply your CQ straight away, in the here and now. Your CQ doesn't begin at work. No, it begins as soon as you wake up. With what intention do you start your day (connecting with yourself)?

What do you do as soon as you walk into your office? How do you greet the receptionist, the catering team, the window cleaner doing his job outside? And here's a tough question: do you actually ever greet these people? (This shows how well you do or don't connect with 'the other.')

And then you walk across to your own office. Do you have a feel for the attitude of your colleagues and the state they're in? Do you notice who's stressed because an important customer will be arriving soon? Who's having a difficult time at home? Are you aware of what's going on? These are all questions that have something to do with your connection with your colleagues on a more personal level and regarding them as human beings (this speaks to how well you connect emotionally).

You should also be asking yourself questions about what people are doing, not only how they are feeling. Who is introspective and has a major deadline coming up? Do you notice how the new team leader is operating? Do people with different functions mix with each other or do function groups stick together? These questions primarily concern the functional side (your colleague as a human *doing*).

Just by reading the book, a number of things will start shifting within yourself. If something moves you, then something has already happened with your CQ. So, embrace every little step. Growing your leadership as a person (human-to-human) *and* as a role (function-to-function) is 5% inspiration and 95% perspiration. Hopefully, this book will provide you with the inspiration you need. But you will have to decide for yourself what you want to do with it. Will you choose to reinforce your CQ? And what will you use your CQ for?

THE STRUCTURE OF THIS BOOK

This book is built around the framework of the Connection Quotient (**Figure 3**). The first three circles of the Connection Quotient will be elaborated on in three sections. Part I is about being in connection with yourself, Part II is about being in connection with the other, and Part III is about being in connection with your team and your organization. The fourth circle (in connection with the rest of the world) is part of the conclusion. In all three sections and the final chapter, I will be looking at the Connection Quotient in relation to the leader as a human doing (functional) *and* the leader as a human being (personal).

THREE WAYS TO READ THIS BOOK

There are three ways you can go through this material.

1. **Workbook.** Read this book first and foremost as a workbook in which you are challenged to extend your CQ even further, and to allow it to grow. This way you will be using the book as a guide for your personal quest. In that case, I would advise you to read the book intensively from front to back. Just follow the structure of the book, including all the assignments. The book works as a methodology from inside to outside, from small to big. I recommend studying the chapters and doing the assignments in a fixed rhythm, for example one chapter every three days. This way you can further develop your CQ in 19 weeks of intensive work.

2. **Book of Inspiration.** You can view this as a book packed with inspiration, letting your fingers be your guide. Browse through it regularly and take a closer look at the parts that attract your attention at that moment. Let the universe lend a hand in your development of your CQ.

3. **Reference book.** Because this book contains so many models and topics, you can also choose to see it as a reference book. The index at the back will help you search for specific subjects, such as levels of conversation, how to develop trust, and leadership styles. Which topic do you need most and what is your attention drawn towards? Which topic is relevant to your organization at the moment or to develop your CQ, and what do you want to know more about? The index will direct you quickly to the pages that cover those specific areas.

POINTS TO NOTE

Finally, there are five points to consider while you read this book:

- For purposes of readability, when 'he' and 'she' are equally applicable, the choice has been made to use only 'he'.

- This book has been written using the themes I have discussed frequently with managers and HR professionals in the commercial sector as a common thread. However, the models, considerations, short theories, sources of inspiration and exercises are also applicable within non-profit and governmental organizations. I am confident that managers and HR practitioners who work across these disparate sectors will be able to translate the examples in such a way that they can be used in their own practice.

- This book explains both the concept/model of the Connection Quotient while helping you to develop and grow your own CQ. When explaining the concept/model I have chosen to write 'Connection Quotient' in full. When I refer to developing your own Connection Quotient I have chosen to use the abbreviation 'CQ'.

- If while reading the chapters you feel that you'd like more inspiration regarding a given topic, I'd invite you to visit **www.marcobuschman.com/cq** for extra resources.

- Perhaps most importantly, CQ is a characteristic of human beings, which is why this is important for everyone and applicable to all. So, whether you're reading this from a functional perspective as a manager, employee or board member, or on a more personal level as a father, mother or friend, I sincerely hope that you will take advantage of the insights I've offered and make your own unique contribution to a connected world.

IN CONNECTION WITH YOURSELF

"The two most important days in your life are the day
you are born and the day you find out why."

Mark Twain

INTRODUCTION

Your CQ is not based on working with functional teams or the functional managing of others within the organization. As we saw in the general introduction, it has another starting point. Your CQ starts with being in connection with yourself. This is also the starting point for creating lasting work relationships. But what exactly does it mean to be in connection with yourself?

THE CONTEXT OF CONNECTION WITH YOURSELF

We are increasingly living and working in a service society. In such a society, you can no longer view the other as just another paying customer. Neither is it just about optimizing the factory and the production processes. More and more, it's about people: about what you have to offer to the other, what the other has to offer you, how you can work smarter together and to what extent you're prepared to grant each other favours.

In other words, employees, clients and suppliers are first and foremost *people*. In all your contacts with them, you are primarily a human being. The more you are your true self in these situations, and can continue to be, the greater the chance that a true connection will take place between you. And based on this connection, 'business gets done' and results are produced.

On the content side, of course a written quotation has to be correctly drawn up, the technical data of services supplied must be accurate, and you have to deliver on time. But at the same time, contact comes before contract. The bottom line is that before a potential customer, a new employer or a new employee engages in a professional connection with you, he will be looking you in the eye. Even though you might match perfectly in terms of your profiles, and the collaboration may seem right on paper, if there's no click and the connection doesn't get established, the deal simply won't go through.

The moment the other looks you in the eye, he will establish: if I encounter problems in the future with this project/this product/this service, do I trust you to resolve those problems for me?

And what applies for clients also applies for employees: are they prepared to follow you? This has partially to do with wanting to follow you as a leader, with respect to the content you present and represent, and also with wanting to follow you as a person.

You work with employees (people). You ask them to be sincere, to be transparent. You want them to voice their opinions and express themselves, even if the insights are at times painful or difficult. And so, you need to act as a role model in this context. It's impossible to *learn* how to be authentic, but you can *re-learn* how to be authentic, if you have somehow drifted away from your core. Remember: you are more than just a functional role. You are more than just your formal function.

All leadership starts with self-leadership, which is why connection with yourself forms the pearl in the framework of the Connection Quotient (**Figure 3** on p12). All trust starts with self-trust. All exploration starts with self-exploration. All observations start with self-observations. All respect starts with self-respect and all doing starts with doing it yourself. My invitation to you is to explore your whole self (the leader as a role/human doing *and* as a person/human being) and to take your whole self with you to your work. Don't leave your human being at home.

ESSENTIAL ELEMENTS CONCERNING CONNECTION WITH YOURSELF

Not only rational

Engaging in a connection with yourself is never purely a rational process, but we live in a world that is largely governed by cognition and logic. You need to stop asking yourself whether you are competent or not. Of course, the content side of your work has to be in place and the foundation has to be solid, but the knowledge level of the majority of people/leaders is generally adequate. They keep up to date with knowledge about their field and the managing/leading of people, as well as having an extensive network.

In his book, *The Speed of Trust* (2008), author Stephen M.R. Covey covers four core themes of trust. Two of these lie in the field of competencies: having sufficient capacities and achieving results. These will continue to be important; you still have to deliver. But that's not all.

Your development as a leader is more than just taking courses to maintain your specialist knowledge and management techniques.

Your true development as a leader does not rely on content, but rather needs to be internally driven – it is the development of your character. It's only when your internal parts are interconnected that you can become complete.

In this context, Covey refers to integrity and intent. Intent is about our motives, our agenda and the behaviour that flows from this. In the above mentioned book he writes: "Trust grows when our motives are straightforward and based on mutual benefit – in other words, when we genuinely care not only for ourselves, but also for the people we interact with, lead or serve."

Integrity here is not only about honesty, but above all about 'integratedness.' This means having the courage to act in alignment with your values and beliefs. So now it's about activating all the different layers you house within yourself: head, heart and hands. This wholeness allows you to work on deepening a connection with yourself. It's about asking yourself bigger, or deeper, questions, such as: what are my fears? What do I find difficult? What are my needs? What are my personal values? What do I want to contribute to? What is the bigger task I have to do in life?

The art is then to make these questions even more concrete: how am I dealing with time, with relationships, with energy, with my work and my private life, with my own emotions and the emotions of others? And how do I *want* to deal with these matters?

The place of emotions

Many leaders find emotions complex to grasp, even scary or taxing. The search for the connection with yourself is sometimes dismissed as silly, but that doesn't have to be the case.

Experiencing emotions and being yourself are part of your birthright. Emotions and our instinct: that's what we come into this world with. After that, under the influence of upbringing, school, training and work, we develop the side of rationality more than that of emotion. We learn to analyse. We are seduced into stepping into a normative straitjacket of good and bad. Or we are rewarded to stay watching at a distance. That's when emotions suddenly become awkward and complex, or we feel clumsy or even at a loss.

But when you were born, you were already a complete person, with the most basic emotions of sadness, fear, anger and joy. Embrace these emotions.

An important lesson here is that of normalization. At work, just as at home, arguments or grief occur. This occurs partly in the form of a rediscovery, when you engage with the connection with yourself. The drive of each individual to be in contact *and* in connection, in whatever way, is immense. It appeals to a primeval instinct. We are a social species.

Sincerity

The Connection Quotient is, among other things, about sincerity. The person who applies his CQ but without being sincere will achieve results only for the short term. The person who looks within himself and does not fully engage with what he encounters there is deceiving himself. Trust in your own ego and believe in yourself. But be sure to accept both the sunny and dark sides in yourself. In the spirit of the celebrated psychoanalyst Carl Jung, I would say, "Life is not about becoming perfect or enlightened, but becoming your whole self."

You can't fake sincerity. The person who simulates sincerity is not in connection with himself. Everyone can feel that. Anyone who has worked with the Connection Quotient and with the source of sincerity for a period of time also sees whether or not someone else has been moved emotionally.

We see ourselves often purely as *human doings*, but we are above all *human beings*. It's important to realize that each one of us possesses both sides, and that it's important to be able to integrate them both.

Especially when you find yourself caught up in the heat of your emotions, reflect how you wish to respond in each situation based on your own values. What are your values? How much integrity and sincerity do you have? And can you be honest with yourself?

Courage

It's often necessary to link courage with being sincere. To what extent do you have the courage to look in the mirror and see your true self? If you can succeed in being 90% okay with all your good sides as well as all your dark sides, you're doing well. Whatever you encounter then will produce many wonderful moments, but it can also be painful. On some occasions you will have to grit your teeth or overcome something.

If you see a mountain standing in your way, and you can't go around it, you probably also realize you can't jump over it in one go. You will have to conquer that mountain step by step, day after day. This book can help you do that. You can already take the first step today. Do you have the courage and the motivation to see your patterns, your difficulties and also ultimately all the sources behind your successes and beautiful moments? This way you may suddenly discover that the mountain you thought you couldn't jump over is already largely behind you.

PUTTING THINGS INTO PRACTICE
Getting started

Putting your CQ into practice is anything but a superficial exercise. It goes further than networking, conducting discussions or making connections on LinkedIn. In addition to courage and inspiration, working on your CQ – and particularly on the connection with yourself – is largely a question of perspiration. Think of it as a muscle that needs to be trained. In other words, it's hard work. A lot of practice and training. Carrying on and persevering. Clenching your teeth and continuing.

You will need the courage and the willingness to look into what it means in your specific case. In my coaching, my rule of thumb for such a process, in which the focus lies on an aspect of the Connection Quotient, is between six and ten sessions. And as a coach, I am aware that I am rarely in the company of the subject at the time of his breakthrough moment. Do not expect to achieve the breakthrough and to see your world transform completely simply by engaging in coaching sessions and reading this book. That breakthrough will be the result of experimenting in practice, by doing it yourself.

The key lies with you. The key lies *within* you. Or, more accurately, you *are* the key.

Enlist the help of others

But creating a connection with yourself doesn't mean that you have to do everything on your own. Ask others to help you. Approach others for feedback and *feedforward*. Ask for social support – whether from your partner, friends or colleagues – when you take steps that may be stressful for you. Make use of your network.

Be aware of the fact that as you are developing, the world around you is developing too. The world will appear differently for you and you will stand differently in the world than before, both in your environment and in yourself. In this development, the people around you will start responding differently to you. Some will react positively, while others will react negatively. This will become apparent, for example, if you actively start breaking through patterns (see Chapter 5), or when you start learning to say no (see Chapter 11). Your colleagues, friends and your partner may become confused as a result of your new way of thinking and acting. This might happen when you stop turning in work weeks of 60 hours or more and start making more time for yourself and your family. Or, when you start talking back more often, instead of accepting everything meekly. Be aware that this change in the responses of others means that you are breaking down a pattern; that you are developing yourself; that you are effectively practising your leadership.

HOW TO READ THIS PART OF THE BOOK

In each chapter, I will offer you a mix of models, ideas, short theories clarifying specific points, and sources of inspiration and assignments, all designed to activate you and your inner compass more often and to get you to continually observe yourself.

All of the chapters in this book start with a personal introduction and are therefore written with the starting point: the leader as a human being. After all, you connect in the first place with other people (customers, suppliers, colleagues) based on yourself as a person. In parts II and III, I also make the distinction that there are chapters that mainly focus on the leader as a person *and* chapters that are written largely based on the leader as a role. In the case of the connection with yourself, this distinction is not so sharply defined, because it primarily involves you.

In each chapter in Part I, I indicate how you can translate your personal insights in the field of, say, deep-seated desires, happiness, trust, your life goal, and making conscious choices involving your day-to-day tasks as leader. Ultimately, what meaning can you give to these personal insights for your work and for your functional role as a leader?

1 Self-reflection
2 Mortality as a source of inspiration
3 A meaningful life
4 Dream big
5 Breaking down patterns
6 Mentally emigrated
7 Feelings
8 Saudade
9 Happiness
10 Strategies for happiness
11 Saying NO
12 Trust in yourself
13 Life goal

Figure 4: Overview of the chapters in Part I

Above all, I wish you the upmost connection with yourself!

CHAPTER 1

SELF-REFLECTION

PERSONAL INTRODUCTION

I have a special relationship with my father, Simon. We share a history of highs and lows. When I was younger, I enjoyed his humour and having him around. Then we drifted apart. My parents argued a lot and finally there was the bitter divorce, a phase I prefer not to be reminded of. I distanced myself from my father and refused to see him for the next eight years. We then got back in touch and built up our relationship again. I now consider him to be a good friend.

In 2010, Simon started up a special project: a book filled with personal stories that he wanted to write in collaboration with 66 fellow authors. He asked me if I wanted to be part of the project. Because the idea of revisiting that emotional period in my life didn't appeal to me, I almost said no, but in the end I decided to accept the invitation.

I am so glad I did. Thanks to him, I have learned a new, playful and powerful method of self-reflection: writing a shadow path.

By writing my shadow path, I have once again learned a lot about myself. And that's something I'd love you to experience too, because self-knowledge is the foundation for self-acceptance and for engaging in a genuine connection with yourself. And from there you can engage in strong connections with others, in both your personal and professional life.

MEETING YOURSELF

Through self-reflection, you increase your knowledge about yourself. By analysing the way you think, speak and act in situations, you become more aware of the beliefs, feelings and thoughts that accompany them. You discover what your deeper drives are and how they determine your identity and your behaviour. The more you practice self-reflection, the more insight you gain into who you are, what motivates you, what comes easy to you and what your challenges and hot buttons are. And that's why self-reflection forms the basis for personal development.

You can practice self-reflection at any time of the day. For example, in your car on your way to work, at lunchtime or in the evening before you go to sleep. Whether you do it on your own or in dialogue with others is completely up to you. Whenever you take the time to reflect upon yourself, you will learn new things about yourself. For instance, ask yourself: am I being honest with myself? Do I dare to confront myself with both my inspiring side and my dark side? By doing so, your self-reflection will certainly contribute to your development, both functionally and personally.

MY PERSONAL SHADOW PATH

A special form of self-reflection is writing a shadow path. My father invited me to write a reflection inspired by a *tanka* (a Japanese form of poetry). The longer I pondered the thoughts and feelings the tanka evoked in me, the more I discovered about myself. When the inner journey of discovery came to an end after a couple of months, I felt disappointed. This was Simon's tanka (translated from Dutch to English, therefore partly losing the rhythm of the original poem):

> I take a step back,
> in front of me
> lies a frog,
> covered in ants;
> without board
> and staff a major
> job's getting done.

The first thing that sprang to mind was that I was behaving more and more like an ant. Additionally, I believed it would be a good thing if more people acted like that: looking for a common goal, putting all of our efforts unconditionally into that pursuit, and prepared to make sacrifices and to actively support each other. Ultimately, to detach ourselves from our ego and to fully connect with the group and the greater good.

Just imagine the impact that would have on the way organizations are structured. What role will managers have then? Will we still need them?

But it also seemed to me that displaying 100% ant behaviour would be extremely difficult, if not impossible.

As I wrote these words, I came to see the dramatic contrast between the desires I used to have and my feelings now. I used to want to be the alpha male. When I was working within the Dutch Royal Air Force, my ideal was to become a general. My next employer was a big IT company and I wanted to be given managerial roles in which people would look up to me. I was determined to become famous, and imagined that people would admire me for the impact I had. And why was that? Almost exclusively because of the external appreciation I would receive. That's when I would really be somebody.

Today I ask myself: if I'd succeeded, would I now be the man who would have inspired me as a child? I don't think so.

So where do I stand now in terms of my development? Somewhere between the alpha male and the ant. My drives have shifted from gaining external appreciation to having an internal desire to contribute to a better world. At the same time, I notice that it thrills me to connect with other people and have a higher goal. I enjoy setting out a specific course and creating impact. Perhaps I'm just an alpha ant.

ASSIGNMENT: Write your shadow path

You've read Simon's tanka and my shadow path. The assignment I want to give you is to write your own shadow path by reflecting on a difficult business decision you were faced with, or a difficult period in your life. Do so through a poem, a piece of music, an artwork or a photograph. It doesn't really matter what medium you choose as your catalyst. Just allow yourself to be surprised by what the act of reflecting evokes in you, and by what you discover about yourself in the process. Transform the insights you have gained from the artistic catalyst into a personal story of no more than 300 words, and share it with people in your immediate environment, both personally and professionally. Sharing your story will enhance its power, and your own power too. When you reveal your vulnerability to others, and show that you accept your inspiring sides as well as your dark sides, you're showing that you are okay as you are.

What do you need to enable you to step over your own shadow path?

CHAPTER 2

MORTALITY AS A SOURCE OF INSPIRATION

PERSONAL INTRODUCTION

Okay, I admit it: I'm scared of dying.

I just don't understand the concept of death. It was strange to think of being born, and to live and breathe in this world for a number of decades, only to disappear again. Forever. I couldn't get my head around that, at least not emotionally.

However, this awareness of my mortality has also had a positive and inspiring side to it. It encourages me – no, it forces me – to think about what is important in life. How do I wish to be remembered by my loved ones? What do I want my wife, my children, my friends and my colleagues to say at my funeral? Even more important: what do I want to have seen myself doing when I look back on my life? How can I best support the people who are dear to me and the people I work with? What do I want my contribution to society to be?

Reflecting on this gives me guidance in my private life, my social environment and in the business context. It helps me, among other things, to make decisions concerning the following questions:

- What things am I going to do (and what am I going to stop doing)?
- Who do I want to connect with and whom do I not (or no longer) want to connect with?

How deliberate are the choices you make? To which goals and people are you connected (consciously or unconsciously)? That's the core question I'll be discussing in this chapter.

WHAT IS YOUR BIGGEST DREAM?

In one of the coaching courses I conduct, I invite participants to ask each other the question: what is your biggest dream? This always produces some special moments. First there's the sense of confusion as the participants think, what is my biggest dream? Do I actually have one? But gradually, as more people have asked them the question, and everyone has heard other people's answers, you can feel the positive energy and mutual inspiration that is being created.

The participants make contact or re-connect with what is important to them. And they immediately make contact with others at a deeper level. Almost everyone is grateful they did the exercise and acknowledge that the question should be asked more often. And yet, when I ask them how often they ask a colleague or a friend this question, the answer is typically: "Well, never, actually."

Why is it that we hardly ever put this question to ourselves and others? And where or when did we lose the art of dreaming, or even daring to dream?

As children, we grew up with dreams. The whole day was filled with them. We lived in our fantasy world, where we could be anyone or anything. We lived in the moment and our actions were based on emotion and instinct. We were primarily human beings.

FROM DREAMING... TO BEING PUT TO SLEEP

From the moment we go to school, we become more and more serious, and have to stick to more and more rules. We are taught that getting good grades is the most important thing to worry about. That of course results in uniformity, competition and emotionlessness, and materialism takes hold of our lives. This process of 'becoming serious' is so powerful that we finally become so obsessed with keeping up with whatever the latest trend is that we don't have time to just sit back and dream, free of any inhibitions. We no longer think about and feel what is really important for us.

We have become action-oriented doers. As a 'human doing,' we forget to ask ourselves whether what we are doing, or about to do, is actually something we really want to do and whether it's appropriate for us (and our qualities). If we're unlucky, we notice too late that we're standing high up on the ladder of society, and that the ladder is up against the wrong wall. And we find ourselves tied up with golden chains, imprisoned in a cage we have created ourselves.

LAUGH YOURSELF TO HEALTH

Don't get me wrong: I'm not claiming that being serious and action-oriented are unhealthy elements in life. What I'm concerned about is that we are sometimes too serious and too action-oriented. Are we able to continue to give the child within us the space it needs? Do we allow ourselves to dream without inhibitions once in a while? I'm always astounded by how much suddenly becomes possible as soon as we do start dreaming.

Did you know, for example, that as children we can easily think up 60 different solutions for a single problem? As adults, we can on average think up between three and six. When we go to school for the first time, we ask some 60 'why' questions a day. When we retire, that figure has gone down to an average of six per day.

Another insight: whereas children will laugh when they feel like it, we as adults first ask ourselves if it's appropriate, and only then allow ourselves to laugh. The result of this is that as adults we laugh less than children. This is a shame, because laughing is healthy for us – it helps us relax, reduces the production of stress hormones, reinforces the immune system, helps us forget complaints and pain, and helps lower our blood pressure. And the nice thing about it is that there are no known negative side-effects of a good bout of laughing.

WHAT IS TRULY IMPORTANT?

So, my advice would be to not wait until tomorrow, next week or next year. Start today by working on what you consider to be truly important, starting this minute. Start dreaming as if your life is at stake and make the conscious decision to primarily carry out only those actions that will contribute to your dream.

Be creative, try things out and learn. And if you fail, then smile, laugh and start over again.

Really, life is now, so adapt your behaviour now. Combine your strengths and qualities as a human being *and* as a human doing. As Gandhi said: "Be the change you want to see in the world."

ASSIGNMENT: The hyphen on your gravestone

Your gravestone is engraved with the date you were born and the date you died. In between those two dates is a hyphen. That hyphen represents your whole life. What colour are you going to give that hyphen?

This assignment will make you more aware of what you find important in life. It will also make clear that you shouldn't wait until tomorrow to make choices (business-related or otherwise) and why you should perform actions that comply with what you really consider to be important.

The assignment lasts about 20 minutes. You can do it on your own or ask someone to supervise you. To gain maximum effect, I recommend that you find a calm, quiet environment to do it in.

1. Close your eyes and focus for a few minutes on the here and now. Become aware of your breathing. Experience consciously what you can hear, feel and smell. And if you notice a thought entering your mind, acknowledge the presence of that thought and then just let it go.

2. Now say to yourself out loud (or ask someone else to do this): 'There is no guarantee that I will still be alive next week, let alone in a couple of years' time.' Allow yourself to take in this sentence for a few minutes. If you want to, repeat it.

3. Then think of your partner, children or a dear friend and say to yourself: 'There is a chance that my partner, children or dear friend will be dead next week, and the chance that he/she will be dead in a few years' time is even greater.' Concentrate your thoughts on this truth for the next few minutes.

4. Now imagine the same thing for a few minutes about a random colleague, a neighbour, the girl at the supermarket cash desk or someone you are having problems with. This person could also be dead next week or in a few years' time.

5. Be aware for a few minutes that each moment of the day, somewhere in the world, someone dies.

6. And while you become conscious of this mortality, think about what you want to leave to this world. How do you want to be remembered by the people around you? What are you passionate about and what do you stand for? What contribution do you want to make to other people's lives and to the society you are part of?

7. Speak out loud about what matters to you in your life. Discuss this with your partner, a dear friend or the person supervising you.

> **Being aware of your mortality increases your chances of making yourself immortal.**

CHAPTER 3

A MEANINGFUL LIFE

PERSONAL INTRODUCTION

In 2008 I had a very scary experience. While I was driving my two eldest children home, I felt heart palpitations, stabbing pains in my chest and experienced difficulties breathing. One minute I was able to breathe briefly and the next minute I couldn't. I was convinced that I had only a few minutes left to live. I became angry, because this was happening in the presence of my children. I didn't want them to become traumatized.

Ultimately, it turned out that I wasn't about to die. After undergoing various tests at the emergency department, they told me that my heart was functioning normally and that I had probably been suffering from a bout of hyperventilation. The cause? Working too hard, too much stress, too little rest and not enough relaxation. In other words, my work-life balance was totally disrupted.

In the years that followed this never-to-be-forgotten experience, I suffered several similar attacks. It was still present in my body, in my system. The attacks were signs of something whose meaning I wasn't aware of initially. Gradually, though, I came to understand that these were calls to make a better and lasting connection with myself. They were a clarion call to consciously reflect on the things that were most important to me in my private and professional life, and to have the courage to commit to them. I learned that if I devoted attention to the important questions and made the relevant choices, the tension in my body would decrease and no new attacks would be triggered.

Luckily, these episodes have now stopped completely. Most of the time I experience calmness, focus and an enduring work-life integration.

The above experience leads me to ask you what your work-life balance looks like. The answer to this question starts with the answer to the core question: what is the meaning of *my* life? That's what this chapter is about.

WHAT IS THE MEANING OF LIFE?

The hyperventilation attacks I suffered got me thinking about what the meaning of life actually is. But the more I thought about it, the more I realized that I was asking myself the wrong question. That's because life is simply life, no more and no less. Just as a table is just a table, and fire is just fire. All these things acquire a meaning only when they are considered in relation to something else.

For example, fire acquires meaning when you use it to prepare a meal or to warm yourself. It therefore has a practical function. You can also stare into a fire, start daydreaming or reflect on life. Fire in this case has a relaxing or reflective function. But fire can also destroy entire cities, claim lives, and create fear. In other words, fire is just fire, yet it has a personal significance based on how you use it or how it intrudes on your health and wellbeing. The same applies to life.

WHAT IS THE MEANING OF MY LIFE?

I no longer ask myself the question, 'What is the meaning of life?' For me, it's much more useful to consider the following question: what is the meaning of *my* life?

One answer might be that I live in order to acquire knowledge. That in itself may seem to make for an interesting life's journey, but ultimately I will then just die as a man full of facts. Beyond the fact that knowledge gives me a lot of pleasure, I can also ask how I can use that knowledge to make a positive contribution to the lives of others and lead them to form meaningful connections both within themselves and with others. To a certain extent, this question has led me to write this book.

AS IT IS IN HEAVEN

Watching and reflecting on the Swedish film, *As it is in Heaven* (Kay Pollak, 2004), can help you answer the question about the meaning of your life.

The film revolves around a world-famous conductor who, after suffering a heart attack, is forced to take things easy. He returns to the village he was born and raised in and becomes involved with the church choir. Not only is he compelled to reflect on unresolved questions from his youth, he also influences the thoughts and actions of many of the people of the small village. Through his unconventional approach, he enriches the lives of the villagers. More and more of them decide to lead their lives consciously, or more consciously than before. As a result, the relationships within the community are transformed, as are those within families, friends and acquaintances.

This film beautifully demonstrates how groups can grow from a collection of individuals into a tightly knit and well-functioning team. I highly recommend watching it.

ASSIGNMENT: Are you of value to others?

In your professional and private life, who has a positive influence on the way you think and act? What is it about this person that is so meaningful for you? What actions have a positive impact on you? And have you told him how much impact he has on you? And vice versa, who do you have a positive impact on? How do you know? How could you create even more value for them? What if you were to ask about what's next?

The assignment is to engage in conversation with five people in your personal environment and five in your professional environment about these and similar questions. What is it about your life and theirs that is so meaningful and impactful? Dedicate at least 30 minutes of active conversation time to each of these people.

What first insights and emotions do these conversations produce? Reserve the next morning or afternoon for some 'me time' to give space to your reflection and learning process. For example, go for a long walk in the woods or on the beach. Perhaps go to the sauna, or simply sit in the garden doing nothing, and see what comes up in your mind and body when you give room to your initial insights and emotions during this 'me time'.

Finally, what actions that you're proud of do you want to carry on doing and what actions do you want to change? Craft a 'start, stop, continue' list. Make the answers as concrete as possible for yourself to increase the chance that you actually take action. Do you have the guts to make that commitment?

Who appears on the outside when you first listen to the voice inside?

CHAPTER 4

DREAM BIG

PERSONAL INTRODUCTION

Over the years, I have done a lot of work on personal development (and I will continue to do so). I have been coached myself and have taken many courses on leadership, team development and coaching.

One course changed my life completely, in a positive way. It was Co-Active Coaching Fundamentals training. This popular coaching methodology revolves around the notion of 'being in action together, and being together in action.' It espouses the idea of all action being grounded in being, and establishing a connection to a larger wholeness.

From the very first day of the course, I knew that this style of training and coaching was a perfect match for me, and I decided then and there that I would one day facilitate the training myself.

I had no idea what was needed to be able to do that, and even less of an idea how I would be able to achieve it. I first had to follow the whole curriculum, including a period of certification lasting six months. Another condition was that I had to follow their leadership programme, which lasted another ten months.

Both programmes demanded a huge investment from me in terms of time and money, but my employer at the time was only prepared to finance part of it. Additionally, if I wanted to be certified by the International Coach Federation, I would have to deliver at least 100 hours of coaching. I had no idea where I would find the time, and conducting training was not part of my role as manager. And even if I succeeded in complying with all the criteria, the chance of being selected as a facilitator for this programme was still quite small.

In other words, there were enough practical obstacles to stop me from even starting to fulfil my wishes. Despite all that, I just went ahead and started, and gradually moved step by step towards fulfilling my dream. Quite a few colleagues thought I was mad, especially when I exchanged my management function for the role of trainer and coach. Yet, the rest is history.

For more than eight years now I have given all five Co-Active Coaching courses. And every day, together with my colleagues at the management coaching group COURIUS, I am adding meaning to being specialists in the human side of change. I can truthfully say that I am living my dream.

The essential question for this chapter is: are you connected strongly enough to your dream/desire so that you will pursue it, despite any pressures from your social environment?

BILLY ELLIOT

The film *Billy Elliot* (2000), set in the 1980s, is about an eleven-year-old boy living in a poverty-stricken mining village with a stubborn father, rebellious brother and a grandmother suffering from dementia.

Billy is forced to take boxing lessons, even though he has no talent for it and doesn't enjoy it at all. One day, when he has to stay late after boxing, he catches sight of the ballet class taught by Mrs. Wilkinson. Something about it fascinates him, and after some hesitation he decides to take part in a ballet lesson.

It doesn't stop at one lesson. Without telling his father, he stops boxing and starts doing ballet. When his father and brother find out that the little money they have is being spent on ballet and not boxing, all hell breaks loose. "Lads do football, boxing or wrestling, not freaking ballet!" they scream at him. "What's wrong with ballet?" he asks, genuinely astonished. Billy is forbidden to dance anymore.

Yet, Billy and Mrs. Wilkinson are determined to do their best so that Billy can audition at the Royal Ballet School in London. He continues to take lessons in secret. When his father finally sees Billy actually dancing, he is impressed, has second thoughts and accompanies him to London so that Billy can audition. He passes the tryout and becomes a professional dancer.

SOCIAL PRESSURE

This film shows how inner desire can be repressed through fear of the reactions from the social context in which you are living or working. Billy discovers his passion for ballet dancing and has a strong desire to follow it through. However, because of his social environment (family, friends, class, milieu), he doesn't dare to openly express it.

Another factor that plays a role here is whether it is possible for him to actually follow his passion due to his financial situation. Billy shows courage in deciding to continue with his dancing. Unfortunately, the fear of being excluded, teased or humiliated results in him pursuing his dream in secret. As such, his development as a dancer is held back.

This social pressure is something that occurs all too often, in both the business and personal spheres. We have desires that we cannot fulfil (partly or at all) due to fear of rejection, in the short term, at least.

Fill in the blanks for yourself:
- You want to move your career in a new direction, but you don't dare to express it because you're scared that...
- You want to express how you value greater transparency, but you're afraid of saying what you think because...
- You can finally take on the leadership position within a team, but you don't dare because...

I'm sure there are many more examples you can think of.

DARE TO FOLLOW YOUR DREAM

What I observe is that there are always enough reasons to think up for *not* doing something. But what reasons are there for actually doing something, perhaps even against the will of the establishment?

Do you allow yourself to be driven by your fear or by your desire? Do you avoid doing something because it's uncommon, or are you allowed to show what makes you unique? Something that can help here is analysing your desire and transforming it into something extra large by visualizing that you are realizing it. What does it look like, and how do you behave then? How do you look, what do you say, how does your environment respond to you, what do you feel when you are doing it, and so on.

Doing this exercise will release energy and courage to enable you to take the first step. After that first uncertain step, each subsequent step becomes a little bit easier.

A much-quoted statement that has to do with daring to pursue your desire is drawn from Nelson Mandela's presidential inaugural speech in 1994. Although this text is often attributed to him, it is actually a quote from the book *A Return to Love* (1992) by Marianne Williamson:

> "Our deepest fear is not that we are inadequate. Our deepest fear is that we are powerful beyond measure. It is our light, not our darkness, that most frightens us. We ask ourselves: who am I to be brilliant, gorgeous, talented, fabulous? Actually, who are you not to be? You are a child of God. Your playing small does not serve the world. There is nothing enlightened about shrinking so that other people won't feel insecure around you. We are all meant to shine, as children do. We were born to make manifest the glory of God that is within us. It's not just in some of us; it's in everyone. And as we let our own light shine, we unconsciously give other people permission to do the same. As we are liberated from our own fear, our presence automatically liberates others."

ASSIGNMENT: From desire to realization

Think hard about the desires you have for yourself that you have given little or no attention to up until now. Make a list of them.

Don't forget to also write down those ideas that sound a bit weird to you when you first think of them. Put the list aside for a few days, and then come back to it and add some more ideas. After a week, choose one idea that you really want to pursue further. Then take ten minutes to visualize what it will look like when you have completely fulfilled that desire.

What has changed? What impact does it have on you and what will the impact be within your team or your organization, for example? What do other people say about you? How proud are you of yourself with this result? How does criticism sound now that you have achieved this result?

Carry out these steps for at least three ideas, even the one that sounds most radical. Then take one of the three ideas and think of one action that you can perform today or next week to move you a step in the direction of fulfilling your desire. This doesn't have to be a big action; it's all about taking that first step.

As soon as you have taken this step, celebrate the fact that you have done it and decide when you will make the next step and what that will be. By constantly taking (small) steps in the direction of your dream, something will happen. As the Chinese say: "Every journey of a thousand miles begins with the first step."

Can you see where your footsteps will take you in the coming months? Pursue your dream and step in your own footsteps!

CHAPTER 5

BREAKING DOWN PATTERNS

PERSONAL INTRODUCTION

In the past, I would do my best to win external appreciation, based on the belief that if others saw me and appreciated me, I would be an actual somebody.

This typically resulted in a rat race that cost me a lot of time and energy and led to personal frustration. Once I received the appreciation, the question (or more accurately, the uncertainty) still remained as to whether that other person genuinely liked me or was simply pretending to do so. I was stuck in a rigid pattern of asking, even yearning, for external appreciation so that I could feel good about myself. Frankly, it was never enough.

Thanks to a series of training courses in the field of personal development, working with personal coaches, gaining work and life experience, and so on, I succeeded in breaking down this dysfunctional pattern, and many other patterns.

These interventions produced some uneasy moments, and my powers of perseverance were severely tested. For example, I can remember the time during a course that I received a *love bombardment*. The other participants told me everything they considered fine and good about me for a full five minutes, and I succeeded in accepting it all. It met my need for external appreciation (although five minutes felt like an awfully long time).

But then came my biggest challenge: for two whole minutes I had to tell the others what I found fine and good about *myself*. Talk about intense! At the end of the assignment, I was left shaking and shivering. And I was so joyful and proud that I had dared to do it. Speaking things out loud helped me to accept who I am.

You too can break down dysfunctional patterns by following training courses. An alternative is to obtain insight into how these patterns occur and employ tools to break them down – to analyse whether you can manage to break them down yourself, and then lead a professional and personal life based more on a connection with your powerful individual core. That's what this chapter is about.

HOW LONG WILL YOU CARRY ON?

Your manager, your partner or your friends may think you should behave differently or adopt a different attitude in certain situations. But that's never going to work, because you happen to be the shy type, you're not someone who will have an opinion ready and waiting. Or, you're someone who happens to be very easily irritated and that's why you regularly say things you regret later. Or, you just happen to be... (think of any number of variations on this theme).

You're not alone in this. Everyone has a pattern about which they say, 'That's just the way I am!' And this statement is correct – in theory. You see your behaviour in a way that corresponds with your limiting beliefs and interpretations. This way, you create calm and structure in your life. After all, anything you can't change will have to be accepted by you and others. So why waste your energy?

By saying 'That's just the way I am!' you're making this explicit. The disadvantage of saying this sentence out loud is that you are justifying your own behaviour and further anchoring the pattern you find yourself in. As Albert Einstein said: "If you always do what you've always done, you'll always get what you always got." The question then becomes whether that's effective.

HOW PATTERNS ARE FORMED

Most behaviour patterns are formed during our youth, or can at least be traced back to it. By then, you have already established general rules that are fairly rigid. For instance, 'I am attractive/ugly/stupid/smart...' or 'People will like me if I keep my opinions to myself.' And then, with these rigid self-affirmations, you continue – often unconsciously – to act accordingly.

It's easy for these patterns to form during your youth because as a child you have the tendency to think in terms of black and white, with very little grey in between. 'Eva's never nice to me' or 'You always disagree with me.' The more often you expressed these convictions and acted in accordance with them, the stronger they pre-determined your behaviour as an adult. Meanwhile, as an adult, you continue to develop new patterns, and these are typically variations on the early patterns.

If you really want to change a dysfunctional 'That's just the way I am!' pattern, you will need to break the vicious circle of experiences, interpretations, decisions, behaviours, responses, which circle back to experiences, and so on.

Let's take a closer look at the steps in this circle.

Figure 5: How patterns are formed

Step 1: Experiences

This is about looking at the concrete situation without attaching a judgment to it. Simply describe the facts as they have happened, as objectively and as honestly as possible. Two examples of my personal experiences (on which I will build the rest of the text):

1. Learning always came easy to me. My parents regularly confirmed this and allowed me to skip a year of school, in agreement with the school.
2. I found it difficult to tell my classmates at the Royal Military Academy that my parents were divorced.

Step 2: Interpretations

You attach meaning to the experiences. This is a process we continually go through both as a child and as an adult. Identical situations are interpreted by everyone in their own, very different ways. And these are then unique interpretations. Two examples of interpretation (building on the previous step):

1. Through the expressed faith in my capacity to learn, I learned to trust my intellect. My interpretation was: I am smart.

2. The longer I kept the divorce to myself, the more difficult it became to be honest about it. I was ashamed of my home situation and that I wasn't being open. My interpretation was: other people don't find me very interesting.

Step 3: Decisions

These are not logical decisions based on objective information. Rather, they are decisions based on emotions, with the decision being made unconsciously. If you follow up on the decision, then it's as if the situation resolves itself automatically. Two examples of decisions (building on the previous step):

1. My decision: if I don't understand a decision, I can analyse the decision and discuss it with the other person. Based on arguments, I then make the best decision.

2. My decision: in principle, I don't say anything about the nasty experiences during the divorce (I don't say very much at all about my youth anyway). Instead, I keep up appearances so that my classmates will like me.

Step 4: Behaviours

If you have (unconsciously) made your decision, then the logical next step is to act in line with that decision. You adapt your behaviour based on the new convictions. For the people in your immediate circle, it won't always be easy to understand why you are behaving differently all of a sudden. Two examples of behaviours (building on the previous step):

1. I engaged in debate easily and did not hesitate to express what I considered to be true. Conversations became edgier and I enjoyed that.

2. I shouted people down. I acted tough and went partying. When conversations turned more personal, I made sure I was the one who asked the questions. That meant that the other person would do the talking, and I didn't need to do my best to show who I was. I only allowed a small number of people to catch a glimpse of my inner world.

Step 5: Reactions

People respond to how you behave. Your behaviour invokes counter-behaviour and has consequences. These consequences enhance the pattern that has been formed. And the self-fulfilling prophecy is born, the pattern proves to itself that it is a 'correct' pattern. Two examples of responses (building on the previous step):

1. A good discussion could be conducted with other rational people. I also observed that sometimes it was not at all a case of the intellect but of the underlying emotions. I noticed that I sometimes found this difficult to deal with.
2. Classmates (and the girls I met when I went out) sensed the distance. We had little or no in-depth conversations. The relationships remained superficial. I had few real friends.

BREAK THE VICIOUS CIRCLE

Reactions of other people not only confirm the pattern, they are also the starting point of the next circle. In themselves they are once again experiences that lead to interpretations and decisions that enhance the pattern and serve to maintain it.

In the case of functional patterns, this is fine, but when dysfunctional patterns are in play, it's time to break the vicious circle. How? First of all, by recognizing how the pattern has developed over time – by studying the different steps in the process critically, and then intervening in one step.

Ask yourself what actually happened and is it necessary to grieve about it? What are the facts and what are personal interpretations? What evidence is there for accepting these interpretations as being true? What have you decided, and do you also dare to let go of these decisions? What behaviour do you demonstrate? Do you have the courage to experiment with new behaviour?

If you implement changes in the previous steps, you will automatically see changes in other people's responses.

YOU ARE NOT ALONE

Breaking patterns that are characterized by the 'That's just the way I am!' mantra is hard work. Additionally, it is confrontational and demands a high level of persistence. Are you prepared to look for your (childlike) convictions and are you then prepared to test and change these?

This way, you create space to experiment with new behaviour. People often call in the services of a therapist or personal coach during such a process.

ASSIGNMENT: Working on your own pattern

I happily admit that I played hide and seek with myself for many years. Just like you, I'm a creature of habit who performs a lot of actions automatically and then afterwards thinks up a wonderful explanation for why I did it. Sound familiar?

I challenge you to investigate three functional and three dysfunctional patterns in your professional life, instead of acting out of habit. What is the current behaviour and what is the behaviour you would like it to be? Analyse why you do what you do by working through the five steps described above. Stop saying 'That's just the way I am!' and instead, based on the insights you gain about your patterns, make a conscious choice either to maintain them or to work on changing them.

**You can't start a new chapter in your life if
you keep repeating the previous chapter.**

CHAPTER 6

MENTALLY EMIGRATED

PERSONAL INTRODUCTION

As of today, I've had nine new jobs in my life, and I have recognized a pattern. If I say yes to a new job, I'll put 100% effort into it. After a while my interest wanes, as well as the pleasure I get from the work. This has a lot do with my urge for autonomy and being independent and my interest in new developments. At some point, I feel an intense desire for a new and more challenging environment.

Interpreting this in a positive way, I would say that my pure optimism leads me constantly to see opportunities for the taking, and I take them. At the same time, you could also say that I withdraw from situations I consider to be complex or difficult. I'm allergic to predictability and being stuck in a rut. For me, that means outright boredom and that's something I can't (or don't want to) deal with. As soon as I see the warning signs, I head for the exit, which results in a feeling of restlessness in myself and my direct environment.

Thanks to these mechanisms, I have succeeded in avoiding situations where I have had to drag myself to work. Before such a situation had the chance to arise, I had found a new challenge for me to put 100% effort into. That might be a new job, but it could also be new responsibilities within my existing job. Increasingly, I have learned to feel more aware and communicate what I want to do (initially, I was more conscious of what I *didn't* want) and to ask for it.

This resulted in the birth of COURIUS, where, together with my business partner Jaco and our associates, I put into daily practise our motto: 'We are specialists in the human side of change.'

The core questions covered in this chapter are: what do you do if you feel increasingly less committed to your work? Do you start moving or do you stay put? And are you more inclined to express what you *don't* want, rather than what you *do* want?

STAY PUT AND DON'T MOVE

I regularly speak to people who are doing work they no longer feel happy with. Despite the fact that it's obvious to themselves and the people around them that they'd rather be working in another environment, they just won't take the initiative. The arguments and justifications I hear include things like: 'The time's not right to change jobs because of the state of the economy,' 'What kind of work could I then do?' and 'I'll never get such attractive employment conditions anywhere else.'

These are all excuses for not having to take the initiative. And the result of all this? An increasing lack of commitment to the work. You can easily recognize these people: physically, they force themselves to turn up at work against their will, but mentally they've already emigrated, with all the ensuing consequences.

The results of mental emigration are visible in three areas: the impact on results, the impact on the social environment, and the impact on yourself. I'll go into all these aspects in detail in the following sections.

THE IMPACT ON RESULTS

At some point, the consequences of mental emigration become evident in the results of the team these people are members of. Less attention and motivation for the work leads to less commitment to the daily tasks. Mistakes occur more frequently, work is put off, and the quality of the work that *is* produced is often below standard. Additionally, more complaints are voiced about new developments or work pressure.

This in turn has an impact on the motivation level of colleagues. And the result is a situation in which:

a. Dissatisfaction spreads through the team

b. And/or, the person complaining becomes isolated

In both cases, the person involved feels justified in being dissatisfied. More often than not, the internal client or the colleague is the one to suffer. As soon as this dissatisfaction begins to spread, it doesn't take long for the situation to become unacceptable.

To what extent do you see your own situation reflected in this scenario, and are you aware of the impact this has?

IMPACT ON THE SOCIAL ENVIRONMENT

Secondly, mental emigration has an impact on the social environment. You start to talk more and more about your work in a negative way, both at home and with your friends. It's crystal-clear that you want to do something else. In the beginning, people listen to your dissatisfaction with understanding and compassion. After all, we all want to do work that we feel is meaningful and that we feel comfortable doing. And we want the same for others.

But, if after a while expressing your dissatisfaction becomes a daily ritual, more and more colleagues, family and friends will experience it as whining. And in more and more places in the immediate environment of the 'whiner', this rigid mentality will not be accepted. Why? Because no action is taken to change the situation.

A lot of people don't realize that they are spewing their dissatisfaction over other people's heads, and what kind of impact that has. What about you? Are you a whiner? If the answer is a yes, what impact does this have on your relationship with your colleagues and those within your personal circle? In the long term this won't be very positive. Something that can help you break through the cycle of whining is to ask yourself what gives you energy. It might be having a conversation with someone else who complains and whines about their work, or chatting with someone who is enthusiastic and enjoys what he does. To whine or not – it's a choice!

THE IMPACT ON YOURSELF

Thirdly, this mental emigration also has an impact on yourself. The gap between how you feel and how you would like to feel widens. At this point, you have a very good idea of what you no longer want, and why you want to do other work. But do you know what you *do* want? Most people find this question a lot more difficult to answer. You will start to blame yourself for not taking action. It's as though you're suffering from the number one social disease, the 'If only I had' syndrome. If only I had a nicer job... If only I had a better boss... If only I had a flexible schedule... and so on.

The more you blame yourself for not taking action, the more internal energy it will cost you. Add to that the negative energy created by the reactions of incomprehension from the people around you and this results in tension and stress. The mental downward spiral has been set in motion;

the process of mental emigration is in full swing. Will you give in to it or will you get in motion?

ACHIEVING THE TURNAROUND

I'm not going to claim it's easy to turn things around. It's unrealistic to expect that you can just make the choice that you're going to start thinking differently, and act accordingly.

What I *am* claiming is that it's possible to achieve this turnaround. This process starts with wanting, imagining and believing that things can change. With this in mind, engage in conversations with others, design a plan and make choices about how you want to carry out this plan.

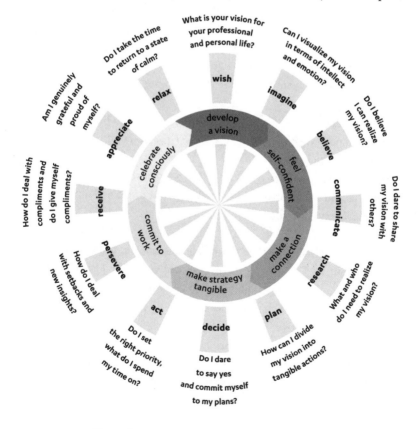

Figure 6: The Spiral of Creation by Marinus Knoope

And then it's all about taking action, persevering (because there will be setbacks, and these are part of the process) and about taking pleasure in the results (including the baby steps) that you achieve.

You can choose to take pleasure in things on your own or you can share it with others, as long as you celebrate the fact that you're in motion. Do you want to know more about these steps and the complete process of turning a wish into reality? Then take a closer look at **Figure 6** on the previous page, based on the work of the physicist Marinus Knoope (*The Spiral of Creation*).

ASSIGNMENT: Get moving!

Have you partially or totally mentally emigrated? What are you going to do: stay where you are or make a decision and get moving? No one else can make that decision for you. If you're thinking it's easy for you to talk, but it won't work for me, then I've got this Russian saying for you to think about: "Those that want to, will see opportunities. Those that don't want to, have their reasons."

If you decide to take action, here are some tips to help you in your quest for a new work environment that will give you energy.

Don't start by looking for a new job. Look for the attributes your new job will need to have. The more insights you gain about these attributes, the better you will be able to visualize what type of job and employer are most appropriate for you.

1. **Make a list of what you like about your current job, and what you don't like about it**. This way you will gain more insight into the attributes of a new job or employer that you consider important. Study different job vacancies and note which of the specified attributes you find attractive, and which you don't. Also ask your family, friends, colleagues and former colleagues what they think of you, and which attributes they think are important for you in a new work environment. Add these insights to your list. What picture are you beginning to form, and what types of functions and work environments match this picture?

2. **Invest in a personality test**, such as the ones offered by Insights Discovery, MBTI or Management Drives. If you've done one of these tests in the past, and you still have access to the report, read it through carefully and discuss it with others. You can also try one of the free tests available on the internet. What have you learned about yourself? What is important to take into account in a new job and new work environment?

3. **Make sure your LinkedIn profile is accurate and up to date**, engage in networking conversations, and start applying for jobs. Apply first to companies that you find interesting and that operate in the sector you're focusing on, but where you probably wouldn't want to work. This will help create a good feeling about yourself, and will help you fine-tune your profile, your letter of application and your actual job interviews. The next step is to apply to companies that you really want to work for.

4. **Dare to be different**. Instead of responding to a job advertisement, you can also write an open letter of application. What do you think would happen if you sent in a short film of yourself, rather than the traditional letter or email? What would happen if you actually physically walked through the doors of an organization and tried to arrange an interview on the spot?

5. **Tell your friends, colleagues and family that you're looking for a new challenge.** By specifying positively what you *do* want, you will be giving others the chance to think along with you. A 'warm' introduction to a prospective employer is so much more effective than a cold call.

If you come to the conclusion that it's time to find fertile new ground in order to grow, pack your bags and start your journey.

CHAPTER 7

FEELINGS

PERSONAL INTRODUCTION

It hasn't always been easy for me to accept my occasionally conflicting feelings. This is something I have had to re-learn in the last few decades.

For example, today I could be watching television in the company of others and a film will move me so much that it will bring tears to my eyes. Or, I could be feeling very happy and I will express my happiness. Sometimes I can spend the whole evening out on the dance floor. Luckily, today I feel less and less compelled to put on a mask – I can just be who I am. What a relief that is!

I have discovered that accepting all my feelings has made life worth living. It means that I'm able to experience being alive, in total connection with myself and with my emotions. And based on this, I can make a genuine connection with others and act in line with my feelings. I dare to be transparent in my relationships and to talk about the fundamental feelings of life: love, fear, joy, anger, grief, surprise, astonishment, shame and disgust.

This chapter is about the importance of making a connection with all your feelings, because they ultimately have an impact on the behaviour you display.

EVERYONE HAS FEELINGS

Are you in the mood for an impossible assignment? Well, try to describe completely what you're feeling *right at this very moment*. And... how's it going?

Of course it's possible to come up with words like angry, tired, calm, relaxed or surprised. But that's just the first layer. These are words that express the emotional state you're experiencing at the moment. But the 'feeling' that lurks beneath that is more difficult to describe. And to make matters worse, we are all unique. So, when you say you're relaxed or angry, you could be describing a totally different physical state than the state described by someone else who also says he's feeling relaxed or angry.

Some people claim they don't experience any feelings. Could the fact that feelings are so hard to describe explain why they say that? Perhaps they haven't learned to express these feelings or they just don't have the necessary words in their vocabulary. Another reason could be that they weren't allowed to express their feelings in the social environment they come from, because it was considered to be a sign of weakness, so those feelings were suppressed.

Whatever the reason for someone to say they don't have any feelings or don't know what they're feeling, the fact is that everyone has them. It's a fundamental law of nature. Whether you recognize them and can express them verbally is another matter.

FEELINGS DETERMINE BEHAVIOUR, AND BEHAVIOUR DETERMINES YOUR FEELINGS

Your feelings determine partly how you behave. For example, what feelings do you experience when you have to phone potential new clients? If you experience feelings of resistance or tension, there's a chance you'll put off making that phone call. And when you finally get around to making that call, how much enthusiasm will the person at the other end of the line hear in your voice, if you're still experiencing those feelings of resistance and tension? A possible solution to this could be to put a smile on your face before you make the call. It's a trick of the brain: when you do this, it will receive a signal indicating that something pleasurable is about to happen. This contributes to changing your emotional state, which increases the chance of your clients hearing a positive energy in your voice. That in turn contributes to creating a connection. They can *hear* your smile through the telephone.

FROM EVENT TO BEHAVIOUR (AND IMPACT)

An event in your immediate surroundings is never the *direct* reason for your behaviour. For example, someone may approach you in a very unfriendly way (event), and this leads to you putting off the work you have to do for him (behaviour).

This looks like a simple cause and effect situation, but it's not the complete story. You've forgotten a step: acknowledging your own feelings and thoughts about the event that forms the basis for your behaviour. This way, a chain of action is created: an event leads to thoughts you have and feelings you experience. These thoughts and feelings form the foundation for the behaviour you then demonstrate, and the impact this has.

EVENT   *leads to*   THOUGHTS & FEELINGS   *leads to*   BEHAVIOUR   *leads to*   IMPACT

Figure 7: Chain of action

Taking the example above, the chain of action could look like this: someone is angry at me (event). I consider this to be disrespectful (thought). I become irritated (feeling) and decide to deliberately delay starting the work I have to do for him (behaviour). The other person starts ignoring me (impact).

Gaining insight into the chain of action from event through to behaviour enables you to take responsibility for the creation of an undesirable situation. Instead of blaming the other person, you try to find out what your contribution is to the situation that has arisen. Once you've done that, you can decide to be transparent about it and adopt a different attitude. And of course, it helps you gain insight into what the chain of action is when it comes to *positive* situations. You can then make your own actions more effective, and you can make these actions repeatable.

ASSIGNMENT: A random act of kindness

The assignment for this chapter is building on the insight that you can influence the behaviour of others through fun and positivity. In the next few weeks, approach people you know (or don't know) with a smile and greet them in a friendly way, without a directly apparent reason. This could be your partner, colleague, manager, client, neighbour, cashier or even a random person on the street. Observe the effect this has on that other person and also the effect on the connection between you and them. Remain curious about your own feelings and about the effect on your own thoughts and actions. I'm curious to know what your findings are.

Allowing your true feelings to manifest themselves exerts a magnetic power on the connection with yourself!

CHAPTER 8

SAUDADE

PERSONAL INTRODUCTION

A few years ago I was introduced to the unique Portuguese word *saudade*. It is a mood state of the soul in which various emotions are experienced, all of whose origins can ultimately be traced back to love. It includes the simultaneous feelings of joy and sadness – a common theme in the Portuguese music genre of the fado.

I was deeply touched by this word and its meaning. It took me back in time, as it still does today.

I recall, for example, my first love, Annemarie, and my special love Ruby. How I loved them, and then had to let them go. I can look back with happiness on what we had and at the same time it makes me feel sad to realize that it's over. Or I think of my dog Pablo, who I spent a lot of time with, walking and playing and just being together. I can relive that joy and at the same time also experience the intense sadness I felt when he died. Or I think of when my knees were strong and healthy, and I was still able to go jogging, which I enjoyed. Today, I can't run anymore and I realize that getting older is accompanied by physical discomforts. The thought of this makes me annoyed and occasionally even angry.

How do you deal with successes and setbacks, and with the emotions that accompany them? Do you express them, or do you suppress them? What impact does it have on your connection with yourself? This is the theme I want to discuss in this chapter.

A SPECIAL FEELING

In English, *saudade* is often translated with words like 'melancholy', 'homesickness' or 'sadness'. But these words still can't convey its true meaning.

To give you a more accurate idea of what this feeling encompasses, we could describe it as: exhilarating feelings caused by a pleasurable memory of something that no longer exists, combined with sadness that the period of joy has gone. It might be a memory of a place you once visited, or of a person or a period from the past.

Despite the fact that there is no English word for this state of mind or mood, we have all experienced these simultaneously conflicting (or should I say complementary?) feelings. The question is, what do you do with them? Do you dare to fully embrace these intermingled feelings of joy and sadness? Or do you quickly suppress them and focus only on the positive feelings in your life?

EXPRESSING ALL YOUR FEELINGS

In my work I meet people who (consciously or unconsciously) choose to 'just' feel happy. I also talk to managers who will quickly try to switch the topic of conversation to a more positive one instead of having to deal with difficulties.

I think that's a shame. After all, by experiencing the sadness and analysing where it comes from, you gain insight into your personal values, your dreams and your wishes. This way, you develop yourself and your talents. The actress Drew Barrymore has this to say on the subject: "In the end, some of your greatest pains become your greatest strengths."

There are so many other inspirational quotes about expressing (and not expressing) feelings and other emotions. Here are three I particularly like:

1. "Tears not cried tire us out. Anger not expressed makes us tense up." (Riane Malfait.) In other words, keeping our emotions locked up inside us is an exhausting process. And it's very likely that when we finally express them, it will be in an explosive way, like an erupting volcano.

2. "What you resist, persists. It is only when you accept something that you can change it." (Neale D. Walsch.) Of course, there are many types of strategies you can adopt to stop you from feeling anything. Emotional eating is one example. The other side of the coin is that it sets a downward spiral in motion that becomes increasingly difficult to break through.

3. "It's not the circumstances that make you unhappy, but your thoughts about them." (Nin Sheng.) Once your negative thinking process has been triggered, the 'self-fulfilling prophecy' is created. To break through this spiral, it's important to separate your thoughts and feelings from the event that is causing them.

There are so many other sayings that deal with experiencing your feelings and embracing them. Which expressions appeal to you, and why?

ASSIGNMENT: Seeing yourself in connection with the past

As I said, we understand *saudade* to mean a mixture of conflicting feelings – of joy and sadness – when recalling places, people or experiences that now exist only as memories. This assignment is related to that.

Find a photo of yourself where you are somewhere between four and six years old. Now take seven minutes to study the photo closely, and to observe the thoughts and feelings this evokes. Just observe, don't judge. Where and when was the photo taken? What do you see when you look at this child? What 'type' of child were you? Which game did you enjoy playing most? What did you want to be when you grew up? Who were the friends you played with? What position did you have within your group of friends? What had you resolved never to do? And what *would* you do if you were grown up? What was your relationship with your parents, brothers and sisters? What do you see reflected in your eyes? What was your favourite meal?

At the end of these seven minutes of observing and experiencing your feelings, take the time to write down your thoughts and emotions. Then read through what you have written and ask yourself: 'Am I today the man or woman that I would have been inspired by as a child?'

By accepting your conflicting feelings, you will become more at one with yourself.

CHAPTER 9

HAPPINESS

PERSONAL INTRODUCTION

I'm an optimist by nature. One advantage of this attitude to life is that by definition I see the sunny side of the situations I find myself in. I can recover from setbacks quickly and I radiate positive energy that motivates others. And when I start up new activities, I don't allow myself to be held back by practical objections.

Of course there are some drawbacks to my optimism. For example, I regularly bite off more than I can chew, because I think it will all turn out fine. This typically results in me setting schedules that are somewhat unrealistic. On top of that, I occasionally forget to take the time to really feel life's pain – to experience it fully and to learn from it.

All things considered, I'm truly satisfied with my optimistic view on life because I experience more benefits than drawbacks from it.

Does that mean I'm generally happy? I can't say for sure. For me, the difference lies in the fact that my optimism generates its own forward motion. It creates a focus and a positive feeling with respect to what's possible in the future. It's a mental state that enables me to see and create opportunities, irrespective of what has happened in the past or is happening at the moment. By contrast, happiness is a feeling that occurs in the here and now.

Increasingly, I notice that when I experience happiness, this feeling has a positive impact on the connection I have with myself and with others. This is what led me to start researching how I might retain the benefits of my optimism and at the same time be able to enjoy more in the moment of what there is *now*. How can I really accept and experience happiness, and give it a permanent place in my life? This is the theme of this chapter.

RESEARCH INTO HAPPINESS

How do you create a true and permanent feeling of happiness? Sonja Lyubomirsky, a leading researcher within the Positive Psychology movement, has dedicated herself to answering this question. She has studied many theories that happiness researchers have come up with.

Those that have been scientifically tested are included in her book, *The How of Happiness.* "Science is not perfect, but it is more reliable than advice based on a limited amount of life experience of a random individual," Lyubomirsky writes.

This chapter discusses a number of her insights on happiness, while the next chapter outlines 12 proven strategies for a happier life.

WHAT IS HAPPINESS?

Happiness is a subjective perception that is difficult to describe and impossible to measure unequivocally. We know when we are feeling happy and when we are not, so scientists talk of 'subjective well-being' rather than 'happiness'.

Lyubomirsky defines happiness as "the experience of joy, contentment, and positive well-being, combined with a sense that one's life is good, meaningful, and worthwhile." She states that most people are inclined to look for happiness outside themselves.

However, many scientific studies show that external circumstances such as a relationship, income, health and living environment determine happiness only to a small degree. These aspects, to which society and many of us attach a lot of worth, are actually not very significant when it comes down to it. Lyubomirsky concludes that these external circumstances ultimately determine just 10% of our feeling of happiness.

HAPPINESS CAN BE INFLUENCED

Based on research with twins, genes and the brain, Lyubomirsky comes to the conclusion that 50% of happiness is influenced by heritage. Your basic level is therefore fixed (with its ups and downs, of course). Which leaves 50% that can be influenced: 10% by the external circumstances and 40% by your thinking patterns and the behaviour you display. In other words, a significant part of our perception of happiness is dependent on and able to be influenced by how you think and what actions you actually take.

Through systematic research, Lyubomirsky has been able to establish which nine thinking and behaviour patterns happy people display, which unhappy people do not (or display to a small degree). She asserts that happy people:

1. Devote a great amount of time to their family and friends
2. Nurture their relationships and enjoy them
3. Express their gratitude for all they have
4. Are often the first to offer people a helping hand
5. Are optimistic about the future
6. Savour life's pleasures and try to live in the present moment
7. Make physical exercise a weekly habit
8. Are deeply committed to lifelong goals
9. Are able to maintain their balance in difficult situations

POSITIVE SIDE EFFECTS OF HAPPINESS

These nine thinking and behaviour patterns provide a first insight into which strategies work to produce a happier life.

By working on your personal happiness, you will feel better, both physically and emotionally. In addition to these benefits, there are countless other side effects. The great thing about these side effects is that they act to further reinforce your feeling of happiness. A kind of self-reinforcing circle is created (that unfortunately also works in reverse).

Not only do happy people experience more joy, love, pride, respect and satisfaction, but other aspects of their lives are also enhanced. Compared with less happy people, they feel more committed to their work and to other people, they are in better physical and mental health, have more energy and more self-confidence, and their level of self-esteem is higher.

So, you're not the only one to benefit from being happy – your partner, family, your living and working environments, and society as a whole benefit too.

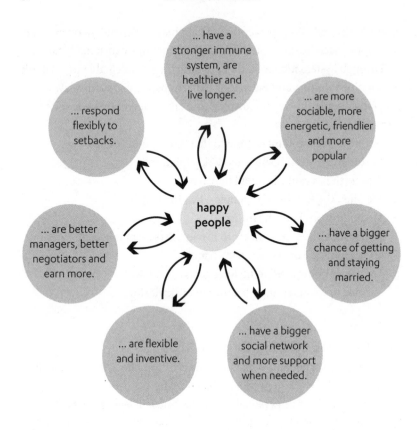

Figure 8: The reinforcing cycle of working on happiness

ASSIGNMENT: Reflecting on happiness

In my coaching practice, I like to make use of inquiries. These are short and seemingly simple questions that, when you start thinking about them, trigger even more questions. The longer you think about the question, the more depth and insights are created with respect to the theme of the question.

Here are six inquiries for you to think about. For the next few weeks, take the time to ponder these inquiries and to engage in conversation with others about them. It's quite revealing to go through your findings on the theme of happiness, and how they influence your feeling of connection with yourself and others.

1. What is happiness for you?
2. Are you working towards being happy, or is it possible for you to be happy?
3. What is your happiness dependent on?
4. What makes the difference for you between being satisfied and being happy?
5. How does it affect you when you see someone else's happiness?
6. How are you actively contributing to other people's happiness?

If you share happiness, it multiplies itself.
That in turn creates permanent wealth for you.

CHAPTER 10

STRATEGIES FOR HAPPINESS

PERSONAL INTRODUCTION

When I am in a state of mental calm, I enjoy what is happening around me and the activities I am taking part in much more. In these moments, I'm effective in my work, calm in my dealings with others, and able to experience happiness easily. This mental calm has a positive impact on my connection with myself and others. That's good for everyone concerned.

With this knowledge, I asked myself how I could experience more calm. My predictable answers are to get enough sleep, engage regularly in physical activity, eat less sugar, take the stairs more often, keep an eye on my weight, practice yoga, meditate and go to the sauna.

While I am writing this book, I am consciously taking action based on these insights. I notice their impact instantly and ask myself why I don't act on these insights all the time. Immediately after asking myself the question, I let go of it. I'm acting on them now, and I'm enjoying it. Evidently, it's important enough for me at this moment. So let me enjoy it instead of putting myself under pressure to do this continuously. This thought alone brings me into a state of calmness.

In the above example, I am acting on 'caring for my body' – one of the 12 proven strategies for experiencing more happiness in your life. Which strategy do you intend to practise? Keep this question at the back of your mind while you read this chapter.

12 STRATEGIES FOR MORE HAPPINESS

In the previous chapter, I outlined a few insights about happiness that Lyubomirsky described in her book. This chapter outlines 12 strategies that she devised , based on scientific research, that noticeably contribute to producing more happiness in your life. They are all open doors, extremely practical, and directly applicable regardless of the phase of life you are in.

Whether you actually become happier or not is all down to you – will you act on them or not? She recommends not trying to tackle all 12 strategies at once. Start with the one that appeals to you most. From my own experience, as well as coaching others, I'd like to emphasize this point; start small and enjoy the impact you create on yourself.

Strategy 1: Express your gratitude

Look around you at what is already there and be thankful for it. So, without investing anything other than focusing your attention on this and consciously dwelling on it, you are already influencing your feeling of happiness. Don't forget to express your gratitude to someone who deserves it. This way, you will influence not just your own happiness, but also someone else's.

Strategy 2: Cultivate and reinforce your optimism

Consider challenges and setbacks life is throwing at you as growth opportunities. By looking for the positive sides of situations, you will start seeing the world as a place full of endless possibilities. Does that mean you have to stop being disappointed? No, of course not. The question is how long will you wallow in your disappointment? Writing down the positive points of the situation you find yourself in can help. This way, you help yourself think about the possibilities rather than the impossibilities.

Strategy 3: Avoid overthinking and comparing yourself with others

It's not much use comparing yourself with others. Instead, it's more powerful to accept yourself for who you are, with all your brilliant and dark sides. After all, if the comparison falls in your favour, this will lead to an unhealthy feeling of superiority. If not, the chances are that you will focus on that and forget all the things you *have* achieved. If this doesn't stop you from comparing yourself with others, ask your friends why they are friends with you and savour their answers.

Strategy 4: Practice acts of kindness

Doing something kind for a friend, colleague, family member or a stranger without asking for anything in return will result in the production of serotonin, our happiness hormone. Whether you planned this kind of action beforehand or it was a spontaneous gesture makes no difference. Apart from the fact that you will start feeling happier yourself, the people around you who witnessed your good deed will also start producing serotonin.

Strategy 5: Nurture social relationships

The happiest people are the ones with intense and meaningful relationships. Australian researchers found that by investing time and energy in strengthening your relationships (and of course enjoying them), you not only become happier, but you also live longer. Studies show that people who are lonely die earlier. So, visit your friends and share your experiences. Dare to be open about your emotions, and share the joyful and vulnerable moments in your life.

Strategy 6: Develop coping strategies

Life isn't always a bed of roses. Rain, thunder and lightning are part of it too. So, it can't do any harm to take an umbrella with you when you go out if you're expecting bad weather… or you can of course decide to stay at home if you want. That's the way it works in life too. If you're expecting to deal with stress, grief or setbacks, think about what you can do to cope with them and take action. As entrepreneur and author Vivian Greene said, "Life isn't about waiting for the storm to pass. It's about learning to dance in the rain."

Strategy 7: Learn to forgive

Being angry at someone (or even worse, feeling contempt for someone) and persisting in thinking about it will have a negative impact on your immune system. Even thinking back to a similar situation in the past will create negative emotions in the here and now. Therefore, learn to forgive, so that you can let go of the anger and sadness you are feeling towards the other person. Those who forgive not only forgive the other person, they make sure that negative emotions no longer control them.

Strategy 8: Create flow experiences

Do you recognize those moments when you're busy performing a task and you become totally immersed in it? The activities and your consciousness coalesce into one. Time no longer exists; you don't feel hungry or sleepy and you are so focused that you are at one with the task. You are experiencing flow! Look for hobbies, tasks and activities that will bring you into that state.

Strategy 9: Savour life's joys

'I'm so busy' is something you hear a lot of these days, and some people even pride themselves on being so busy. We rush from one event or task to the next, without enjoying the moment or the result. And so, life loses some of its shine and you reduce the chance of being happy. In other words, slow down now and then, stop to reflect on that joyful moment or that result you achieved, enjoy it and celebrate it. What becomes possible when you accept that slow is the new fast?

Strategy 10: Commit to your goals

How do you eat an elephant? Bit by bit. It's the same with achieving your life goals. What are the most important goals or sub-goals for you at the moment, the ones you want to put all your energy into? Dare to make choices and make an effort to make them work. Break down you bigger goals into smaller steps and execute. Remember, each step forward is a step towards your happiness.

Strategy 11: Practice religion and/or spirituality

People who practise a faith or are involved with spirituality are generally happier than those who don't. A feeling of deeper connection with life on Earth and beyond (whatever that may be) can help to establish meaning and purpose. But it's not necessary to join a church or become part of a spiritual movement. You can start by being open to the possibilities of spirituality and by reading more about it.

Strategy 12: Take care of your body

A healthy body is a breeding ground for spirituality (your life goal), for emotional energy (your feelings) and for mental energy (your focus). Can you succeed in taking action and maintaining it while using this as a base? Studies of people who are clinically depressed show that regularly doing physical exercise leads to more feelings of happiness.

Think carefully about what you eat and drink, go to the gym or take walks regularly, meditate or practise yoga.

ASSIGNMENT: Achieving happiness

What are you going to try in order to experience more happiness in your life? If you choose one of the 12 proven strategies, then choose the one that appeals to you most. And don't be afraid to ask others to join in.

**Happiness is not down to chance, but rather to
how much you're prepared to commit to it.**

CHAPTER 11

SAYING NO

PERSONAL INTRODUCTION

Being able to say no is an essential skill for true connection. If you are in connection with yourself, you know exactly what you want. And in order to live this desire (to say yes to it), you have to have the guts to say no to people, initiatives, plans, etc., that do not contribute to moving you further along your chosen path. It's something that friends, coaching clients, managers and course participants constantly struggle with. We all find saying no difficult at some point or another.

I regularly have problems saying no. For example, I find it difficult to say no to anything sweet, to a cold beer after a hockey match, or to a challenging question by a client of mine. That is the case even though I know that I won't be the only person to benefit by daring to say no. My behaviour is an example to others of how important it is to look after yourself.

If more and more people start saying no, this will inevitably create the occasional conflict. But this isn't such a bad thing, because conflicts are simply a part of life and are just a collision between different truths. They arise when you and someone else apparently consider the theme so important that the both of you are prepared to fight for it.

In my opinion, you have to be more alert and be more concerned when no one ever says no and no conflicts ever arise. Are you really in connection with each other then? In other words, the theme of this chapter is to express yourself and say no if necessary.

REASONS TO SAY NO

Why do you sometimes find it difficult to say no to your partner, your friends, your manager, to sweets, television, relaxation, other people's tasks or working overtime? There could be a variety of reasons. A few of the explanations I hear regularly are: 'It's impolite,' 'It could damage my career,' 'It's not collegial,' 'I'd be acting selfishly' or 'It's just not done.'

I'm sure you can think of more yourself. Take a few minutes to reflect on the arguments you use for not being able to say no, not wanting to say no, or not being allowed to say no.

All of these have one thing in common: you have decided to consider them important, and therefore you will not say no to what is being asked of you. By doing this, you have said yes to what's being asked, consciously or unconsciously. Increasing your awareness in this area – it's about choices you make again and again – is the first step in learning to say no. Saying no actually means making a choice!

MAKING CONSCIOUS CHOICES

How consciously do you make your choices in life? To what extent do you analyse what you say yes and no to? When you say yes to working overtime every day, for example, are you aware that you are saying no to your family, relaxation and rest? Or when you say yes due to the irrational fear that you will be seen as not being collegial, do you realize that you are saying no to your independence?

You can also look at it from the opposite perspective. After all, by saying yes to your dignity and trust in yourself, you are saying no to your fear of losing your job and no to powerlessness. Or by saying yes to personal development, you are saying no to stagnation and doing the same work for the rest of your life.

Learning to say no therefore starts by rigorously analysing what you say yes and no to when you make choices. As soon as you become aware of this, the so-called blind spots or habits will become evident and you will create the energy to dare to make a choice. This way, actually saying no comes a step closer.

ACTUALLY SAYING NO

Once you have analysed every yes and every no, and you have made a choice, the next step is having the guts to actually say no. You can think up all kinds of theories for it, but it's all about taking action. Think of saying no as a muscle that has to be strengthened. This won't happen by simply talking about it, but by taking action and practising, even though you may be concerned about what will happen if you did say no.

In my experience, the fear of the consequences rarely matches actual outcomes. People constantly tell me that it really wasn't as bad as they thought it would be; the manager or the partner actually understood.

The question that consistently comes up in the end is whether you want to give in to your often irrational thoughts about what may go wrong, and then to say yes to something you don't really want. Or, are you prepared to take the risk, and do you have the guts to follow your thoughts and feelings and say no to something you don't want? Would you rather be the architect of your future or the victim of your past?

ASSIGNMENT: Say yes to saying no

In the next three weeks I want you to say no ten times a day. Don't worry, that doesn't have to be in earthshattering situations. Start small. Try it if someone asks you to get them a cup of coffee, or to bring them something, or if someone in a shop asks you if you have some small change, for example. Consider how you are feeling at the moment you say no and be aware of what is happening in your immediate surroundings. It's not about the result, but about strengthening your 'no' muscle. Neither the muscle nor the skill of saying no will grow simply by talking or reading about it.

Say no to the good things, so that you can say yes to the best things.

CHAPTER 12

TRUST IN YOURSELF

PERSONAL INTRODUCTION

I'm an optimist and I have faith in the sincere intentions of the people around me. I'm aware that in certain circumstances people will behave with less sincerity. The question is then how do I deal with that?

For me, the answer is that I maintain my trust in their sincere intentions. Why? Well, let's imagine that I conduct a hundred conversations with different people, and I try to be as open and vulnerable as possible in all of them. Of those conversations, 98 would make me very happy because they provided depth and honoured my trust, reinforcing my connection with the other person. But that means there would be two I felt unhappy about because they abused my trust, which led to a mutual feeling of distrust.

Am I expected to stop being so open and vulnerable just because of the fear for those two negative experiences, thereby missing out on those 98 wonderful experiences? Or, do I accept that I'm going to be disappointed in life once in a while and focus on enjoying the many wonderful experiences it will bring? The answer for me couldn't be clearer: I focus on the warmth and therefore assume that the people around me have sincere intentions.

In other words, I choose to give others my trust. Not only for the warmth, but also because it's a key ingredient for creating long-term relationships. Yet that starts with having trust in yourself. That's the basis. And that's what this chapter is about.

THE SPEED OF TRUST

Stephen Covey wrote in *The Speed of Trust* that trust is the key to success in both business and personal relationships. He shows that displaying trust is a core competence for a manager who wants to be successful in this century. This is how he puts it:

"There is one thing that is common to every individual, relationship, team, family, organization, nation, economy and civilization – one thing which, if removed, will destroy the most powerful government, the most successful business, the most thriving economy, the most influential leadership, the greatest friendship, the strongest character, the deepest love. Yet it is the least understood, the most neglected, and most underestimated possibility of our time. That one thing is trust."

THE PRODUCT OF LONG-TERM RELATIONSHIPS

Trust is the key to seeking and creating long-term relationships with employees, clients, business partners and investors. Previously characterized as a 'soft' concept and a matter of 'gut' feeling, it has become a pivotal management characteristic that yields measurable results.

Covey demonstrates this by establishing a link between trust (and the speed with which it is gained) and the costs of an economic relationship. The higher the level of trust, the quicker business will get done, reducing the total costs for both supplier and customer.

Conversely, the lower the trust, the more time it will take to do business and the more delays will occur, making the total costs higher for all parties concerned. For example, think about the payroll costs for hiring specialists, account managers, lawyers, secretaries and managers when concluding a contract. There are additional costs for maintaining extra stock and interest payments. And we mustn't forget the latent costs associated with not daring to deviate from agreed procedures and contracts, or the time spent on gaining internal and external consensus (and sometimes even arguments).

FOUR CORE THEMES

To be able to build trust in a relationship, whether in the business or personal context, a key condition is the ability to exhibit trust in others. The crucial step that precedes this is the ability to trust oneself. It goes without saying that you can't give anything or expect something from someone that you can't give to yourself or don't possess to begin with.

To lead a life of trust, you need to focus on four core themes: integrity, intentions, capacities and results. The first two are concerned with your character (Human Being), while the latter two are concerned with your competencies (Human Doing).

trust	
character	competencies
integrity	capacities
intentions	results

Figure 9: Four core themes that lead to trust

Theme 1: Integrity (character)

Integrity is all about how congruent you are as a person in your thinking, words and actions. Do you 'walk your talk' and do your actions reveal what you consider to be important? And do you display these sides of yourself even when your opinion differs from the prevailing norm? Integrity is more than being honest. It's about thinking, choosing and acting based on your personal values, norms and convictions.

Do you have the courage to stand up for your principles – in all circumstances and every situation?

Theme 2: Intentions (character)

When we talk about intentions, we are talking about what your genuine goal is when you engage in a relationship. What are the motivations and agendas that drive your actions? Are they open or hidden? Again, the more visible your true intentions are, the quicker you will be able to build trust. If, for example, you tell the other person that they are free to make their own choices, while in reality you actually want them to do what you say, it won't be long before the other person notices this and it will have an impact on the trust experienced within the relationship.

Do you analyse your true intentions and express them, do you specify the actions you will take to achieve these intentions, and do you provide an honest explanation after the fact if you are questioned about them?

Theme 3: Capacities (competencies)

Do you have the knowledge, skills and resources to fulfil what you promise? We're talking here about a combination of talent, attitude, skills, knowledge and style. And that's not something you gain simply by studying for a couple of years. It's a process of lifelong learning in which you acquire new knowledge, continuously reflect on your own behaviour, and actively work on personal and professional growth.

How honest are you with yourself about the amount of knowledge, skills or resources you have and don't have?

Theme 4: Results (competencies)

Finally, trust in yourself ensues through achieving tangible results and being proud of them. By explicitly communicating these results (instead of assuming that the results will automatically be noticed) you create credibility with regard to yourself and others.

From personal experience, I know that many people become nervous when it comes to presenting their achievements. They feel as though they are boasting, and it triggers a fear that others will consider them arrogant. The internal critic rears its ugly head. Do you want your actions to be influenced by this?

Do you have the guts to feel proud to express to yourself (and others) the fantastic results you have achieved?

ASSIGNMENT: Mirror yourself

Working on the core themes of integrity, intentions, capacities and results will create a feeling of trust and connection with yourself. That's the foundation for creating trust and connection with others. The next assignment often evokes feelings of resistance. But if you allow yourself to get into the spirit of the assignment, unexpected insights can occur.

This exercise consists of two phases. Start by sitting in front of a mirror and looking at yourself for at least 30 minutes.

Phase 1

Spend the first ten minutes just observing who you see, what your face looks like, what you see in your eyes (after all, the eyes are the window to the soul). Play with your facial expressions and watch what happens. How are you sitting? Are you satisfied with the way you look, and what would you like to change?

Carry on observing, even if you start feeling some resistance. See what you look like when you are dealing with resistance. Whatever comes up, don't judge yourself for it. Stay open and see what comes up. What do you look like when you are in a state of calm, pleasure, joy, resistance, unhappiness, sadness? Remain curious about the way your inner state translates into your physical attitude.

Phase 2

For the next 20 minutes, carry on looking at yourself while you ask yourself questions related to the four core themes. To help you, here are a few questions you can ask yourself:

- What will I not give in to? (And how do I express that?)
- How do I react when I am being deceived? (And who am I deceiving?)
- When do I make use of my power? (And how do I react to power?)
- How do I turn distrust around? (And do I dare to trust myself unconditionally?)
- When do I shout myself out? (And when am I allowed to be vulnerable?)
- What must I forgive myself for? (And what have I come to terms with?)
- What still frustrates me? (And am I prepared to do something about it?)
- What achievements am I proud of? (And who have I shared them with?)
- What makes me powerful? (And am I using that in my work?)
- What do I want to achieve in my work? (And does my manager know that?)
- What secrets do I have? (And why am I keeping them secret?)

Having worked through this exercise, what have you discovered about yourself, both personally and professionally? What are you going to do with these insights?

Kindness in words creates trust. Which words do you say to yourself?

CHAPTER 13

LIFE GOAL

PERSONAL INTRODUCTION

What do you really stand for? What do you consider to be really important? What do you truly believe in? What is your life goal?

All of these questions are difficult to answer, yet it's vital to spend time reflecting on them. That's because your answers will give direction to both your life and the actions you take in your life.

For me, I want to contribute to humanizing society and workplaces by raising the consciousness level of people. Based on the strong connection with themselves, they will proceed to make contact with others. This results in deep and respectful connections, both personal and professional, which generate a multitude of opportunities. A connected world is created that says yes to allowing room for differences in being, thinking, religion, skin colour, faith, sexual orientation, etc. A world emerges in which professionalism, quality of life and sustainability go hand in hand. This is what I believe in and this is what I want to make a contribution towards.

To help me achieve my life goal, I gave up my management position in 2003 and underwent a career switch. I started working as a trainer, team coach and executive coach. At the same time, I decided to offer coaching to people for free, or at greatly reduced rates, so that everyone would be able to make use of my services. I also started to write and distribute short articles designed to inspire others.

Another tangible result of pursuing my life goal: the book you now have in your hands.

In other words, connecting to a life goal gives you direction, which results in professional and personal choices and actions that you just can't say no to. What is your life goal? Keep this question in the back of your mind while you read this chapter.

WHAT DO YOU REALLY STAND FOR?

Your time on this planet is limited, so spend it wisely.

This begins by formulating a life goal (or a purpose, as some people prefer to call it). What do you want to achieve in terms of your work, your relationship, society or, for example, your work-life integration? How satisfied are you with your attitude, your behaviour, your emotional stability, your strength, your readiness to help others, etc.?

These kinds of questions, and the assignment at the end of this chapter, will help you gain more insight into your life goal and help you assess how to go about achieving it. Depending on your answers, this means taking action. A first active step is to formulate and articulate your life goal and/ or set activities in motion to help you to achieve – or to better help you to achieve – your life goal.

GETTING INTO MOTION

When you are healthy, your bills have been paid, you have a fine relationship and you do good work, you will usually feel pretty good. In times when the basic needs are taken care of, it's relatively simple to take responsibility for reflecting on and achieving your life goal. That is, if you make the choice to do so.

When you are depressed, anxious, stressed, the circumstances are initially less favourable for implementing such changes. It demands courage to act and to grow mentally, emotionally or spiritually; courage to get into motion and initiate actions in line with your life goal – with no guarantee that these actions will produce what you hope for or expect. And, perhaps this negative disposition is just what you need to get the change into motion. After all, the most wonderful insights and opportunities are the result of experiencing the deepest troughs.

PAUL POTTS

Paul Potts is a fine example of having the courage to go after your life goal.

Paul was a mediocre man with little self-confidence who sold mobile phones for a living. On the side, he performed as an amateur opera singer. Then, while undergoing an appendix operation, a tumour was discovered, after which he was involved in an accident, bringing his singing career to a standstill. But singing remained the joy of his life. His life goal was to become a professional opera singer and inspire people with his music – in his own words, this was what he was "born to do."

But, given his situation, how could he ever expect to achieve such an unlikely goal?

Paul took action and enrolled for the TV talent show *Britain's Got Talent*. He auditioned on 7 June 2007. When he appeared on stage, what the judges and the audience saw was a rather plump, shy man with crooked teeth and a sagging face. The second he started singing – goose bumps.

Paul won first prize in the show, and he is currently singing all over the world, earning a living with his passion for music. He has also had his teeth straightened. He remains a modest and charming man with both feet firmly on the ground, and he is intensely happy. He is living his life goal.

LIVE YOUR LIFE FORWARDS, UNDERSTAND IT BACKWARDS

With hindsight, it's easier to think things through and understand what led you to the situation you find yourself in now. You're able to identify the connections between the actions and the outcomes, and you can see the bigger picture. As the Danish philosopher Søren Kierkegaard wrote: "Life can only be understood backwards; but it must be lived forwards."

In order to be able to take action, you need trust in the future, and you have to know why you want to move in a specific direction. This 'trust' and 'knowing' is derived from your powerful life goal. It therefore serves as a framework against which you can test your intuition, heart and head, and then get into motion.

Be aware, though, that formulating your life goal is not the same as formulating a concrete goal. Your life goal is the bigger picture (do you dare to truly dream/think big?), while goals lead to concrete actions (a manifestation of your life goal in the short term).

ASSIGNMENT: Connecting extremes?

Read the following questions and add four questions of your own that are relevant for you at this moment. Immediately afterwards, make a promise to yourself that you will open the book at this page every day for the next two weeks. Choose a different question from the list each day, and take it as your theme throughout that day.

1. Is the life I am living someone else's, or my own?
2. Am I dragging myself to work every day, or do I look forward to going in?
3. Is my life based on fear, or is it based on courage?
4. Do I follow my head and my rational thinking, or do I follow my heart and my intuition?
5. Do my emotions control me, or do I control my emotions?
6. Do I give up quickly or do I persevere?
7. Do I think in terms of limitations or of opportunities?
8. Do I work based on control, or based on trust?
9. Do I see myself as a victim of circumstance, or do I take responsibility for my actions?
10. Are my actions based on choices determined by circumstances, or are my actions based on choices aligned with my life goal?
11. Your own question #1
12. Your own question #2
13. Your own question #3
14. Your own question #4

You will notice that each question contains two extremes. These are intended to create a scale within which you can position yourself, with your personal and/or professional environment as a reference (do you notice a big difference between the two?). For example:

| I am living someone else's life | My position (professional/personal) | I am living my own life |

It's not about whether your position is good or bad, although you will undoubtedly have your own judgment about it. It's more important that you reflect on whether you are satisfied with your position. What do the insights tell you about your life goal and the extent to which you are living your life in line with it? What is your true life goal?

**Find your life goal by connecting with what takes place
in both your head *and* your heart.**

PART II

IN CONNECTION WITH THE OTHER

*"We have two ears and one mouth
to listen twice as much as we speak."*
Confucius

INTRODUCTION

The second part of this book deals with the connection between the other and yourself.

The theme of the first part – being in connection with yourself – was about the relationship with yourself. Now it's about entering into a relationship – however long or short – with someone in the outside world.

THE CONTEXT OF CONNECTION WITH THE OTHER

In Part I, I demonstrated that in today's world, and the pervasive service society, the focus is switching to people collaborating with each other. In view of the fact that the human side has become essential, the Connection Quotient starts with the connection with yourself.

In Part II, the focus lies on being in connection with 'the other.' Moving from one person to two has more impact on your CQ than the tenfold increase to the team context at a later stage, or the hundredfold increase to the scale of a whole organization. Why is that?

Every functioning of a team, every functioning of a leader, and every intervention in an organization can ultimately be reduced to the communication between an extremely limited number of people – more often than not, the collaboration between just two individuals. The connection with the other is therefore the most elementary and smallest entity to which many other and bigger collaborations can be traced back.

Whether you study long-term collaborations between organizations and suppliers, mergers between companies or alliances between countries, all of these can be boiled down to a meeting and a connection between two people. Bankruptcies, commercial split-ups or the dissolution of partnerships form the other side of the coin.

These situations can also be traced back in many cases to a lack of understanding, a lack of communication, or a lack of connection between, often, just two people. Just do a web search for the terms 'power struggle' and 'CEO' and you'll be inundated with machos tearing each other's hair out. The same dynamic emerges, whether it's about the battle at Volkswagen between Chairman Ferdinand Piëch and Chief Executive Martin Winter-korn (in 2015), or about how Steve Jobs was publicly ousted after losing a power struggle with the then-CEO John Scully in 1985. You'll find the same regarding the American merchant bank Morgan Stanley with Greg Fleming and Colm Kelleher (in 2016) – the leading players in this soap opera – or Wim Vanhelleputte versus Anthony Katamba, board members of the telecom company MTN Uganda (in 2019).

The connection all these examples have with each other is that the protagonists lacked the capacity to restore the connection with the other in the power struggle.

IMPORTANT ELEMENTS IN MAKING A CONNECTION WITH THE OTHER

The ego dismantled

In the connection with yourself, you are the focal point. Your 'self' is explicitly different from your ego, as used in words such as 'egocentric' or 'egotistical.' The difference between your 'self' and your ego influences the connection with the other.

If your ego was playing a major role in your daily thinking and acting, then it wouldn't have come to the surface when you engaged in the connection with yourself. This is because you were your own judge. However, in this second domain of connection with the other, you start having an opinion about others, and others have an opinion about you. The 'size' of your 'self' then suddenly has an impact on the Connection Quotient in your relation with the other.

How much mutual trust is generated if you are constantly positioning yourself above the other in terms of importance? What is the impact on the relationship if you take credit for other people's achievements rather than acknowledge their roles in them? In relation to this theme, business management expert David Maister drew up his 'trust formula' in 2001. He states that the degree to which you gain other people's trust is the result of:

Credibility	+	Reliability	+	Intimacy
(Having expert knowledge)		(Being dependable & consistent)		(Creating emotional closeness)

On a ten-point scale, the sum of these three factors can be a maximum of 30 (10 + 10 + 10 = 30). But this total can be reduced if one other factor is not taken into account. That's because you have to divide this total by the degree to which you are focused on yourself, as well as the degree to which you are focused on your own interests. Maister calls this factor 'self-orientation' (**Figure 10**). If your self-orientation is geared towards placing yourself in the spotlight – to the value of 10, for example – then the equation becomes:

$$\frac{10 \ + \ 10 \ + \ 10}{10} = \frac{30}{10}$$

| Trust = | Credibility + Reliability + Intimacy |
| | Self-orientation |

Credibility	Reliability	Intimacy	Self-orientation
is concerned with the *words* you speak, using your professional knowledge and honesty as a foundation.	is about the *actions* you perform, with at its foundation: how you deal with the agreements you make.	is about inviting *emotions* within your relation, with at its foundation: being able to experience the safety to speak freely.	is about *caring* for others, the foundation being a focus on yourself versus genuine focus on the other.

Figure 10: David Maister's trust equation

Can you imagine the impact this can have? The score of 30 will be drastically reduced to three. It doesn't matter how much relevant knowledge you have, or how well you honour all your agreements, or if you create an atmosphere within which the other dares to speak their mind.

If the other person has the feeling that you are acting primarily out of your own interest, and they don't sense that you are also caring for them, the trust factor is reduced enormously. This will lead to the other person – despite high scores on credibility, reliability and intimacy – not considering you to be trustworthy. Conversely, if you always maintain focus on the common interest, and in your self-orientation you focus minimally on your personal interests, your trustworthiness will suddenly rise astronomically. In that case, the denominator can become less than one. Obviously, this will result in immense leverage on the trust that people have in you. Because:

$$\frac{10 + 10 + 10}{0.1} = \frac{30}{0.1} = 300 \quad \text{or even:} \quad \frac{10 + 10 + 10}{0.01} = \frac{30}{00.1} = 3000$$

These calculations are of course rather cognitive in nature. And I don't want to reduce human relationships to an exercise in filling in the blanks. At the same time, this equation does demonstrate the exponential effect on trust as soon as you can consistently focus on the common interest, detach yourself from your ego and act in accordance with that.

Working on a healthy form of self-orientation is a key factor in achieving a good and lasting connection with the other.

The birth of a relationship

In the connection with the other, for the first time, a relationship arises in which you are no longer in total control. Irrespective of how independent a stance you want to adopt, in the connection with the other, by definition, a dependency exists. In every contact with the other, you have to constantly re-appraise the relationship. Who talks, who listens? Who gives, who takes? Who follows, who leads? How much distance do you maintain, how much proximity are you looking for?

What is your relation with the other in various situations? What meaning do conflicts have for you? Are you typically the persecutor or mostly the victim? How do you talk to the other? Do you do so as an adult full of self-knowledge, or do you suddenly catch yourself saying something in the role of a hurt child or a critical parent? In that contact with the other, are you predominantly occupied with shielding yourself or with looking for something?

Connection with the other *and* autonomy

From the perspective of the Connection Quotient, autonomy can be seen as having the courage to choose to have a connection with yourself, and from there to consciously engage in a connection with the other.

These connections exist side-by-side and do not necessarily cancel each other out.

That's because the person who's in connection with himself thinks and acts based on a deep self-awareness. You choose to be loyal to yourself and to remain so. In the connection with the other, you do not automatically have to be self-sacrificing. You are not making yourself dependent or subordinate because you stand for your personal values, vision and humanity, among other things. At the same time, you are curious and you are open to what the (temporary) relation with the other demands of you and what it has to offer you. A dance is thus created in which you take turns looking at what effect the other is having on you and what you are evoking in the other.

Connection with the other, and maintaining your own autonomy, are therefore not mutually exclusive. This means that you make a connection with the other with all the power and firmness you have *and* are. This way, you observe what happens when you consider your unique (temporary, in principle) connection as a new entity, with each maintaining their own autonomy. In so doing, you can both ask yourselves the following:

1. Am I getting enough autonomy?
2. If not, shall I ask for (more) autonomy?
3. And if that does not succeed, shall I demand my autonomy?

For the leaders and managers I work with in my coaching practice, these three questions regarding autonomy are a recurring topic of conversation. They no longer feel or experience their own autonomy. They have lost the connection with themselves. It is an exciting and essential topic because the renewed claim for one's own autonomy requires that you are mentally strong yourself.

To what extent do you allow yourself to be influenced by the question of what the other will think of you if you allow and demonstrate this autonomy? Or even worse: do you allow yourself to be influenced by the fear of the answer to this question?

The other as a mirror

You can only really learn about yourself in connection with the other. The other functions mercilessly as a mirror to lay bare the themes you hold within you. It could be that you are predominantly occupied with shielding something. Perhaps you are occupied with keeping yourself (or something within yourself) from making a connection. Another possible pattern is that you are looking for something in your contact with the other. If you need the other for confirmation of yourself, or you want to constantly engage in battle with the other, your life will be an exhausting one. In the latter case you have to be better than the other to be able to feel good. That means that the connection with the other has become a dependent relationship. Or, if you are constantly trying to do well in the eyes of the other, and you are constantly afraid of being rejected, then you are probably suffering from the *disease to please*.

All of these patterns have one thing in common: the way you speak to the other says something about the quality of your connection. And often, below the surface there lurks the question of whether you are someone in the eyes of the other as a result of what you *do* (human doing), or are you simply worth knowing because of who you *are* (human being)? I very much hope for you that it's a combination of both these things.

From drama triangle to supportive connections

The drama triangle is an example of a special set of dynamics in which you can find yourself by being involved in connections with the other and/or others. The drama triangle consists of three positions that reinforce each other. First, you have the persecutor (aka the villain): someone who gives another person the blame. There's a big chance then that the person who gets the blame will feel like the victim (the second position). The third position is that of the rescuer. By virtue of their mutual relations, these three positions are held in balance. In fact, the persecutor in turn becomes the victim because the rescuer of the first victim transforms into the persecutor of the initial persecutor.

However, by making a connection with the other, you can turn the drama triangle around, into a healthy set of dynamics. As soon as the persecutor specifies his own boundaries instead of blaming others, he has created clarity. By replacing aggression with assertiveness, you shift from the domain of anger to the domain of strength. Instead of using adverse pronouncements ('You can't trust them'), you act on the basis of respect for yourself and others.

SELF-CONFIDENCE
Research your own actions/thoughts.
Is it really true? Is this correct?
Can it be done differently?
What more can I do?
Ask for help.
Experiment, but accept the consequences.

POWER
Defines own boundaries.
Respect for yourself and others.
Connection through being assertive.

researcher

FULFILMENT
Caring and concerned.
Allows others to make choices.
Teaches others to become more independent and more skilled.

creator of clarity

coach

SUPPORTIVE CONNECTIONS

DRAMA TRIANGLE

persecutor

rescuer

Accusing others.
They can't be trusted.
Seeks contact through anger.

AGGRESSION

victim

Resolves issues for others.
Relieves others of tasks.
Seeks contact through pity.

FRUSTRATION/DESPAIR

The fact that I have problems is due to the other or to circumstances.
I cannot take action or make choices myself.
Contact based on self-pity.

DEPRESSION

Figure 11: From drama triangle to supportive connections (Source: SQ Bewust)

You can escape the position of victim by further analysing your own actions and thoughts.

Is it true if I say that I couldn't do anything about it myself? Is it true that the other person was to blame, or the circumstances? Or is it possible for me to look at the situation differently? Can I succeed in asking for help instead of drowning myself in self-pity? What would happen if I focused on what I can do instead of constantly searching for evidence to prove I am unable to choose or undertake something myself?

The invitation is to experiment and to accept the consequences of your own actions. As a result, your position as victim (in the domain of depression) shifts to that of the researcher (in the domain of self-confidence).

The position of the rescuer can be turned around by refusing to accept the responsibility for the other, by no longer resolving the issues of others by relieving them of tasks or by seeking contact based on pity.

Instead, teach others to become independent and skillful themselves, and allow others to make their own choices. Adopt a caring and concerned attitude when you do this. Instead of acting based on frustration and despair, we must act based on fulfilment (not to be confused with satisfaction). In the domain of fulfilment, your position shifts from the rescuer to more of a coach.

APPLICATION IN PRACTISE
Focus attention on the here and now
A condition for creating powerful connections is to focus on the other in the here and now.

It's only when you can be physically and mentally completely present in the moment that a true meeting can take place in the here and now. That's when you can reflect on and respond at both the level of content (human doing) and the level of feeling (human being), based on what there is *now*. The other will feel and experience it, and it will help build mutual trust. By doing so you are sending out the message: I see you, I take you seriously, I want to understand you, and I am here for you. This requires you to be fully present and therefore to temporarily let go of thinking about the past ('If I had only…') and the future ('I would like so much to…').

Let it clash, let it flow
In collaborations with others, you will notice that sometimes there will be a clash, and at other times things will flow. If things continually clash, in the long term this will often lead to the connection being broken. There may be various causes for this. It may be that you hope or want something completely different from what the other hopes or wants – a mismatch in expectations.

It can also be that you and the other are actually the same, and you therefore repel each other like opposite poles of a magnet. For example, think of a situation in which you both want to be dominant over the other. Or, perhaps, a time when you both want to adopt a subordinate attitude with regard to the other. Because you both want to follow the same pattern, you are both waiting for the other to make a move.

In contrast, if things are flowing, there are no obstructions and the connection will be able to find its own way. There is a will to collaborate, to find out where the connection reinforces each other's autonomy and to achieve powerful results together. To this end, diversity and a different approach to thinking and acting, amongst other things, are embraced. Being different leads to new insights and solutions for business issues.

Learning from the other

There are many people who, over the years – thanks, for example, to therapy, leadership training, coaching sessions, 360-degree feedback sessions, or via a *vision quest* – have developed a more complete picture of themselves.

The obvious question is, of course, what are you going to do with those insights? How will you use these to make a difference in your contact with the other person? Simultaneously, the connection with the other is also a useful source for confirming an insight or discovering something new about yourself.

For instance, what do you learn about yourself in the connection with the other? What do you become irritated about and what does this tell you about yourself? What do you recognize in the other that is important for you, which results in you becoming attracted to him? How is it that the contact between you runs smoothly on the one occasion, and that on another occasion you would prefer to be left on your own? And, in this situation, are the mutual dynamics and your own thoughts, feelings and actions open for discussion in an honest and transparent manner?

In the case of the above-mentioned clash, this works as a de-escalation, while reinforcing a flow. In both cases, the result will be a deeper connection and more self-insight for both parties.

The other, myself and the context

It is wise not to consider the relation between the other and yourself as purely two-way traffic. Add the context as a third factor. The context can pertain to both the work situation (for example, KPIs, work agreements and goals) and the personal situation (family, sports club, community). By including the context, you realize that the connection with the other is not a goal in itself. The connection is a means of contributing to the context in the correct way. If the context is clearly defined, you often suddenly realize what you have to do within that relation and the context.

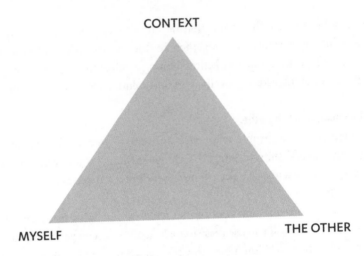

Figure 12: Connection between myself and the other in relation to the context

In the fourteen chapters in Part II, we will be looking particularly at the connection between the other and you, within the context. And then, we will look for that which connects and enriches you both. We are looking for the '1 + 1 = at least 3. How big do you dare to dream?

HOW TO READ THIS PART OF THE BOOK

As in Part I, Part II again contains many assignments, theories and sources of inspiration. They will help you to further explore and develop yourself in connection with the other.

The first seven chapters in this section have been written predominantly from the viewpoint of the leader *as a person* (Human Being). The last seven chapters have been written largely from the standpoint of the leader *as a role* (Human Doing).

Each chapter again starts with a personal introduction. In these introductions, I will indicate how, based on your personal insights – concerning, for example, the way you deal with conflicts, trust within a relationship, friendship, empathy and listening skills – you can weave these into your daily practice as a leader.

In each chapter, a lot of attention will be paid to the question of how you can get the acquired insights to work *for* you in your organization.

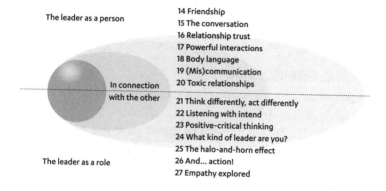

Figure 13: Overview of chapters in Part II

I wish you an excellent connection with the other.

CHAPTER 14

FRIENDSHIP

PERSONAL INTRODUCTION

Most people can count how many best friends they have on the fingers of one hand. Well, that's true for me in any case. I've got three: Anton, Erwin and Gerhard. They're the friends I've shared good and bad times with, the people I feel comfortable with, with whom I can laugh and cry. They accept me unconditionally for who I am, regardless of whatever I do.

At least once a year, the four of us go off on a trip together. One of these trips took us to Prague, where we had a wonderful discussion about our friendship, accompanied by large glasses of beer and multiple sausages. We talked intensely about what had kept us together for the past 25 years – and what irritated us about each other. The honest and open conversations we had, including the laughter and tears, served to make our friendship even more intense.

I'm convinced that conducting these kinds of sincere discussions (even though they can be tense), either in a private or professional context, is crucial if you want to create and maintain lasting connections.

THE HUMAN BEING AS A SOCIAL CREATURE

Let's imagine you've got everything you could possibly wish for: a lovely house, more than enough money to live on, vacations whenever you want and good health. At least, it seems that you've got everything you could want… but you don't have anyone to share it with. Is it then possible for you to still be happy?

Not according to the American psychologist Roy Baumeister (1995). He asserted that contact with others is crucial within our existence. In fact, we have the primeval need to belong, and to engage in a long-term relationship with people we can trust and who we can have fun with. It is one of our strongest drives. Baumeister showed, among other things, that our fear of being rejected and of being left on our own is greater than our fear of dying. And, he suggested, this is something we actually think about several times a day.

The fear of being alone can also be explained as a matter of evolution. Being part of a group gave us a greater chance of survival. Aside from this practical aspect, friendships also have many other positive effects. For example, Australian researchers have shown that having good friends contributes to a healthier and longer life (Giles, et al., 2005). The same applies to having good family relations. However, the link between good health and friendships is much stronger than that between family members.

Another study (Miller, 2014) shows that not having friends is just as bad for your health as smoking and being overweight. Friendships are a matter of life and death!

KEEPING FRIENDSHIPS OPEN FOR DISCUSSION

Breaking up friendships is an art in itself. While you wouldn't think twice about driving a hundred kilometres to see a true friend, a short telephone call with a friend who's less close to you may prove irritating. At the end of the call, you may feel you have less energy than before you made the call. And the next time that person calls, you deliberately don't pick up the phone. Or, you say, 'Let's arrange to meet soon', but – consciously or unconsciously – you put off contacting them for as long as possible.

If you notice that a friendship has become less intense, do you discuss that with the person concerned? You don't want to hurt that person's feelings, but the other side of the coin is that it's costing you energy. Would you rather bring the relationship to an end radically, or allow it to die a slow death? Either way, ultimately, you will not be doing the friendship justice. On top of that, there's a chance that you will hurt someone's feelings. Is it worth it to you?

FRIENDSHIP AND LEADERSHIP

As a leader, you are expected to engage in a functional connection with your colleagues. Your role exists (as is the case with teams and organizations) to achieve results.

To this end, rational frameworks such as goals, tasks, responsibilities and authorities are defined for and by you. Additionally, organizations and teams consist of people who collaborate within the rational frameworks you have created. And wherever people work together, issues will arise concerning themes such as trust, diversity, respect and dealing with conflicts – all things that you as a leader will also need to focus attention on. At their core, these kinds of themes are about emotional connections. As I indicated earlier in this chapter, this is a deep-rooted human need.

As a leader, you are thus expected to create and maintain both your functional *and* your emotional connections. And that's not something you can do purely through logical reasoning. You will have to engage with your connections with your whole being. The distinction between the function and the individual as a whole is purely artificial. The connection therefore takes place based on the leader as a role *and* on the leader as a person.

If you bring your whole being into your role as leader, and make maximum use of your CQ, your relationships in the workplace will not be purely businesslike. You will be working increasingly with elements that typically play a role in regular friendships. For example, there will be the desire to work on the basis of trust, engaging in sincere connection, knowing that you can rely on each other, and being able to express your opinion about the other person openly and honestly – and to discuss this at an early stage if the work relationship shows signs of tension. This way, your leadership contributes positively to the relations on the work floor in terms of health – both yours and that of the other person.

ASSIGNMENT: Friendship on the work floor

What is the current state of your friendships? How sincere are you about the quality of the relationships?

Have an open and honest discussion about this with a few of your friends. Ask them why they are friends with you. What is it about you that attracts them, so that they are willing to spend time and energy in your relationship? And what would they like you to change, or display more or less of? Next, switch roles and ask yourself these same questions. Express your thoughts and feelings explicitly.

Compare the insights about your friendships with those of your work environment. In your work, do you, as a leader, make use of elements that characterize your personal friendships? Do you make a conscious choice to use or not use these elements in your work? Which element could you (or would you dare to) make more use of in your relationship with your colleagues or clients? And what impact does this have on your connection with the other person?

Friendships can't be forced: friends need to continue to invest in the connection with their whole being.

CHAPTER 15

THE CONVERSATION

PERSONAL INTRODUCTION

A client of mine summarized my style of working with the metaphor: "You're a velvet fist." He appreciated the velvet, and he appreciated the fist.

But my style hasn't always been successful with all my clients. For example, I remember working with a management team that was experiencing high turnover. The CEO described himself as a true team player, yet in meetings I observed a different side to him. True, he would ask questions, but only to gather information and form his own picture of the situation. Based on this, he would tell the others what to do in a directive manner. That's not really the picture that comes to mind when I think of a team player.

During a meeting in which the whole team was present, I explicitly mentioned this pattern I had observed. He took it as a personal attack, which led to an awkward situation that lasted some ten minutes. After that, the meeting continued as normal. Later, I was told by the client organization's HR manager that I had been declared persona non grata by the CEO. It was a moment both of pain (I wanted to achieve a connection with everyone and to provide added value) and of pride (I was aligned with my core values), as well as being a learning moment (considering his character, it would have been better to discuss his pattern in a one-on-one).

The way in which this CEO conducted discussions is an example of the first of the four levels of conversation. At the moment I confronted him with this, I myself was stuck at level 2 – not the ideal combination, as we shall see. This is especially significant when you consider that to create lasting connections, you need to be operating at levels 3 and/or 4. Interested in learning more about this topic? Then read this chapter.

CHIT-CHAT

It's Monday morning and you walk into the meeting room:
- "Hi Peter, how was your weekend?"

- "Great, and yours?"
- "Fine, thanks. What's on the agenda today?"

And the conversation then switches immediately to work.

Sound familiar? We call these sorts of exchanges of pleasantries 'chit-chat.' Communication occurs based on unwritten rules. The example above is a ritual that takes place when people meet, and there's a range of variations on the theme. For example, the common response to the question 'How are you?' is 'Fine, thanks.' But what would you say if you're not feeling all that well? In chit-chat, you would keep it to yourself because telling the other person how you're really feeling 'is not done'. And, you have to ask yourself whether they would even listen, or care, if you told the truth.

Chit-chat has its role during the first contact, and for creating a connection between individuals. To deepen the connection, though, other conversations are usually required.

FOUR CONVERSATION LEVELS

The academic Otto Scharmer (2009) has plotted out four levels at which conversations take place. These levels – downloading, debate, dialogue and presencing – require you to approach each other with increased degrees of openness, leading to an increase in the intensity of the connection.

Level 1: Downloading

An example of a conversation at the first level is a meeting where questions are asked with the specific aim of extracting information. For example, the project manager who wants to know if the project is on schedule starts asking questions about the progress being made. He may indicate that he's only interested in the answer to his question and doesn't want to hear any disagreements or other issues. His aim is to form his own picture, based on the answers he receives and his experience from the past, and to make decisions and issue instructions based on this.

During the download conversation, a sort of question and answer game develops – almost an interrogation, in fact. This typically has a negative impact on the connection. In general, it leads to the answers being less open and transparent. And the bigger the gap between what is said in conversation ('We're on track') and the truth ('We can't seem to solve the problem'), the bigger the chance that the wrong choices will be made.

Level 2: Debate

Then there's the second level of conversation: the debate. At this level, the participants say openly what they feel and think, rather than simply going along with the prevailing idea of the other person. Deviating standpoints are possible. In fact, these standpoints are positively encouraged because they can help persuade the other party to accept your better idea.

However, if your own insights are so important for you that you have no intention of deviating from them, this second level also has a darker side. Instead of a truly open and honest conversation, a debate can arise, complete with deeply entrenched standpoints. The aim of the debate becomes convincing the other party that you are right. You listen purely with a view to identifying elements that are incorrect, looking for any flaws in the reasoning so that you can undermine their argument. A struggle ensues in which rhetorical tricks are exchanged. Instead of playing hard on the ball, it's the individual that gets hit hard. The result is one winner and one loser, the relationship becomes rigid, and in the long term it is no longer tenable.

Level 3: Dialogue

The third conversation level is that of the dialogue. Here again, there are various viewpoints, but this time you will be listening with the aim of understanding the other person. You will no longer be trying to 'beat' the opposite viewpoint but instead listening with empathy and genuine interest. This will provide you with new insights. The next step in a dialogue is to continue to try to see what these new insights mean for your own viewpoint. At this third level, you are essentially looking through the eyes of the other person rather than being preoccupied with defending the standpoint you have adopted at all costs (level 2).

If you're not used to engaging in a true dialogue, you may find it extremely difficult to make the transition from level 2 to level 3. A dialogue requires a willingness to really listen to the other person in a non-judgmental way. It requires you to detach yourself temporarily from your own truth and to go in search of the truth in the other person's words. By doing this, you are acknowledging his thoughts and opinions (which doesn't necessarily mean that you are accepting that the other person is right).

Once you know the other person's views, the reasoning behind them, the motivations that lie at their root, the pain from the past, the interests, the motives, etc., you can then look for the commonalities. And, you can jointly make them explicit and leave them to one side. You then look for the differences and determine what these differences mean. You look for solutions together.

This temporary release from your own train of thought and convictions may feel like a defeat for you and your own 'position'. If you are already in a conflict situation with the other person, this transition will be even more difficult to make. People often find themselves at an impasse, thinking that the other person has to acknowledge them first before they start listening to him. However logical this emotional reaction may seem, if you really want to resolve the conflict, one or both of you will need to let go of the need to feel acknowledged and be willing to make the transition to level 3. If neither party succeeds in doing this, there's a chance that the conflict will remain unresolved and both of you end up being losers.

Level 4: Presencing

And then, we have the fourth conversation level: presencing. At this level, all parties let go of their own opinions and self-reflections. The conversation is about what the group considers important without the topic of discussion necessarily being explicitly mentioned. A feeling of a unique and deep connection between you and the other participants is created, resulting in you being able to let go of reality completely. The aim is to create new insights in collaboration with the others, with the connection and open conversation style as the starting point.

Relations and groups are able to constantly return to this conversation level the more often they have experienced it. You could compare it to the feeling of connection or bonding that exists with good friends. Even though you haven't seen each other for years, as soon as you meet, you hit it off and that special bond is there again.

ASSIGNMENT: Yesss! A conflict!

A conflict is something to celebrate, because it is an indication of commitment. It is a sign that someone in your professional or personal life is willing to adopt a viewpoint. Apparently, the topic is important enough to fight for. If you then engage in a conversation to resolve the conflict, you raise both the conversation level you are speaking at and the intention with which you are speaking. That greatly increases the chance of a positive result.

The way in which you run through the process, from conflict to resolution, contributes to building up a lasting relationship.

Who do you have a conflict with at the moment? Take a good look at the conversation level you (and not the other person) are conducting the conversation at. What would the conversation look like if you were speaking at the next level? Take action and ignore the emotional blockage that keeps you stuck at the current level.

Let's stop talking and start having conversations.

CHAPTER 16

RELATIONSHIP TRUST

PERSONAL INTRODUCTION

In the past, I was strongly driven by the fear of rejection. The result was that I showed my respect for people by pleasing. But this isn't really showing respect. It's more of a (subconscious) rational behaviour I adopted in order to get something in return. I gave because I wanted ultimately to gain emotionally.

Today, when I give respect, it's no longer predominantly about me. At least, not generally. Of course, I have my ego moments. For instance, when I'm on stage I enjoy being the centre of attention, but I've discovered how much I enjoy genuinely seeing others for who they are, and respecting them for that. Being able to contribute to this gives me tremendous energy. So yes, I do become a better person through it. The difference is that it's no longer my primary motivation, but more of an enjoyable by-product.

What this turnaround has brought about, among other things, is that I have learned to trust myself and to respect myself for who I am, including both my positive aspects *and* my dark ones. The more I can trust myself, the less confirmation I need from others. In other words, if I genuinely respect myself, I can also genuinely respect others.

This impact on myself has an impact on others. It contributes to building trust in the relationship.

Stephen Covey specifies 'showing respect' as one of the 13 behaviours that lead to relationship trust. Relationship trust is the logical next step after trust in oneself and is essential if you want to create lasting connections. And as a manager, you work with people with whom you enter into a connection and contribute to their engagement in mutual connections. From this perspective, it's important to know more about this topic. This chapter will give you valuable insights.

BEHAVIOUR AS A BASIS FOR RELATIONSHIP TRUST

Covey states that trust is the most essential ingredient within every relationship.

Today, changes occur increasingly quickly. And so, commitment on the part of employees and managers is more crucial than ever. This way, the value we should attach to mutual trust increases even more. According to Covey, it's the most important, and yet most undervalued, ingredient for business success.

In Chapter 12 ('Trust in yourself'), I described the four core themes that form the basis for self-confidence: intention, integrity, capacities and results (Covey, 2008). In this chapter, I describe the 13 behaviours that create trust in relation to another person (also based on Covey's ideas). This is about the behaviour you demonstrate. But before you start reading, I want to give you a few tips on what to watch out for:

- Just as with using your core qualities, when we look at behaviours, using any of them excessively will not be effective
- The 13 behaviours complement each other, creating a balance in your actions and an impact on the other person. For example, always 'talking straight' will result in the impact of the bull in a china shop. By adding two behaviours – 'listen first' and 'demonstrate respect' – you will create an effective mix.
- The first five behaviours deal with your own character. Abusing one or more of these five is the quickest way to disrupt mutual trust.
- The next five behaviours deal with your competencies. It's good to know that demonstrating these behaviours is the quickest way to build up relationship trust.
- The last three behaviours are a combination of both character traits and competencies.

Character	Competence
1 Talk straight	6 Get better
2 Demonstrate respect	7 Confront reality
3 Show loyalty	8 Clarify expectations
4 Create transparency	9 Practise accountability
5 Right wrongs	10 Deliver results
11 Listen first	
12 Keep commitments	
13 Extend trust	

Figure 14: Thirteen behaviours that create relationship trust

Behaviour 1: Talk straight (character)

Be open and honest. Speak the truth and try not to appear better than you are. If, for example, you've done something wrong, don't try to think up a smart reason that will let you off the hook. Just truthfully mention why you didn't keep to your agreement. And, don't forget that a half-truth is a lie.

Behaviour 2: Demonstrate respect (character)

Demonstrating respect means showing sincerely that you accept someone as being a worthy and valued individual. It has nothing to do with some-one's functional position, or whether he can be of use to you. Whether someone is a manager or a cleaner, a team leader or a receptionist, they all contribute to the success of the organization. Demonstrating respect is often a question of the little things: looking a person in the eye, saying thank you, holding the door open for someone, or addressing them by their first name.

Behaviour 3: Show loyalty (character)

If your employees have achieved a fantastic result, do you give them the honour they deserve for their work? Or, do you steal the spotlight for yourself? Be sincere, stand for and behind your colleagues, and be proud of them. Tell them explicitly, and tell others. Conversely, be reserved in your criticism of your colleagues in the presence of others. If you do need to be critical or negative about others, do this when the person in question is present, or discuss beforehand what you intend to bring to the table.

Behaviour 4: Create transparency (character)

Did you know that six out of ten employees are not satisfied with their manager? This often has to do with a lack of transparency, perhaps because the managers don't admit their mistakes, or don't dare to. Or, it can be because they aren't open about bad news within the organization. Instead, you need to be crystal-clear wherever possible. Be transparent about those things you might be afraid that you can't be transparent about. And remember that being transparent yourself is an invitation to others to create more transparency in their contact with you.

Behaviour 5: Right wrongs (character)

If you make a mistake, accept responsibility for it. Explore how you can put it right. Don't wait too long but establish what you can do immediately. Don't forget to say a genuine 'sorry'. You may find this awkward, but if you can manage to put your ego to one side, it will pay off big time.

Behaviour 6: Get better (competence)

Are you the kind of person who wants to continue learning throughout your life; who dares to take risks, asks for feedback and learns from his mistakes; who expresses his gratitude when he receives feedback? By adopting this attitude in life, you will not only learn more, but you will also be an example to others. That's a wonderful foundation to enable a team and organization to become increasingly powerful.

Behaviour 7: Confront reality (competence)

Everyone goes through difficult times now and then. The question is, what do you do in such a situation? Do you beat around the bush and put off doing the tasks you should be doing, or do you tackle the difficult tasks straight away? Don't bury your head in the sand, but say explicitly what you find difficult, look for assistance and start resolving the situation.

Behaviour 8: Clarify expectations (competence)

What do you expect from your employees? Make clear-cut agreements about what needs to be done and the corresponding behaviour. If you express your expectations, don't forget to check with the other person whether they have understood, and that they know they can act on them in their own way. Be as clear and concrete as possible. In other words, make them SMART: specific, measurable, achievable, relevant and timebound.

Behaviour 9: Practise accountability (competence)

Take responsibility for your own results and hold others accountable for their responsibilities. If things aren't going the way you want them to, don't point the finger at others, but take action yourself. Don't walk away from your agreements. Be open towards others holding you accountable for your responsibilities.

Behaviour 10: Deliver results (competence)

The road to hell is paved with good intentions. Intentions are fine, but ultimately, it's all about results. That's why your team and function exist. Build on a solid track record by delivering what has been agreed upon, within the time and budget allocated. Don't over-promise and don't under-deliver.

Behaviour 11: Listen first (combination of character and competence)

What happens in terms of leadership and your possibilities as a leader when you stop transmitting? What becomes possible when you ask questions and listen to the answers instead? If, instead of delivering a monologue or debating, you create a dialogue? If you are sincerely willing to understand the non-standard viewpoints and insights of others? If you adopt this attitude, you will be working on the third level of conversation (dialogue) as described in Chapter 15.

Behaviour 12: Keep commitments (combination of character and competence)

'Agreed is agreed.' I tend to hear this kind of statement in environments where agreements are not automatically fulfilled. Fulfilling simple agreements is generally not that much of a problem, but it's a different story when it comes to more complex or politically sensitive issues. When you find yourself in such a situation, be honest and transparent. If you already know beforehand that you won't be able to keep a promise, or you realize at some point that you won't be able to fulfil it, just go ahead and admit it. Be the one to come up with solutions and be open to other people's ideas for solutions. Focus on the future, and on how to deal with the situation from now on in as constructive a way as possible.

Behaviour 13: Extend trust (combination of character and competence)

Show that you fundamentally trust people instead of basing your actions on minimizing risks. People who have fully earned your trust can give it you in abundance. When it comes to those who are still earning it, give them just a little more than they're used to. With those you're not sure about – for instance, if there's a question about how effectively they'll collaborate – base the trust you extend on the situation, the risk and the credibility you experience. At the same time, don't forget to continue to trust your gut feeling.

ASSIGNMENT: Extending relationship trust

Relationship trust derives from behaviour you demonstrate. What you do, both privately and professionally, ultimately has much more impact within your relationships than what you say. Or, as the old expression goes: 'Empty vessels make the most noise.'

This exercise asks you to reflect on how you respond to the behaviours specified above.

Read through all 13 behaviours and rate yourself on a scale from one to ten. You can also ask someone else to tell you how they rate you. A one means that you don't demonstrate this behaviour at all, and a ten means that you act completely in line with this behaviour. When your list is complete – and if you've had one compiled by another person – note how satisfied you are with your current scores. Is there a difference between your list and that of the other person? If so, there's a real opportunity for you to gain insight into your blind spot.

For all behaviours, make a note of how you would like to score in six months' time. And then, start experimenting with your behaviour. What are you actually going to do? Who will you ask for feedback on the impact of your changed behaviour on his relationship trust?

Trust is of immeasurable value. Will you be the first to give it?

CHAPTER 17

POWERFUL INTERACTIONS

PERSONAL INTRODUCTION

After graduating from the Dutch Royal Military Academy, I was trained to become an intercept controller and learned to guide fighter aircraft to their aerial targets. I guided Dutch pilots and those of our NATO allies – via radar and radio – during aerial defence manoeuvres and aerial combat.

The job came with high levels of responsibility and extreme peak loads. I enjoyed it initially, but I realized very quickly that it wasn't the career for me. The focus lay too much on developing routines and 'just' executing your task. I yearned for a job with more variety and dynamics.

During my period as an intercept controller, I developed an interest in business and began studying the subject at the Radboud University Nijmegen in my spare time. My manager at the Defence Department knew about my education, as well as my dissatisfaction with being an intercept controller. So, he gave me the opportunity to work on an organizational change.

In addition to a valuable lesson in leadership ('Give people responsibilities that match their interests'), this was a perfect chance to apply the knowledge I was acquiring and to learn more about how organizations work.

As an enthusiastic amateur in the field of organizational change, I constructed ambitious plans and deadlines to implement the changes. And, I expected that others would cooperate in executing these plans out of a sense of loyalty, especially if they had agreed to them. The reality was of course much less simple.

What I learned during that period is that organizations are made up of people, and people want to be seen and heard when it comes to implementing change. That means you need to get onto the work floor, make contact with them and engage in a dialogue. These conversations create the opportunity to build your message based on their answers and create a basis for change.

I also learned the distinction between nice interactions and powerful interactions. In this chapter I want to share with you my most important insights.

MULTIPLE INTERACTIONS A DAY

Interactions form the basis for creating a connection with the other, organizing work, making joint decisions, etc. Your whole day is a constant stream of interactions. And the more powerful these are, the more impact they will have on the connection and collaboration processes. To support you in creating powerful interactions, I have selected eight tips you can apply right now.

Tip 1: Getting from 'but' to 'and'

Some words in our language have an enormous impact on the effectiveness of our interactions. For example: 'You did a good job, but next time, make sure you deliver on time.' By using the word 'but', the focus switches to the second part of the sentence and this is perceived as a judgment. Or, as the old expression so beautifully puts it: *Everything before 'but' is a lie.* It's more powerful to make use of the 'and' word. This has a connecting influence and lends a positive charge to the second part of the sentence. 'You did a good job, and next time, make sure you deliver on time.'

Tip 2: Getting from 'why' to 'what makes'

Another word that has a lot of impact on the effectiveness of interactions is the 'why' word. For example: 'Why did you choose Laura as your replacement?' It gives the other person the feeling that what he did wasn't right and that he has to justify his decision. And yes, of course it depends a lot on your tone, your intonation and your non-verbal communication whether or not the question you start with 'why' is received in this way. It's more powerful to start your question with 'what makes.' For example: 'What made you choose Laura as your replacement?' 'What makes' usually comes across as being more positive. This construction is typical for an inquiring and researching attitude, inviting a reply and maintaining the connection.

Tip 3: Getting from 'would not' to 'would'

A lot of people have trouble answering the question of what they would like to change about their work. If they have an answer, they very soon start talking in terms of what they don't want anymore. For example: 'I wouldn't work overtime anymore.' These 'would not' answers generally fail to produce any positive energy. Instead of specifying what you want to get away from, it's much more powerful to indicate where you want to get to. For example: 'I would like to work from home every Friday afternoon.' You can almost feel the energy in that statement. If your conversation partner starts talking about the 'would not' side, stop them in mid-sentence and ask: 'And what *would* you like to do?'

Tip 4: Getting from 'we' to 'I'

When talking with team members about what works well and what could be improved – for example, in the collaboration within the team – people very soon tend to switch to talking in the 'safe' mode. By this I mean that instead of saying what they really think, they make use of generalizations. Instead of 'I don't take people to account,' a team member will say: '*We* don't take each other to account.' The general statement is of course important. But, it doesn't alter the fact that the more someone formulates in the 'I' form, the more responsibility he takes for his actions and the greater the chance that he'll actually start to make changes himself. Therefore, if people are talking in general terms, ask them to talk from their own point of view, starting with 'I.'

Tip 5: Getting from passive to active

As soon as the subject turns to personal responsibility, a lot of people switch to talking in the passive voice. They say: 'A lot of gossiping is happening, something should be done about it.' This is quite a passive, not very concrete, statement. But it *is* based on a good observation. It becomes a little less passive if someone says: 'I should really do something if people are gossiping.' There is a positive intention embedded in this statement. Build on this constructively. The vagueness of the follow-up allows a person to remain passive and not take action. You can easily change this if you say: 'From now on, I'm going to ask anyone who starts gossiping to justify their behaviour.' This is what I call making results-based use of active language. So, next time you're in conversation with others, ask them what they will do.

Tip 6: Getting from behaviour to intention

One reason irritations arise is that other people demonstrate behaviour that you consider unacceptable. For example, an employee might keep asking you whether the next step in a certain project is the right one.

You could call that person to account by telling him that this really has to change. But it's unlikely that he will change his behaviour. It's more powerful to ask him what he intends by constantly raising this question: 'What makes you always check the next step with me?' This way, you will discover what motivates him and you can start a conversation around this. You are tackling the core problem and not just its external manifestation.

Tip 7: Getting from the general to the specific

Good feedback contributes to the growth of the other. A statement such as 'You did well' isn't really helpful. It's too general and doesn't tell the other person what you are talking about. What is meant by 'did' and what does 'well' mean exactly? It's more powerful to specifically indicate what you have observed, what the other person should continue doing, and what could be improved. For example: 'Your report about yesterday's incident is factual and clearly formulated. This gives me confidence in you. And next time, I'd like to see you also suggest a possible solution.'

Tip 8: Getting from compliment to acknowledgement

If someone hands out a compliment, it's usually about a result that has been achieved. For example: 'Great that you managed to supply the data today.' These compliments are important – carry on giving them and ensure that you mean them. Yet, acknowledging someone's qualities would be even more powerful and would really hit home. So, instead of only focusing on the functional behaviour, you need to mention explicitly the qualities you see in the other person. For example, 'You are trustworthy' or 'You are genuine.' This way, the other person is seen as a human being and not just as a production machine.

ASSIGNMENT: Eating a bit of elephant

How do you eat an elephant? Bit by bit. Relating this to personal development, the essence is as follows: instead of focusing on implementing many changes all at once, and wanting to execute them perfectly, choose a single change that you want to implement. Choose a change that you know you are interested in, or that you expect will have a big impact on the desired goal. Once you've chosen the change, take action.

Experiment and reflect until you understand the essence of the change and the change has become part of your thinking, attitude and behaviour. Then choose the next change, and so on.

If you re-read the eight tips above (I'm sure you can add a few of your own), which single tip will you start experimenting with in your interactions? What makes you choose that particular approach? What impact do you expect this will have on yourself and the other if you start to apply it in practise?

How and when will you actually start? What does that look like and who can help you achieve it? And now... action!

Open and honest interactions are an inexhaustible source of connection and form the basis for organizational change.

CHAPTER 18

BODY LANGUAGE

PERSONAL INTRODUCTION

I love dancing. When I go out, you'll see me on the dance floor for most of the evening. It puts a smile on my face, I enjoy it intensely and my behaviour quite often also evokes a positive response from others. What I'm doing is engaging in a wordless conversation.

My youngest daughter, Erin, has also been infected by the dance bug. She dances literally all day long. She started with toddler dancing and then went on to ballet. From the age of eight she's been dancing in a hip hop group together with 20 girls and two boys. They take part in contests, performing solo, in duets, and with the whole group. It's fantastic to see how she gets totally immersed in her dance. I'm so proud of her.

When the TV programme *So You Think You Can Dance* is on the air again, you'll find me on my settee. Full of admiration (and occasionally envy), I'll watch the dancers showing off their talents. And what I notice every time is that although some of the participants are good dancers, I'm not moved by what I see. With other performances, I sit there with tears in my eyes. What is it that makes the difference? It's not about the technical movements, but rather about the emotions that the dancers put into their movements.

Sometimes I feel as though I'm watching an instruction book, and sometimes a dancer tells me a whole story. He expresses it all through his body language, and when that happens, it's amazing to watch.

Body language is an important aspect when it comes to genuine connection with the other. If you can feel a story, really experience it and then start to talk, you will not only be telling it word for word, but your whole body will become part of it. And this has a huge impact. That's what this chapter is about.

NON-VERBAL COMMUNICATION

What percentage of our communication do we express non-verbally? A brief search on the internet will unearth a range of answers. It could be 70%, 80% or even 90%, depending what you read.

Trainers and coaches will refer to research done by, among others, Professor Albert Mehrabian (1981), indicating that 93% of our communication is non-verbal, and just 7% is the result of the words we use. Does this mean then that words are of little importance? Can we stop learning foreign languages because we will be able to understand what the other person means just from their body language? Of course not.

What consistently happens with the data from Mehrabian's study is that the conclusions of his research are quoted out of context.

ESSENTIAL QUESTION OF MEHRABIAN'S STUDY

The essential question posed by Mehrabian's work was what people base their trust on when they observe differences between verbal and non-verbal signals in the person they are engaged in conversation with, when the other person is talking about his *feelings* or his *opinion* about a specific topic? For example, when you tell your colleague you agree with his proposal, but you say this with a taut mouth, using short sentences and mumbling, frowning and looking away, what message will your colleague pick up? Does he believe you, based on the words you use, or does he form another opinion based on your non-verbal communication? Mehrabian's study revealed that in these kinds of situations, in 7% of the cases the opinion of the listener is formed based on words, 38% on tonality (speed of speech, tone level, volume) and 55% on the facial expression.

So, when you talk about your feelings and opinions, the person you talk to tends to primarily believe you based on what they think they're observing in your non-verbal behaviour. That's the message from Mehrabian's study. This relationship can also apply in all other types of conversations, but it is not evident from the study.

What can we conclude from this? It means that if you're engaged in a conversation in which you want to make a good impression, and increase the chance that people will believe what you're saying, you should ensure that your verbal and non-verbal behaviour are in alignment with each other.

WORDS ARE IMPORTANT

Let me stress again that words still play a major role in communication (and not just 7%!). For example, if you're giving a presentation where you're trying to get a message across, then it's important that what you say expresses the content accurately. In fact, it is even claimed that in one-to-one sales talks or negotiations, words are much more important than we generally assume.

It's been said that, globally speaking, verbal communication counts for half, non-verbal for one-third and tonality for the remaining one-sixth. Although intuitively I would agree, I haven't managed to find any information to substantiate this. If you happen to have proof, I'd like to hear from you!

LEARN TO READ BODY LANGUAGE

Based on a person's non-verbal behaviour, you may not believe them, despite their eloquent words. Or, quite the opposite may happen – even though someone's story isn't that well-structured or convincing, you may feel you can trust him. The better you're able to read body language, the better you'll be able to assess the meaning of what someone is saying.

To get started, search the internet to explore this topic. You'll find a lot of background information and you can do several tests to see how accurately you can read body language.

ASSIGNMENT: Modelling your new you

This exercise is based on a technique from neurolinguistic programming (NLP), called modelling. The technique is based on the principle that if someone else can do it, I can learn to do it too. Once you know what you want to learn, you look for experts in your environment who can already do it. And then you perform three steps: observe, code and install.

1. **Observe**. Who are the people in your business environment who are experts in engaging in powerful relationships with others? Observe these people in the coming weeks. How do they stand, what distance do they keep with respect to others, what hand gestures do they make, how quickly and with what intonation do they speak, what do

you see happening in their faces, and so on? Speak to these experts to hear what they think, what their convictions are and what emotions they experience.

2. **Code**. What pattern do you notice in your observations of these experts and their conversations? Which inner strategies did you hear, how did they use body language, how did they make contact, etc.?

3. **Install**. Apply the same coding. Simply copy and paste, as if they are your own lines of thought and actions. Think, feel, observe, talk, stand and breathe just like the experts. Be curious about the impact on yourself and the person you're addressing. What has changed in your thinking and behaviour? How does the other person respond to the new you? Do you create the same powerful connections as the experts? If not, repeat steps 1 and 2 and fine-tune them until you're satisfied with the results of your efforts.

Can you see the difference between someone with a heart without words, and someone with words without a heart?

CHAPTER 19

(MIS)COMMUNICATION

PERSONAL INTRODUCTION

My son Frank has been diagnosed with Asperger Syndrome, and I'm still learning what that means.

Simple communication protocols that are 'normal' to you and me are harder for him to understand. For example, one Saturday morning I was holding the electric toaster in my hand, and while he was eating his sandwich, I asked him if he wanted to eat some more. Of course, what I was asking was if he still wanted to use the toaster, or if I could put it away. Yet, because of the literal way in which he thinks, he interpreted my question differently. He told me that he still wanted to eat his sandwich (which he was holding in his hand). All in all, a wonderful example of miscommunication.

In our family, we're learning about the impact of Asperger on each of our lives – and even more so, on that of my son. The upside of this is that we're all learning how we can communicate effectively with each other, and we keep learning that communicating doesn't automatically mean understanding.

In all the interactions with the people I have contact with, both privately and professionally, the chance of miscommunication is always present (and it actually also happens with some degree of regularity). Conversely, it's important that I continue to consciously check whether the other person and I understand each other, especially when we're discussing a topic that's important for either or both of us.

This basic attitude helps to create genuine and lasting connections between people. This chapter covers this insight in detail.

WATCHING PEOPLE

Isn't it fun to sit on a terrace and watch the people go by? And, of course, we form an opinion about them based on their facial expressions, the way they use their hands, the way they walk, the clothes they're wearing, their perfume, etc. This is actually what we do all the time. We are constantly interpreting what we see, hear, feel, taste and smell, and we decide for ourselves that this is the reality. *Our* perception is *our* reality.

WE THINK IN IMAGES

The same things that happen on the terrace also happen with language. We use language to communicate with each other, and in doing so, we occasionally miss a beat because we assume the other person understands what we mean. Sometimes this works fine, and at other times it doesn't.

Our brain converts the spoken or written language from the external world into meaning and images, while attaching an *emotion* to it based on experiences. For example, if I ask you what the word 'dog' means, you will immediately have a picture in your mind (for example, of a pit bull). And if I then ask you to give a unique definition of the word 'dog', you will come up with something fairly accurate. But the question is whether your definition also applies to *my* dog. When I think of a dog, I picture Pablo, the black-and-white cocker spaniel with long drooping ears and short tail I grew up with. The fact that we both attach a different image and a different meaning to one specific word can therefore lead to confusion. This is where the core of miscommunication is born.

FEELING ALSO PLAYS A ROLE

Leaving aside the image and meaning I have in my mind, the word 'dog' evokes a feeling of happiness. I think back to when I used to take Pablo for walks in the woods. Alternately, someone who was bitten by a dog in their youth could associate the word 'dog' with very unpleasant feelings as a result of that experience. This emotional experience then has an influence on his way of thinking and communicating about the topic.

Even in the exceptional situation that you and I attach the identical meaning and image to one word, each of us can experience a different emotion, based on a different experience. This will, by definition, influence our communication.

The chance of miscommunication is further increased through the fact that attaching meaning, images and emotions to words generally occurs completely unconsciously. Observe what happens while you read this chapter. You don't need to think about the meaning of the words; you understand what you're reading immediately. And as you read the text, you develop an opinion about it and attach an emotion to it. This all happens automatically!

As a short test to underline this statement, read the following text and observe your thoughts and feelings:

I cndluo't bvleiee taht I culod aulaclty uesdtannrd waht I was rdnaieg. Unisg the icndeblire pweor of the hmuan mnid, aocdcrnig to rseecrah at Cmabrigde Uinervtisy, it dseno't mttaer in waht oderr the lterets in a wrod are, the olny irpoamtnt tihng is taht the frsit and lsat ltteer be in the rhgit pclae. The rset can be a taotl mses and you can sitll raed it whoutit a pboerlm. Tihs is bucseae the huamn mnid deos not raed ervey ltteer by istlef, but the wrod as a wlohe. Aaznmig, huh? Yaeh and I awlyas tghhuot slelinpg was ipmorantt! See if yuor fdreins can raed tihs too.

Was that so difficult? When you're talking to someone, be aware of how quickly the words flow from one to the other. Are you constantly consciously thinking about what you're going to say and which words you're going to choose, or are you sometimes surprised at what comes out of your mouth?

LSD IN, OMA OUT!

Is it theoretically possible to understand each other completely? I don't think so. But, we can strive to understand each other as well as possible. What can help is the notion of 'LSD in and OMA out': (listen, summarize and deepening questions in; opinions, my truth and advice out). Trust your gut feeling and bring things out into the open. Be curious about the other person's thoughts and feelings. This way, you will be helping to build lasting relationships.

ASSIGNMENT: Do you understand what I mean?

How often do you ask the following question: do you understand what I mean? And how often are you asked this question yourself? The next time you're asked this, ask yourself consciously whether you really understand what the other person is saying (you know what the other person means), or whether you have largely interpreted it based on your own meaning, images and emotions (you think you know what the other person means). In the latter case, you say no and you continue asking questions about the meaning, images and emotions the other person has concerning the topic under discussion.

In the case of miscommunication, talking even more rarely leads to the solution; first ask a question.

CHAPTER 20

TOXIC RELATIONSHIPS

PERSONAL INTRODUCTION

I met my wife, Cindy, during the turbulent period of my divorce from my first wife. Two months later, Cindy was pregnant, and nine months after that our daughter Erin was born.

The years that followed were to prove extraordinarily tough for us both. We got to know each other better, exploring our positive sides as well as our dark sides. Partly due to the fact that our characters are so different, you could rightly describe our relationship at that time as 'sporadically unstable.' Thankfully, we have never stopped investing in our relationship. Even now, we still have to force ourselves to make the time and effort to engage in discussions (who doesn't?) to ensure that we don't lose contact with each other and to clear the air.

During that initial stormy period, Cindy and I learned about the work of psychological researcher Dr. John Gottman, and the four types of toxins that cause personal relationships and team relationships to become unstable. Thanks to his model, the dysfunctional pattern we found ourselves in became crystal-clear to us. All four types of toxins were present in our relationship, to an unhealthy degree. Recognizing and acknowledging this gave us both the opportunity to do something about it.

I'm becoming increasingly adept at recognizing the dysfunctional patterns in myself and in my relationships with others, both in the personal and professional sphere. I'm also finding it easier to apply the antidote. Of course, I still make mistakes. I'm only human after all.

Gottman's insights (1994) – reflecting on your own pattern and striving to change it – are among the basic ingredients for maintaining sincere and lasting connections with your family, your friends and your colleagues at work. This chapter describes Gottman's insights in more detail.

WHAT MAKES RELATIONSHIPS WORK?

Gottman has spent more than 25 years conducting research aimed at answering the question: what makes relationships work? His insights enable him to predict with a great degree of accuracy whether a relationship will prove to be a long-term one or not.

By focusing on how couples communicate with each other, both verbally and non-verbally, one of the conclusions he comes to is that couples that have a ratio of at least 5:1 of positive expressions of communication versus negative ones have a greater chance of enjoying a long-term relationship. Examples of these positive expressions include showing interest in each other, asking questions, being empathetic and friendly, and giving compliments and acknowledgements. Negative examples are expressing anger, consciously upsetting the other person, expressing criticism or being outright antagonistic towards the other person.

What is the ratio of positive versus negative expressions at work? What I often see is this ratio in reverse. If something isn't going well, this will be explicitly mentioned. In other words, someone is held accountable and an opinion is expressed, or occasionally people will talk behind other people's backs. But, if something is going well, this will be rarely commented on and few people will actively express their appreciation. If you ask people about this, they will often say: 'It's normal when things go well, so we don't have to pay special attention to it', or, 'They're paid to do their work, aren't they?'

FOUR TYPES OF TOXINS

Gottman also demonstrated that it's fine to have conflicts within a relationship, since expressing your anger in a constructive manner clears the air and restores balance. However, this does not apply when a 'toxin' is a regular ingredient within these conflicts.

Gottman distinguishes four types of such toxins: criticism, defence, stonewalling and contempt. His research reveals that if one or more of these types of toxins are consistently present, 80% of the relationships will end in divorce. And when attempts to restore the balance in the relationship are regularly rejected, the chances of the relationship being terminated are as high as 90%.

Toxin 1: Criticism

There's a difference between expressing a complaint and venting criticism. With a complaint, you indicate what behaviour you find difficult to deal with. But criticism goes further, putting the personality or character of the other person under discussion and indirectly implying that he has to take action and change his behaviour, placing the problem firmly on that person's plate.

For example, 'I'm upset you haven't called that client to make an appointment,' is a complaint. But 'I can't believe you still haven't called that client yet, that's really irresponsible,' is an example of criticism. You can generally recognize criticism when words such as 'always' and 'never' are used, and formulations such as 'Why are you so...' and 'It's typical of you to...'

Toxin 2: Defensiveness

It's a fairly natural reaction to become defensive during a conflict. However, even though it's logical, it doesn't contribute anything to the quality of the relationship. This defensive attitude is often the result of the tension that's being felt at the time. Instead of trying to understand the other person, you are denying your own responsibility, making excuses or responding to a complaint with another complaint.

For example, you repeat yourself without engaging in a dialogue to establish what the other person is trying to clarify. You can also recognize this situation if you hear expressions such as: 'It's not my fault that...'; 'That's not true...'; 'Yes, but...'; 'You're the one who...'; or 'It's not fair...'

Toxin 3: Stonewalling

In the case of what Gottman calls stonewalling, instead of responding to the problem or conflict, you detach yourself from the relationship, either physically or mentally. Although it can occasionally be meaningful to react in such a way, if it happens on a regular basis it is destructive for the relationship. Different forms of this behaviour include: changing the subject, looking away, going away, isolating yourself or remaining silent.

Toxin 4: Contempt

Contempt is one step up from the first toxin (criticism) and means that someone has no respect for the other person. A sure sign of this is being deliberately insulting towards your partner. It's often about bringing down someone or their self-esteem. Examples of this are the use of swear words or malicious humour, making sarcastic comments or parodying the partner. Example: 'I do my best all day to organize things for the children and do the housework, and all you can do when you get home is slump onto the sofa and turn into a shapeless heap of a human being. You're so pathetic! I can't understand what I ever saw in you!'

ANTIDOTE

Although Gottman's study focuses on relationships within marriage, the insights gained can also be applied to friendships or relationships at work. If, for example, one or more of these toxins are at play within a team, there's work to be done.

So, what can you do in a situation in which the above-mentioned toxins are present? Here are six practical strategies:

- Identify the 1-2% of truth in what the other person is saying and communicate this explicitly to him. Acknowledging the content will often open up the path to better appreciating each other's insights.
- Try to pinpoint the complaint that lies at the root of your own, or the other person's, criticism and make this explicit. So, rather than saying, 'Your whole day is planned full of meetings, you only think of others,' you could say, 'You've been consistently missing our feedback sessions.'
- Acknowledge your role in the situation and accept responsibility for it. Express what your contribution to the situation is, without expecting anything from the other person in return.
- If you realize you're in the wrong, be sincere and say that you're sorry, however hard it might be to admit it.
- If the situation has become really tense, a time-out may do the trick. Once you've made sure that you've both calmed down, you can take up the conversation where you left it. Be sure to make clear that both of you want the time-out; if this doesn't happen, it may be considered as stonewalling.
- Bring things out into the open if you notice a toxic presence in the collaboration or relationship. Make agreements with each other about how you both want to deal with the situation.

EMOTIONAL BANK ACCOUNT

In any interpersonal action, a positive or negative 'deposit' is made into the joint emotional bank account. This has a direct impact on mutual trust, mutual respect and the willingness to be open to different ways of thinking or communicating. That's why building up a 'positive' balance – through attentive listening, showing interest, giving compliments and acknowledgments, thinking win-win, being appreciative, forgiving the other person, receiving feedback, etc. – is a powerful antidote.

When reflecting on the emotional bank account, it's wise to take the following aspects into consideration:

- Every relationship, whether a private or professional one, has two emotional bank accounts: yours and the other person's.
- Every emotional bank account is unique.
- Not all types of deposits or withdrawals are comparable. Just as it's true that losing someone's trust happens much faster than gaining it, withdrawals are generally bigger than deposits.
- Something you regard as a deposit may not necessarily be considered a deposit by the other person. Be aware of what the other person considers important, and what he considers to be deposits.
- The quickest way to restore a good balance in the accounts is to stop making withdrawals and start focusing on deposits.

ASSIGNMENT: From toxic to toxin-free

Determine how much one or more of the four types of toxins occurs with some degree of regularity within your team, friendships or relationships (business or personal).

Be honest here about your own contribution. If a certain toxin is consistently present, decide how you want to deal with it. Are you willing to invest in order to improve your relationship? Do you have the courage to make your insights open for discussion, and do you want to experiment with an antidote? Or, are you content to leave things as they are, with the chance that the relationship will terminate sooner or later?

Whichever choice you make, make it a deliberate one. And if you want to change, don't wait until tomorrow – take action today!

Communicate your appreciation and respect for the other person every day. You can always find something to appreciate in the other person, whatever the situation.

CHAPTER 21

THINK DIFFERENTLY, ACT DIFFERENTLY

PERSONAL INTRODUCTION

I've been playing field hockey all my life. It's a wonderful, energetic sport that's developing continuously. The Hockey Association here in the Netherlands is constantly looking for ways to make the game more attractive, which is why they introduce new rules every year. Sometimes these are minor changes; other modifications are more radical and have a huge impact on how the game is played.

Here are a few examples: abolishing the offside rule; introducing the self-pass after a foul; and the use of a video referee during major tournaments. For me as a player, this means I have to adapt to a new reality every year.

Needing to adapt every year is no big deal for me, because I enjoy adjusting my private and professional lives to new circumstances. I love change. Change keeps me alert. In fact, I find it boring to do the same things over and over again.

The nice thing about change is that there's something new to discover and that produces new results. In this context, Einstein's definition of the concept of 'insanity' resonates with me: "Insanity is doing the same thing over and over and expecting different results."

How do you cope with changes? Do you avoid them, or do you instinctively meet them head on? What impact does this have on the connection you engage in with others? Hopefully, this chapter will challenge you to think differently and act differently.

MARC LAMMERS

Marc Lammers is an innovative coach who led the Dutch Women's Hockey Team to a world title (2006) and an Olympic title (2008). To achieve these fantastic results, he made use of coach foundations that can be directly applied to the development of organizations: focus on qualities, encourage conflict, assign responsibility and dare to innovate (Lammers, 2007).

Coach foundation 1: Look for qualities

'Look for qualities' means that instead of looking at what someone is *not* good at, look for their strengths. Once you've both identified these, you can decide how these qualities can be used optimally within the team and the organization.

This line of thought is directly linked to Appreciative Inquiry, a method devised by the American academic David Cooperrider, which is becoming increasingly popular among organizations. Instead of focusing on problems and weak points within the organization, and trying to resolve them, the focus lies on what *does* go well, and how the organization can make even better use of these strong points. Lammers made a provocative statement regarding this: "In the Netherlands, coaching is 80% focused on limitations. The result is uniformity. A score of four (out of ten) becomes a six, and an eight becomes a six too."

To what degree does this apply to you? Are you trying to develop the limitations of the other person in your daily work? Or, do you try to make optimal use of his qualities?

Coach foundation 2: Encourage conflict

'Encourage conflict' doesn't mean that you have to start physically fighting with each other. It means you encourage one another to tell the truth and share insights. Conflicts within teams are part of everyday business. In fact, they open the way to achieving better solutions.

This is also emphasized in the work of psychological researcher Bruce Tuckman (1965; 1977) regarding the stages of group development. He identifies five phases of development: forming, storming, norming, performing and adjourning. The second phase is where conflicts arise, as team members are trying to establish their position within the group, and the form of collaboration is being debated. This inevitably leads to struggle when ideas are ranged opposite each other.

It's essential then for the team members themselves to learn how to resolve these conflicts. In your role as manager, give them the room to do this, while remaining objective.

Coach foundation 3: Assign responsibility

'Assign responsibility' means that you avoid being directive and do not hold any monologues designed to persuade. Rather, your aim as manager is to make your team members feel personally involved with the goal and the path to achieving it.

This is the only way to get people to pursue the goal with passion. You achieve this level of commitment by asking your team members questions, involving them in the decision-making process, and allowing them enough space and responsibility. It demands a coaching style firmly rooted in healthy curiosity.

This coaching style involves a willingness to let go of your own ideas in favour of the best solution. You put your trust in the path your team members propose. How much responsibility do you give your team members? Do you give them a false sense of participation, or do you have the courage to let go of your own ideas and follow the path they have chosen?

Coach foundation 4: Dare to innovate

The fourth point of departure is 'dare to innovate.' This means having the courage to abandon existing patterns of thought and trying something new. A crisis signals an opportunity, and if you want to be better than your competitors, you'll have to take action. "Not adapting means standing still. Stay that one step ahead of your competitors by continuing to develop through technology and study," Lammers says.

Remain curious about developments inside and outside your specialist area and ask yourself how you can integrate these into your own business or work. Challenge your colleagues to think up ideas that deviate from existing lines of thought, and make sure you can take a well-reasoned decision before rejecting the idea or continuing work on it.

Do you give off-the-wall ideas a chance or do you reject them based on your gut feeling?

ASSIGNMENT: Which of the four?

You learned about four coach foundations in this chapter. For each of these, I've outlined a short assignment. Which assignment is the most challenging for you? Do you have the guts to go for it?

Assignment 1: Look for qualities
Start a discussion with a colleague about his personal qualities and how he can use them within his work environment. If he says that he finds that difficult, interrupt him immediately and repeat the question: 'How can you make the best use of your personal qualities for your work?'

Assignment 2: Encourage conflicts
How do you view conflicts? Do you allow them to arise or would you rather avoid them? The challenge is to express an explicit opinion about a specific topic, preferably in a conversation with someone whose opinion on that topic will differ from yours. Then, open up the conversation and allow the other to express his way of thinking, as well as create space to express your thoughts.

Assignment 3: Assign responsibility
If a colleague approaches you with a question, warn him that in your conversation with him you will only be asking questions, and not offering any solutions. Ask the other person to interrupt you if he notices you giving advice. In other words: LSD in, OMA out (Chapter 19).

Assignment 4: Dare to innovate
Give a meeting an energy boost if you notice that the energy in the room is ebbing away. If you need some inspiration in finding games you can use in workshops, meetings and the community, visit **https://www.slideshare.net/vickthorr/100-energizers** where you will find 100 examples.

By thinking differently, believing in your convictions, and adapting your behaviour accordingly, you will change the future.

CHAPTER 22

LISTENING WITH INTENT

PERSONAL INTRODUCTION

After my parents' divorce, I made a promise to myself that this would never happen to me. Unfortunately, after a relationship lasting 13 years, in which we brought up two young children, I made the choice to divorce my wife.

Needless to say, this had an enormous impact on my ex-wife and myself, and above all on our children, Laura and Frank. One of the reasons was that I chose to focus on my personal development rather than on co-parenting. On the one hand, I'm now enjoying the benefits of that decision in both my private and professional life. On the other hand, I look back on my choice with regret. At the time, I didn't act on my responsibility towards my kids.

In the first few years following my divorce, I was constantly asking myself whether I'd been right to choose to divorce, due to the impact on the children. Every time, the conclusion was the same: yes. It was the first time in my life that I had ever chosen 100% for myself. I have learned to accept the consequences.

With the benefit of hindsight, I think I would have organized my divorce differently (inasmuch as anyone is able to organize a divorce on their own). I was predominantly occupied with myself in that turbulent period and paid little attention to the wishes and desires of my ex-wife. The connection had disappeared completely because I was listening on level 1 and less on levels 2 and 3 (explained below). If I had listened primarily on levels 2 and 3, the divorce would have happened differently.

Would this have affected how the children experienced the divorce? I think so, but I will never know for sure.

In this chapter, I will explain the three levels of listening and the impact they have on the connection with the other.

ALLOW ROOM FOR STRUGGLE

A man is observing a butterfly trying to escape from its cocoon. The struggle seems to be taking a long time, so the man decides to help the butterfly. He takes a small pair of scissors and carefully cuts open the cocoon. But, instead of flying freely, the butterfly falls to the ground, makes some disjointed movements and finally lies motionless. It has starved to death, having spent too little time struggling in the cocoon to develop the muscle power it needed to be able to fly.

This is exactly what some managers do with their employees. They consider it their task to solve problems for their employees. If someone comes to them with a problem, they ask questions so that they can comprehend the matter and then they explain how it can be resolved. This often involves an action plan full of concrete actions. All the employee has to do is execute the plan.

However good his intentions are, what this manager doesn't realize is that he is training his employees to think less. If there are any problems, he's essentially saying, just drop by and you'll be taken care of. This way of working may make the manager feel good, but it is to the detriment of the employee and ultimately to the manger too.

DIRECTIVE VERSUS COACHING

Eric is a manager who loves helping his direct reports. In spite of this, he regularly gets complaints about his style of support. Instead of asking any questions, his response is to work even harder, to exert even greater control over his employees.

Eric decides to seek advice from a coach and is amazed by what happens during his session. After explaining his situation at work, he doesn't get a ready-made answer about what needs to happen. On the contrary, the coach asks him questions, and instead of pushing Eric in a particular direction, he allows him to make his own choices. But he does challenge him to engage in conversations with his direct reports in the coming weeks.

His coach calls this 'designing the relationship.' The coach also gives him a wise lesson to think about. It's a theory on 'the art of listening' – that it's possible to listen at three different levels (Whitworth, et al., 2004).

Level 1: Internal listening

Level 1 is internal listening. Instead of listening to the other person and trying to understand what it means to him, you're too involved with your own story. You are listening to your own thoughts and feelings. What do I think about what the other person is saying? Based on your own frame of reference, you form an opinion about the best thing to do in this situation.

Level 2: Focused listening

Level 2 is focused listening. Here, you constantly ask questions because you really want to understand the other person's situation. You listen to the answers, and new questions continually arise. The other person gradually starts to recognize what the real question is and what the possible solutions are. Based on this deeper understanding of the issue at hand, he is able to make his own choices.

Level 3: Intuitive listening

The third level is intuitive listening. You listen to what the other person is saying, while listening between the lines to what isn't being said, and what the likely meaning is. What's important for the other person in this situation and what does your own intuition tell you? If you openly express these kinds of things, you introduce a deeper level into the conversation.

Listening at level 3 makes the other person increasingly aware of the essence and of what he thinks about this. What's important here is that you don't consider your insights to be the truth – that would take you back to level 1 again. Yet, you continue to be curious about what your insights do to the other person.

LISTENING WITH INTENT

Finally, the coach gives Eric something to think about. If he engages in a conversation with a direct report, that person will mostly be active at level 1 (he is reflecting on his own problem). As a manager, Eric should be acting predominantly at levels 2 and 3 (the basis for coaching leadership). By engaging in a conversation with each other in this way, you are practising what the coach calls 'listening with intent.'

ASSIGNMENT: And... switch!

Which level do you normally operate at when you are listening during a conversation? Are you able to consciously switch between the three levels? In the coming weeks, experiment with this and experience the differences and the impact on the connection with yourself and the other person.

This assignment demands a high degree of self-management and mental determination, and will undoubtedly cost you extra energy in the beginning. But, I'm convinced it will result in a deeper connection.

Listening with intent is a basic skill required to be able to engage meaningfully with the other.

CHAPTER 23

POSITIVE-CRITICAL THINKING

PERSONAL INTRODUCTION

When I'm conducting leadership or coaching training, I often get asked the question: 'How far can I go as a manager when it comes to inquiring about someone's private situation?' My answer's always the same: 'As far as you've both agreed to go.'

As a manager, it can feel awkward to ask someone about their personal situation. On the other hand, the person may find it very comforting to be able to tell someone their story.

Our team at COURIUS regularly spends time together. In addition to work-related discussions, we talk about our personal experiences and values, as well as sharing what's happening in our private lives. We also evaluate how the collaboration is going, ask ourselves if we would like to see some changes and, if so, what they might be.

Are the discussions within our team completely open and transparent from the moment we start collaborating? I would very much hope so, but I/we have to continue to grow together.

What helps here is that everyone's intention is positive. We all want to work together on a basis of complete honesty and integrity. We are prepared to 'risk' being open to each other. We have the courage to express what's going on in our minds. We're also confident that we'll always be able to come to an agreement together, even though we're not always completely satisfied with each other. This way, we are true to our motto of being 'hard on the content, and soft on the connection.'

How do you make use of the insights of others in your role as manager? This chapter is designed to get you to think about just that.

A CAGE FULL OF MONKEYS

Consider for a moment a cage full of monkeys. Suspended from the ceiling is a banana, and directly below it stands a ladder. It doesn't take long before a monkey approaches the ladder, but as soon as he places one foot on it, all the monkeys get hosed down with water. A little later, the same monkey, or a different one, tries it again, but with the same result – all the monkeys get sprayed with water.

Before long, if another monkey wants to climb the ladder, he gets stopped by the others.

Now let's remove a monkey from the cage and replace it with a new monkey. The new monkey sees the banana and heads for the ladder. It's immediately sprung upon by all the other monkeys. After one more try, he realizes what's going on – if he starts to climb the ladder, he will get beaten up. Now we remove a second monkey and introduce a new one. The newbie walks in the direction of the ladder and gets beaten up. The previous newbie joins in enthusiastically with the beating.

A third old monkey now leaves and a third new one enters, and so on, until all the monkeys that witnessed the hosing down have been replaced. But, no monkey ever goes up the ladder again.

NEW EMPLOYEES ARE A SOURCE OF INSPIRATION

Although this story is more of a parable than a scientific experiment, it does illustrate an essential fact: every time a new employee arrives at the department, there's a wonderful opportunity to achieve improvements in the organization and its processes. Because they have no background knowledge about the work processes, they will ask questions out of curiosity, or they will come up with proposals to implement changes. Why do we have so many meetings? Why do we take minutes of these meetings? How about if from now on we hold meetings based on an agenda? Why are we executing this task and not department XYZ?

New employees see things with fresh eyes and are curious about the how and why of certain choices. As a manager (and also as a colleague), you can respond in one of two ways.

You can view these newcomers as a nuisance and discourage any discussions: 'Don't ask so many difficult questions, just get on with your work.' The logical result is that they leave the company very quickly or stay grudgingly, accepting the straitjacket of the department. Or, you can decide to view the new employees as people with a positive-critical attitude who are able to expose these blind spots. They will see issues that you're no longer able to see, because you've been working in the department for too long. You and your team members have developed a certain degree of organization blindness.

SCHEDULE A CONVERSATION

Instead of being reactive and waiting until new employees come up with questions and proposals, you can actively invite them to approach you with their ideas. Encourage them to question what they see and experience within the team. After a month has gone by, plan in a conversation centred around the questions of what works well in the department, what should be maintained and what they suggest changing. And during this conversation with the newbies, make sure that you listen and don't start explaining or defending why things are done the way they are.

Of course, this doesn't mean that you're not allowed to give any explanations during the discussion. If there is a need for clarification or some background information, go ahead and give it. But observe whether your tone is a defensive one or if it encourages the other person to continue to share what he has noticed. If you succeed in adopting this way of listening naturally, you will notice that even employees who have been working in the organization for many years are usually full of ideas for smart changes.

LISTENING WITH CURIOSITY

Stephen Covey (1989) also stresses the importance of listening with curiosity. In his popular management book, *The Seven Habits of Highly Effective People*, his fifth habit is to seek first to understand, then to be understood.

The key to effective communication, he suggests, is suspending your judgment and not giving in to the tendency to offer your own opinion too quickly, or to only half-listen to what the other person is saying. Attention, non-judgmental listening, putting yourself in another person's shoes and acknowledging their viewpoint are the first steps on the path to true understanding.

ASSIGNMENT: Looking for positive-critical sounds

Many collaborations are characterized by actions based on unvoiced assumptions and existing routines. This exercise is intended to remove those internal and somewhat lazy and convenient 'elephant paths' from your relationship, and to enhance the relationship.

Schedule meetings of at least 45 minutes with new and existing employees to exchange thoughts and ideas about your connection. Take the time to gain insights into each other's way of thinking, to discuss the manner of collaboration, and to make agreements about this. This way you increase mutual understanding and work towards raising the trust in the relationship. This is a precondition for a lasting connection within teams and organizations.

- Here are a few questions you could ask during your meeting:
- What expectations do we have about our collaboration?
- How do we experience the mutual connection?
- What are key personal values for you and me?
- How do we hold each other to account regarding agreements we make?
- What irritates you and what irritates me, and how can we deal with these irritations?
- How can we discuss sensitive topics openly?
- What do you think about how work is organized here, and what do I think about it?
- What things astound you at work?
- If you could change something in the collaboration, what would that be?
- How often do we arrange a one-on-one meeting?
- Do we discuss our private lives, and shall we set up guidelines for this?

This list represents just a fraction of what you could discuss with each other and what you could make arrangements about. At the end of each session, evaluate what this time investment has produced for you both. If these meetings work out well, make scheduling the next meeting a mutual responsibility. From that point on, either of you can initiate this meeting.

I'm curious to know which insights (new or existing) you acquire.

What happens in the connection if you decide that a positive-critical attitude on the part of the other person is a sign of involvement?

CHAPTER 24

WHAT KIND OF LEADER ARE YOU?

PERSONAL INTRODUCTION

I believe that organizations around the world, whether they are one-man businesses or huge multinationals, should use part of their knowledge and profits to improve society. This way, we take responsibility for the quality of the environment we live in. For me this means making a contribution to society that will encourage living through connection.

For many years now, I have been living this vision on a small scale by coaching people either for free or for a small fee, because I knew they were unable to afford it. Actually, since we founded COURIUS, we have reserved part of our profit for the support of socially engaged organizations. We will also donate part of the profits from the sales of this book for the same purpose. And, while writing this book, we launched a foundation in order to support these organizations, financially and by providing knowledge about the human side of change.

I don't just have a vision. I also know which steps I need to take to transform my vision into concrete products and services. This demonstrates that my dominant leadership style is that of the magician. Curious to know what I'm talking about here, and find out what your dominant style of leadership is? Well, that's what this chapter is about.

WHAT IS YOUR NATURAL STYLE?

What is it that makes people want to follow you? What is your natural style of leadership and what other styles from the categories below do you have access to? What happens when you're under pressure – which style do you then naturally adopt and how satisfied are you about that? Which styles would you like to develop further?

These are just a few questions you should keep at the back of your mind when reading this chapter. Whatever answers you give, don't forget that there are no good or bad answers. After all, each style has its own pros and cons, and depending on the situation you're in, they can produce better (or worse) results.

For example: if fire breaks out in a shop, would you want the staff to enter into a discussion with you about all the different methods there are for leaving the building quickly, or would you prefer that they manage themselves and tell you what to do?

A WORD OF WARNING WHILE READING THIS CHAPTER

The seven styles are based on insights from a leadership development course I deliver around the world for the French technology and consulting firm Capgemini. They were developed by the Artgym leadership academy, provide insights into how you think and act when managing others.

The model is, logically, a simplification of the real world. Look at it more as a tool through which you can view and explore your leadership.

My assumption is that everyone has one or two dominant styles, but also uses all the other styles to some degree. The question is, to what extent do you choose to use each style when you engage in connecting with the other?

It's important to keep in mind that the people I mention as examples for each style use more than just their one dominant style when connecting with others. By using them as examples of a specific style, I give you an indication of the way of working that is appropriate for that style.

The visionary

The leadership of the visionary is based on his picture of what the distant future will bring. He possesses the power of imagination and a grand vision (dream) that he pursues relentlessly. Nobody can cause him to doubt the truth of his way of thinking. What motivates him is executing his vision, inspiring others and, with them, undertaking actions to realize his ideal. If no actions are taken, feelings of frustration and disbelief may be aroused in him: how is it possible that the others can't see this vision of the future and not take action? Two examples of this style are Dr. Martin Luther King, Jr., and Nelson Mandela.

The magician

An important driving factor for the magician is translating his (grand) vision into practical products and services for customers. The magician is looking to facilitate transformations and produce real innovative solutions, not just achieve small-scale breakthroughs, and so is prepared to take risks and to manage others, even aggressively. But his inexhaustible enthusiasm may be experienced as overwhelming and chaotic. Two examples of this style are Sir Richard Branson and Steve Jobs.

The emperor

The emperor is characterized by a top-down style of creating clearly defined goals and structures so that predefined results can be achieved in a calm and orderly way. It is a hierarchical approach, with the intention of uniting people and focusing on a single, well-defined goal. 'I know what is good and what needs to be done,' 'I am the head, and you are the hands' and 'Execute what I think up' are a few of the expressions that correspond to this style of leadership. The consequences of this attitude are that no discussion or questioning is tolerated, losing face is unthinkable, and being 'in control' is essential. Two examples: Kim Jong-un and Vladimir Putin.

The warrior

The leadership of the warrior is based on action. His motto is: 'Let's get it done.. He is courageous and driven by his spirit of adventure and justice. If there is a mission he believes in, he will fight for it. His manner is direct, aggressive if required, and he acts on his instincts. If mistakes are made, that's nothing to worry about in the short term, as it's better to make a mistake and learn from it. But if the same mistake is made more than once, his tolerance for faults will disappear, and he can become hostile towards his own people. Two examples of this style are Theresa May and Elon Musk.

The orator

The orator has a great capacity to express himself clearly and coherently, and an ability to empathize with others, using their language to get his own message across. He is also a master at relating his own life story, to create an emotional connection with the other. What motivates him is exerting his influence and the sincere belief that his message is of crucial importance for everyone. Where the visionary lives predominantly in the future, the orator makes sure he lives in the present. But, as a result of his way with words, he can come across as superficial, manipulative and inauthentic. Two examples of this style are Barack Obama and Oprah Winfrey.

The guru

The guru is admired by others and is viewed as someone with much knowledge and many insights, who shares these with the world. Followers go in search of him and are eager to learn from him. He himself is driven by curiosity – the more he knows, the more questions he has. Where ego plays an important role in the previous leadership styles, the guru is not interested in himself but in the role he can fulfil in the bigger picture. Yet, his willingness to question his own way of thinking can be perceived as elusive, distant and condescending. Two examples of this style are the Dalai Lama and Mahatma Gandhi.

The giver

The giver is motivated by serving the other and achieving higher goals together, often operating from behind the scenes and not in the spotlight. This leader ensures that others can operate from their strengths and have access to the resources they need, making sure that the honours for any achievements go to those who deserve them. But, he can sometimes go too far, taking on the role of martyr. Two examples of this style are Mother Teresa and Lady Diana.

ASSIGNMENT: Leadership in style

Which examples of leaders do you know that match the different styles? Research their lives and discover what you can learn from them. Which forms of the Connection Quotient do they apply? Translate the lessons to your own situation and define three concrete follow-up actions you can take yourself.

**Providing effective leadership to others
starts with giving leadership to yourself.**

CHAPTER 25

THE HALO-AND-HORN EFFECT

PERSONAL INTRODUCTION

Among the less enjoyable tasks I had in my role as manager was the annual 'ranking session,' when we as a management team came together to discuss all the employees.

We would decide who the top five talents were and which five employees ended up at the bottom of the list, setting in motion the 'moving towards farewell' trajectory. Seen as a purely business-driven exercise, I could appreciate the necessity of these sessions. Still, from the human point of view, I felt some resistance and loss of energy, particularly due to the way the process was designed.

I, like the other managers, was expected to have an opinion on a large group of employees, despite the fact that I only spoke to some sporadically and did not know much about their true contribution. In the discussions, arguments were put forward that were clearly based on personal preferences. Some employees were ranked higher because they were so-called 'good guys,' but how fair is it to allow these personal preferences weigh so heavily in a process that has such an impact on the careers of others?

We should have challenged ourselves to arrive at a more balanced choice. If someone is 'nice,' what does that mean and what facts make him 'less nice?' And, conversely, what are the qualities of a less nice person, what can he contribute and what can we learn from him?

The situation in which we sometimes allow ourselves to be influenced unconsciously is known as the halo-and-horn effect ('halo' in the sense of angel and 'horn' in the sense of the devil). In this chapter, I will explain this effect and its impact on being in connection with another person.

LABEL INFLUENCES OBSERVATION

Psychologist and academic Edward Thorndike (1920) demonstrated that we tend to attribute characteristics to a person based on just one character trait, and we assign that person a label. And, because we like to be proven right, in all our interactions with that person we are constantly looking for 'evidence' that shows our label is correct. This label causes us to not only to observe things differently, but to also adapt how we behave in the relationship.

In the 'halo' relationship we are more likely to encourage contact, while in the 'horn' we will tend to keep our distance.

APPEARANCE INFLUENCES OBSERVATION

But it's not just the labels that influence our behaviour; the outward appearance of the other person also plays a role, causing us to even attribute certain character traits to people based on how they look.

The academics David Landy and Harold Sigall (1974) conducted a study in which participants were asked to judge the quality of an essay. Each essay was accompanied by a photograph of the supposed author. These 'authors' were divided into three categories: attractive, reasonably attractive and unattractive. They found that the essay was assessed differently depending on the photo. Attractive authors were given a higher mark than the unattractive ones and the control group. In the case of well-written essays, the difference was one point on a scale of one to nine, and in the case of badly written essays there was as much as a 2.5-point difference.

EMOTION INFLUENCES OBSERVATION

In addition to assumed characteristics and the appearance of a person, external influences – such as the opinions of our friends or the media – and our emotional state also have an unconscious influence on our observations, thoughts, opinions and behaviour.

THE HALO-AND-HORN EFFECT

When making conscious and unconscious judgments about people, we are often influenced by the halo-and-horn effect.

In the case of the halo effect, you will see this person in a generally positive light. This can be a result of someone's actions in the past, but can also be triggered by a memory or association that has nothing to do with that person. For instance, if you view a colleague through the halo effect, you will notice a positive response in yourself when you see him approaching, find yourself willing to help him if he has questions and be able to forgive him easily when he makes mistakes, not blaming him for the error.

The horn effect is the opposite. Consciously or unconsciously, you place people in your 'allergy zone' based on their actions or as a result of characteristics that don't have anything to do with them directly. You just don't like working with them, and you'd rather avoid them. When they do something positive, you tend to quickly forget about it.

HALO AND HORN INFLUENCE OBSERVATIONS AND MEMORIES

So, the halo-and-horn effect influences how you view a person in your direct environment, resulting in how you remember him.

Here's a simple test to demonstrate this. Think of someone who is in the halo category (someone you like). What five positive characteristics does this person have? You'll probably find this fairly easy to answer. But now try naming five negative characteristics about this person. I'm pretty sure it will take you longer to come up with these.

Next, think of someone who is in the horn effect category (someone whose behaviour you're allergic to). What five positive characteristics does this person have? You'll probably notice how difficult it is (perhaps even impossible) to name five. But, if I had asked you for five negative characteristics of this person, you probably would have been able to answer straight away.

HALO AND HORN INFLUENCE THINKING AND BEHAVIOUR

The halo-and-horn effect also influences how you respond to a situation involving these people.

For instance, if someone you know within your halo effect category comes in and slams the door behind them, there's a good chance you'll think he's just had a bad meeting and will calm down soon. Fifteen minutes later, he's sitting on the corner of your desk, drinking coffee with you and having a chat. Very likely, you'll think: 'See, he's okay now. That's good.'

Now think of the same situation with someone you know who is in the horn effect category. He also comes in and slams the door shut. This time you're likely to think: 'That's typical of him. It's going to be one of those days. Why can't he close the door in a normal way?' He too brings you a cup of coffee 15 minutes later, sits on the corner of your desk and starts telling you a story. The chances are that you will now be thinking: 'What does he want from me?'

Sound familiar?

LOOK FOR BALANCE IN EXAMPLES

Understanding the halo-and-horn mechanism will help you in your role as manager. It will help when you are drawing up an annual review, considering people for promotion, or on other occasions when forming impressions and judgments play a role. Be aware that how you think about your employees is influenced unconsciously by factors other than their actions. This has an impact on the examples you cite and conclusions you draw when you assess them 'objectively.' Your employees have the right to a balanced assessment. So, make sure you always actively look for a balance between their strong points and their points for improvement, independent of how you perceive them.

ASSIGNMENT: I can feel your halo

Ask yourself the following questions about your employees to better understand the halo-and-horn effect on your relationships at work and as a manager:

- For which employees are you conscious that the halo-and-horn effect plays a role?
- What impact does this have on how you approach these employees and how you conduct performance review interviews?
- How much time and space do you set aside for them? At the same time, why is the halo-and-horn effect a factor in their case? What does this tell you about your framework of thinking and acting?

- What is it that you apparently find important in work and what don't you like dealing with?
- Finally, if you have a conversation with someone (either privately or professionally) and you know that person is in your horn effect category, consider beforehand the positive characteristics of this person. This technique makes you aware and helps you to enter conversations in a more neutral frame of mind.

Are you aware of where the angel stops and the devil begins — for yourself, as well as for the other person?

CHAPTER 26

AND... ACTION!

PERSONAL INTRODUCTION

One thing about me is that I enjoy taking part in discussions about new insights and ideas. And, I love combining them with existing theories and using them to construct overarching models and business opportunities.

Once that preparatory work has been done, actions will be generated automatically. There's really no need to agree on these in detail. At least, that's what I think. But things always work out differently in practice.

Other people might need to be given more direction and clarity, and I have to give it to them, or create it in conjunction with them. If I'm being perfectly honest, I also need this direction and clarity myself, otherwise I go off in all directions.

As soon as I get a new idea or insight, I focus on it totally. In that context, I've explained to my business partner, Jaco, that I don't have an action list, but an intention list. I don't always do what I've agreed to do. Sometimes, that makes me a difficult person to work with, especially if the other person has an 'agreed is agreed' mindset. I have a lot of respect for the way Jaco deals with that. When he really wants something to be done, he simply asks me to put the action on top of my intention list. For me, that's a clear signal I need to take action.

My personality results in situations where a question I receive doesn't always lead to an action on my part. More generally, many times, the reason why a question doesn't result in an action is that we don't devote sufficient time to discussing the importance of the question. I know that if I'm really convinced about the question, I will actually take action.

How do you do that – emphasize the importance of a question? That's the theme of this chapter.

WHO IS THE GUILTY ONE?

Why doesn't he just do what I've asked him to? Have you ever asked yourself that question? And do you then blame the other person?

Then I've got good and bad news for you. The good news is that it could be the other person's fault. The bad news is that the reason your question doesn't lead to action being taken could be you.

Are you curious to find out how this works? There are two common reasons for this, and five following assumptions based upon the first possible reason.

FIVE STEPS THAT LEAD TO ACTION

The first reason someone doesn't do what you ask of them is that a lot of people assume that the link between the two is simple. Asking someone a question doesn't necessarily mean that it will lead directly to an appropriate action.

Between thinking of an action and it actually being executed by the other person lie a number of intervening steps. These steps are often implicit – they are often assumptions. If you observe that no action is being taken, it's a good idea to check these five assumptions.

	Steps required to initiate an action	Verification question
1	Thinking something doesn't mean that you have said it.	Have you actually asked (when did you do that)?
2	Saying something doesn't mean that the other person has received or heard what you said.	Has the other person really listened to you (and how do you know that)?
3	Hearing or receiving something doesn't mean that the other person has understood it.	Does he understand what you are asking (can he, for example, repeat in his own words what you have asked him)?
4	Understanding something doesn't mean that the other person has agreed to do it.	Does he want to take responsibility or does he simply acknowledge what you've said (do you ask for a commitment)?
5	Agreeing to do something doesn't mean that the other person will execute it.	Which agreements have you made about deadlines, feedback and progress reporting?

ARE YOU LISTENING TO ME?

The second most common reason that a question doesn't lead to action has to do with how people listen.

The ability to listen is one of the core skills you need to achieve a high Connection Quotient. In Chapter 15, listening was approached from the perspective of an interaction between the other and yourself ('How do we listen to each other?'). In Chapter 22, listening was approached from your own position ('How do I listen to the other?').

What I want to add in this chapter is the approach to listening from the position of the other person ('How does he listen to me?').

1. **Not listening.** While you're talking to the other person, he is busy doing other things or his thoughts are elsewhere, and he just doesn't hear you. Despite this, you carry on talking. It happens all of the time! The next time you're in a meeting, have a good look around you.

2. **Pretending to listen.** The other person is hard at work at his laptop while you ask him a question. While continuing to concentrate on what he's doing, he replies in mumbles, but he has no idea what you've just said. He may not even have looked at you, but continued to stare at his screen. Familiar? You're probably guilty of doing the same once in a while, too.

3. **Listening selectively.** This is where the other person is listening to you through a filter, deciding which information is important or of interest, and only asking questions to clarify something if necessary. The rest of the information passes by unnoticed.

4. **Listening attentively.** The other person is now listening in order to understand. What are you saying, exactly? He tries to understand what you expect from him. The emphasis is very much on the facts. He listens to what you are saying and draws his own conclusions.

5. **Listening with empathy.** Now the other is listening to the words and the facts, as well as observing your body language, intonation, volume and other non-verbal signals. This way, he is able to read between the lines and therefore obtains a fuller picture of the situation.

ASSIGNMENT: Field study in the meeting room

I'm not against having meetings, but I do have serious doubts about the effectiveness of holding a lot of them. They should certainly not last longer than an hour. After that, participants often become disengaged and lose the energy to try to understand different viewpoints... or even to defend their own.

How long do you think a good meeting should last?

The assignment is to observe how you and others around the table act during meetings. Which listening style do you adopt, and which styles do you observe in others? And, when agreements are made regarding the results to be achieved, are the five checks that I formulated earlier in this chapter carried out?

Of course, it's not only about observing. If you notice that opportunities for improvement arise – which help the meeting to proceed more effectively and efficiently – put them on the table and discuss them.

**Getting people to act is one big game of questions and answers.
How good of a player are you?**

CHAPTER 27

EMPATHY EXPLORED

PERSONAL INTRODUCTION

As an introduction to the chapter on empathy, I'd like you to make acquaintance with a beautiful song – I Love Myself – by the comedian and musician Harrie Jekkers.

It's one of my favourite songs, purely because of the lyrics. It explains how it's only possible to engage in a connection with another person if that connection is based on the connection with yourself – a message I agree with completely.

Ask yourself: how can you genuinely love someone else if you aren't capable of genuinely loving yourself? Watching him perform the song (https://www.youtube.com/watch?v=JmtPXcsItqs) you may not understand the Dutch lyrics, but the singer puts so much into the performance that I'm sure you'll be able to feel the message without understanding the words. (I do include an English translation below.)

After reading this chapter, ask yourself what sort of empathy you experienced while listening to the song.

I love myself, nobody ever sings that
I love myself, nobody ever says that
But I love myself, is still what I'm going to sing
Because I love myself, just myself, and I really mean that!

I love myself, because I can be trusted
I love myself, because I can count on me
I love myself, because I can always rely on me
I love myself and I'm never going to let myself go!

I'll stay with me, and not just for a while
I'll stay with me, forever
I'm even willing to give my life for me
I'll stay with me, till death us do part!

I love you, is something I say now and then
I love you, darling, and I really mean that
But I only say I love you in front of the mirror
So I love you comes right back to me!

I love myself, myself, myself and nobody else
Because I'm the nicest person I know, by far
I feel I don't need to change myself
I love myself, myself, just the way I am

'I love you' usually means:
Darling, here are my problems, go and solve them
I'm living in a hell and you should offer me heaven
You give away your hell, no way, get the hell out of here!

Because loving someone else is what you need
For you're not able to love yourself enough
Just love yourself, independent of the other person's care
For true love, believe me, always begins with loving yourself

Because 'I love you' isn't the key to deep connections with the other
It's 'I love myself', even though that sounds so bad and crude
So when you say I love you to the other person, based on the love for yourself
You are giving that person something truly priceless

I Love Myself, Harrie Jekkers

CORE SKILL

One of the core skills you will need to engage in a connection with the other is the ability to show empathy. It's no coincidence that a lot of attention is focused on developing this ability to empathize within leadership courses. But which form of empathy is then being developed?

According to journalist Daniel Goleman (2007), there are three forms of empathy: cognitive empathy, emotional empathy and empathic concern. Ideally, these three forms would be developed, and the manager would apply all three effectively while engaging in a connection with the other.

COGNITIVE EMPATHY

In the case of cognitive empathy, the focus is on understanding how the other person is feeling and what and how he's thinking. This is predominantly a rational approach, whereby asking questions and listening to the answers you come to understand the other person's perspective. If that perspective is not functional, you could try to change this via conversation and coaching techniques.

For example, if someone finds it difficult to give feedback to others, you can ask him a few probing questions. You may learn that he is afraid of hurting other people's feelings. Instead of saying that he doesn't need to be afraid, you can also try to change this non-functional perspective by connecting with the values he considers important. Let's imagine he considers personal growth to be very important. In that case, you could present him with the perspective that giving feedback is an opportunity for growth for the other person. And, if you learn how to give feedback, you also grow personally yourself.

Research shows that managers who are able to analyse the perspectives of their employees accurately are also able to get the best out of them. So, it's good to realize that cognitive empathy isn't only helpful for getting people into motion who are inhibited in some way, it also encourages people to carry on doing what they're already doing.

By enhancing the perspective, you are acknowledging the other person in his thinking and doing, and you are sustaining the action.

EMOTIONAL EMPATHY

With emotional empathy, you experience/feel the emotions of the other person as though they're infectious. Brain research has shown that we do this through the presence of mirror neurons. If another person performs a specific action, these paths are also activated in your own brain.

If, for example, you notice that someone is feeling sad, you may also feel tears welling up in your eyes. The key here is that you connect with the other person's inner world. You can develop this skill by learning how to slow down your responses, becoming introspective in the peace of the moment, and experiencing what you are feeling in such a situation.

Emotional empathy is useful in operational and managerial functions. A relationship of trust arises based on the connection with the other, and you can work well together. But, there is the danger that you will be sucked into the emotions of the other. In that case, the emotions of the other will start to control your life.

If you want to prevent this from happening, it's important to close yourself off functionally. On the other hand, too much detachment and self-protection lead to distance, and possibly to reduced effectiveness. Finding the right balance is something you will need to investigate.

EMPATHIC CONCERN

Then there's what Goleman calls empathic concern, where you feel a natural compulsion to support someone in need. The option of not helping simply does not exist, as you also consider his growth to be crucial. You want to help the other person become better in his function by, for example, giving him feedback or taking time to support him in performing his tasks. You make time to do this.

The danger here is that you go over the top and forget about yourself. All of your energy is devoted to the development of the other and you don't have any time for your own tasks. Again, it's about finding the balance between what's good for the other person and what's good for yourself.

ASSIGNMENT: A small act of kindness, but a huge amount of joy

Think about ways you can do something for a colleague at work without asking for anything in return. It doesn't have to be something of epic proportions – it can be a small act of kindness, such as holding the door open for someone, helping him carry his things, giving constructive feedback on a task or asking how you can help him.

Once you've thought about what you can do, spend a week putting these thoughts into actions. Try to perform as many small acts of kindness as possible. During the week, and at the end of it, reflect on your feelings and those of the other. What impact have your acts had on the connection with the other, and what have you learned about the three types of empathy?

Acting with a little more empathy is good for ourselves, the other, the team, the organization and the world.

PART III

IN CONNECTION WITH YOUR TEAM AND YOUR ORGANIZATION

"Coming together is a beginning, keeping together is progress, working together is success."
Henry Ford

INTRODUCTION

After connecting with yourself (Part I) and connecting with the other (Part II), I will now focus on the connection you engage in with your team and your organization.

How do you leverage your CQ within the relation with your own team, across teams, and inside and outside the organization? This is an important theme because teams and organizations are formed to achieve results, and you achieve these results by collaborating with others within the group.

You make use of the Connection Quotient here as a kind of lubricant to add depth to the dimension of rational collaboration: emotional collaboration. The better you are able to retain and connect the people involved, based on the rational *and* the emotional, *and* get them collaborating on a common goal, the more powerful your results will be.

THE CONTEXT OF CONNECTION WITH THE TEAM AND THE ORGANIZATION

Developing the Connection Quotient at the level of teams and organizations is essential. This is true both from the perspective of task-orientation (the rational side of organizations: they exist in order to achieve results) and relative to people-orientation (the emotional side of organizations: they are composed of people).

The next two subsections will briefly explain these two factors, emphasizing how important the Connection Quotient is if an organization wishes to become – and remain – successful.

The importance of being task-oriented

The most important tasks demand a high Connection Quotient. Business guru Ian Altman (Altman, 2015) outlines what he considers the top ten challenges today's organizations face if they want to become and remain successful. Here's a summary of his first five points:

1. Organizations that perform excellently focus on creating lasting relationships with customers. The customer is increasingly accustomed

to connecting online with the rest of the world. He, together with other customers, wants to learn how he can make optimum use of the product or service prior to and after its purchase. He also wants to keep up to date on new developments and get prompt answers to his questions, independent of time and location. To meet these growing needs, more and more organizations are creating communities that connect customers with the organization *and* the other customers.

2. Smart companies embrace Millennials, a huge demographic born in the 1980s and '90s that is coming into its earning- and purchasing-power prime. They are today's new employees. For them, experiencing a connection is important. Author Brad Szollose (2010) emphasizes that this group especially buys products from organizations that focus attention on issues that they consider to be important. They want to connect with and work for organizations they can truly be proud of, and where they are encouraged to grow personally (PwC, 2011).

3. Innovative organizations invest consciously in supervising and involving employees who work offsite. Work is becoming less location-dependent, with alternatives that range from working from home to residing offshore. This means, among other things, that your employees working remotely have to be managed, encouraged, corrected, coached and connected differently. Increasingly, this statement is relevant for the leader: it's not about what happens when you're around, it's about what happens when you're not.

4. Top companies focus on the qualities of their employees (strengths-based leadership). Research by Gallup (2006) shows that the productivity of companies grows by 21% if employees are committed. A powerful way to get committed employees is to give them the opportunity to make use of their qualities. Employees who can do this on a daily basis are 6% more committed than those who don't get this chance.

5. While margins on commodity products will drop further, services will add value. Today's client is used to purchasing his product online, so competing in terms of speed of delivery is impossible. 'Order before

23.00 today, delivery tomorrow' has become a standard for commodity products. The added value lies in the connection prior to, during and after the purchase. How does the organization distinguish itself and what services does it deliver?

Notice that you can derive every one of these points from a further implementation of the power of the Connection Quotient.

Additionally, research shows that during the last two decades, the time that employees spent on collaboration has increased by 50% or more (Cross, et al., 2016). This same study also shows that three quarters of the working day is spent on communicating with colleagues. For both these activities, the Connection Quotient is essential.

In other words, for many of the business challenges of today, the Connection Quotient is the answer.

The importance of being people-oriented

The Connection Quotient is key to overall welfare and retention. The welfare of people (employees/colleagues) is largely dependent on the quality of the Connection Quotient. For example, research by the HR consulting group Meurs HRM (RTL Nieuws, 2016) shows that feeling connected with your colleagues and your organization is a much-underrated factor. Estimates by the Netherlands Society of Occupational Medicine indicate that 70-80% of sickness absence is not directly related to illness.

By organizing work differently – for instance, connecting with each other differently – it is possible to greatly reduce sickness absence. In addition to doing what you have the talent for and being offered the possibilities to structure your work in your own way, feeling connected with the company and colleagues plays a crucial part.

Research by Gallup (2006) also illustrates what makes the Connection Quotient so crucial within companies: employees don't leave the organization, they leave their manager. Even if an employee feels connected with the organization and its products and services, it's that employee's manager who has the most influence on the employee's state of mind and, ultimately, on his commitment to whether or not he wishes to continue working for the organization.

This will become increasingly important with the imminent talent scarcity on the labour market. How managers are able to make and retain a connection with their employees (through a high Connection Quotient) should be key within any organization's hiring and retention policy. In this context, one question that will need to be answered is how you retain and motivate the new generation of employees (Millennials and Generation Z, born in the mid- to late-'90s) and high potentials?

THE IMPORTANCE OF THE CONNECTION QUOTIENT AS A CONDITION FOR NEW LEADERSHIP

Working on innovations, embracing new markets, engaging in alliances or retaining rare talent can all be placed in the bigger context of leadership through the Connection Quotient.

Among other things, we are talking here about bridging:

- Hierarchical differences (vertical connection)
- Distances between employees and teams (horizontal connection)
- The boundaries between your own organization and other organizations (connection with external parties and stakeholders)
- Differences in insight based on demographics (connecting subgroups)
- Geographical differences (connecting different regions and 'glocalization')

vertical	horizontal	stakeholder	demographic	geographic
Across levels and hierarchy	Across functions and expertise	Beyond the boundaries of the organization, with external partners	Across diverse groups (e.g. gender, ethnicity, nationality)	Across regions and locality

Figure 15: The importance of the Connection Quotient as a condition for leadership for the future (Source: CCL)

Research by the Center for Creative Leadership (CCL, 2012) shows that leaders consider these five forms of the Connection Quotient extremely important for the future of leadership, and therefore for their impact on the organization. But, if you ask these leaders about the degree to which they themselves are effectively able to apply the Connection Quotient, only a small group actually believe they are able to do this very well. There is a gap between acknowledging that the Connection Quotient is important and being effective in applying it. This is what CCL refers to as the *critical gap* (**Figure 16**).

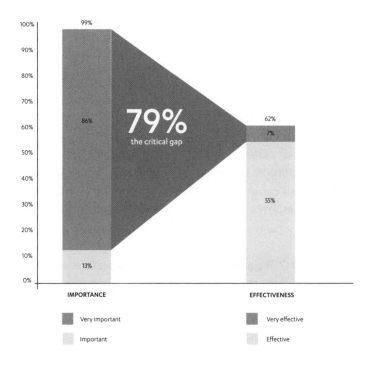

Figure 16: The critical gap between urgency and own effectiveness of the connection quotient at team and organization level (Source: CCL)

Leaders find the Connection Quotient – or more specifically, the bridging of all kinds of differences in the context of teamwork and organizations – extremely important, and they consider themselves inadequately equipped to make use of it.

IMPORTANT ELEMENTS WHEN CONNECTING WITH THE TEAM AND THE ORGANIZATION

What are the important elements required to achieve the Connection Quotient for teams and organizations as a whole? The result of this quest to achieve their CQ will provide insights into what needs to be taken into account when creating the Connection Quotient at team and organization level.

The ultimate answer is an illusion

Just as the context is important when establishing a connection with the other, the same applies for the connection with the team or organization. Depending on the context within which the team or the organization operates, the Connection Quotient will be designed accordingly. There is no 'one size fits all' solution for creating powerful connections.

As a leader, you should reflect (rationally and emotionally) on what your need is and what you consider important. Research and experience the needs of your customers, team members, stakeholders and others, and what they consider important. You can then link these insights with each other, attach meaning to them and act within the connection based on your findings. This way, the Connection Quotient is situationally dependent on the context within which the involved parties are operating.

Effective leaders? The presence of individual top performers?

No single cure-all exists that enables teams or organizations to flourish. Research has shown (Duhigg, 2016) that while leaders do have certain character traits in common, these character traits do not always guarantee that teams perform well. (See the last chapter 'The power of the Connection Quotient.') Neither does the presence of intelligence, excellent talent or individual high performers fully explain why some teams perform so well. So, if you should happen to be thinking that all you need to do to form your top team is to fill it with top performers, think again.

Collective tissue in teams and organizations

Research by Woolley, et al. (2010) shows that in successful teams, a kind of overarching, collective intelligence exists that cannot be traced back to separate individuals. These are character traits that can be wholly assigned to the group and not to the individuals themselves. This has to do with what we refer to as the connection at the team level or the organization level.

The leader at the centre versus the team/organization at the centre

To what extent are team leaders in connection with one other? It's important to hold the fabric of the team against the light of the Connection Quotient. After all, the way in which a team is organized has a major influence on the degree to which the Connection Quotient can, will and is allowed to develop. Let's imagine that there are ten team members who only communicate with the leader and only connect with him (**Figure 17**), as opposed to ten team members who communicate with each other and connect optimally with each (**Figure 18**).

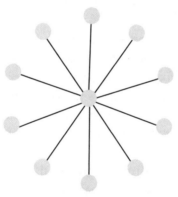

Figure 17: The leader at the centre — 11 junctions, 10 connections

Figure 18: The team/organization at the centre — 10 junctions, 45 connections

In the situation in which the leader is at the centre, there are 11 junctions (ten team members plus the leader) and in the most extreme case just ten connections are formed. All communication and connections pass through the manager. In the second case – when the leader gives others space – there are still ten junctions (the team members) but 45 connections are now possible. In this situation, as a leader, you allow the activities to be performed by the team members and trust their mutual relationships and capacities (head, hands *and* heart). You will find that mutual task allocation, decision-making, prioritization, conflict resolution, giving and asking for feedback and more will be done effectively by the team itself. If a leader is able to give the necessary space to ten people as a group, he is able to realize a massively powerful increase in the Connection Quotient (in this example, up to four and a half times as big).

Focusing inwards versus focusing outwards

In the above example, in which the team or the organization is given the lead role, it's not a question of the leader taking a step back but of actively giving others space. As a result, the leader is also able to fulfil his role differently. After all, if there are countless loose lines running to the leader (**Figure 17**), he will be constantly tempted to focus inwards. By contrast, if the leader succeeds in treating everyone else on the team as full members, and even expresses the wish that everyone takes ownership (**Figure 18**), then he can increasingly focus on the connections that lie outside the team. For example, connecting with other teams, developing new services, or accessing other customer segments. In that case, as a leader, he will only need to intervene, at most, when exceptions to the rule occur. This might be when a decision is escalated as a result of strategic considerations, or when a conflict has arisen that the team itself cannot resolve. If the leader is able to ensure that the functional layer has been taken care of by the team itself, this will create time for the leader to discuss the emotional layer (passions and frustrations) and the unique, personal side of the individuals (talent, drive, unique opportunities and circumstances). He can then link this unique yield to opportunities in the market.

Complexity versus simplification

As soon as the number of connections increases, as in **Figure 18**, the situation also becomes more complex. The leader who wants to manage this complexity will soon come up against obstacles. The more the number of connections increases, the more you will *have to* learn to trust your people. Instead of wanting to manage everything, it makes more sense to adopt the servant perspective by asking how you can support the employee in order to realize your tasks and goals. This supportive style of management leads to a totally different dynamic than seen in **Figure 17**, where the ball is always in the leader's court.

Trust versus distrust

The key often lies in a simplification of the collaboration by applying simplicity instead of making more agreements and getting more things done with fewer rules. *Less is more.* The question you have to ask yourself is: am I able to create a context in which I can say, 'I trust you'? How often does it happen that we lose ourselves in legal contracts or in detailed task and process descriptions? Is it possible to do this more simply, without losing sight of the finesses, the clarity and the unforeseen scenarios? What is prudent risk management, and where does the tipping point lie between wanting to manage risk and leading based on distrust?

Perhaps it's necessary to apply 'the small within the large' – smaller units that can work independently within a bigger context – in order to maintain a connection with the essence and to introduce (or re-introduce) the human element.

Freedom within the hierarchical structure

Anyone seeing **Figure 18** for the first time might be tempted to think it's a representation of a network organization. But this isn't necessarily the case. The connections drawn could also be plotted on a hierarchically structured organization, straight through all the layers, structures and boundaries. Vis-à-vis the Connection Quotient, the question within this hierarchically designed structure becomes whether you feel encouraged to engage in connections with colleagues, and with people outside the organization whom you consider to be personally important to connect with… or not?

The Connection Quotient within each valid functional structure

If we study the origins of the majority of organizations, we see that the classical build-up in hierarchy is often based on the implicit concept of mankind as a managing and controlling entity. This structure does not always go well when new forms of collaboration and managing are introduced that emphasize letting go and trust.

Based on this development in thinking and doing, new organizations are arising, such as Buurtzorg Nederland. Within this Dutch home-healthcare organization, small self-steering teams are responsible for the planning and execution of their tasks. Several teams are supported by a regional coach and there is just one small main office.

However, the classical hierarchical structure must not necessarily be abolished completely. It's about offering a way of connecting within each valid functional structure. This can be the case at the team level or organizational level. The organization chooses a functional team or organization structure. Within such a structure, how do you engage in a connection with each other, to help your clients and to achieve the results you have agreed on with each other?

Figure 18 is a supplement to a hierarchical structure. It is an invitation within the classical construct, or any other structure, to reflect on the following question: how many connections do you engage in to be optimally effective as individual, team and organization? Does that look more like the situation depicted in **Figure 17**, or the one in **Figure 18**? Which one do you prefer and what is required to achieve this desirable degree of connection?

PUTTING THINGS INTO PRACTISE

Functions, teams and organizations are put in place to achieve results. Period.

The key question in Part III is: how do you do that in connection with your own team, across teams, and inside and outside your organization? I will explain this below, while at the same time giving a few guidelines and tips on how to apply this in practise.

Working with multiple screens

As a team coach while developing teams, in theory I can choose to follow a pre-defined scenario in detail. This way, I will be 100% sure that everything will be said and done that my client and I have established as important. At the same time, the chances are high that I will fail the final evaluation assessment. Why? Because I only followed the process in technical terms rather than responding to questions that arose during the execution.

For example, no attention was paid to the wishes and needs of the team members. And, when disturbances occurred, I failed to react adequately. Following the predefined scenario has become the goal, instead of the goal that had been agreed on.

What is expected of me when developing teams is that I constantly weigh up the situation and analyse the following:

- What do I see happening to people individually?
- What do I see happening at the team level?
- Do I encourage someone to put their point across strongly or do I cut him short?
- When does a group attempt to avoid the heat in the kitchen, and when is it a case of a repetition of moves?
- Which issues/topics do people avoid and what is the real underlying issue?

Sometimes something is necessary at the team level, sometimes at the individual level or at the organization level, so to what extent do you have all screens in view? And, which one will you then choose to stand behind, and why? What is now required to achieve the agreed goal and how do I act accordingly – with integrity?

This way, for you as a leader and for me as a team coach, the Connection Quotient produces a reality full of multiple screens in the arena of teamwork or within the scope of an entire organization.

The reason for existence and looking for the optimal situation

As a leader, you are continually making trade-offs. In one case it's important to stick to agreements that have been made, or to apply a standard procedure. In another, it's more important to ignore the agreements or to deviate from standard operating procedure. Your actions are governed here by your own perceptions. You link everything that you discover at the team or organization level, or what discussions reveal (either intentionally or unintentionally) to the reason for existence of the team or the organization.

Once you have verified your findings, taking into account all the various levels and perspectives, check how things are for the rest of the team or for those elements of the organization that may be affected.

Take appropriate action. And, of course, you'll occasionally get things wrong. In that case, ask yourself: what can I learn from this and how can we ultimately improve here? Do so even when you've encountered business frustrations, blunders within a team or when an element of the organization fails.

Nelson Mandela said once: "I never lose. I either win or learn." Can you manage to think this way when you don't succeed in achieving the optimal situation?

The human issue behind a technical problem

A lot of the problems we come across on the work floor appear at first sight to be technical questions. 'The computer isn't working' or 'The update wasn't installed on time.' If you then dig a little deeper ('Why wasn't that update on time?') and you ask the question 'Why is it that...' a few times in a row, you will start to notice something. In a lot of cases, behind the technical problem there's a human factor involved. For example, the person responsible for installing the update is a perfectionist, has never done it before, is afraid to make mistakes, feels a huge responsibility for the impact on the organization if things go wrong. He's afraid of what others will think of him if things do go wrong, has had no training, asked for some supervision but didn't receive it, gets stressed out about it and therefore reported sick on the day he had to install the update.

The same applies to finding solutions. By asking a few in-depth questions about the completeness and effectiveness of the solution, you will in the first instance be delaying the decision-making process. And, by increasingly fine-tuning the solution, you will see that the definitive approach that results from this process is a more permanent one, or that it tackles the problem more directly at its core.

Solving issues rationally and emotionally

Typically, when problems occur, a technical solution is not enough. You will also need to take into account related questions at the personal level. For agreements involving collaboration, is there a need for extra training, or disturbed work relations that need to be resolved? This will save time in the long run because the problem will then be structurally resolved both rationally and emotionally. With a strong connection between the participants in the discussion, a mutually endorsed approach, and a psychologically safe environment, it becomes easier and more logical to discuss the human factors and root causes, in addition to the technical problems.

Rate your team on five key values

In addition to the perspective based on leadership, we can also draw conclusions at the level of the team itself. A study by Google (Duhigg, 2016) revealed the collective character traits of teams. These are traits that can be assigned to the team as a whole; ones that cannot be explained by simply studying the individual level. So, it's about how a team functions as a collective. The research shows that when mediocre employees learn how they can collaborate well in a team, they get things done that a team consisting solely of high performers would not be able to get done.

According to Google, there are five key values that make this possible. Team members:

1. Perceive collectively that their work is important
2. Have the feeling that their work is personally meaningful
3. Need clearly defined goals and roles at all times
4. Can rely on each other and are aware of this
5. Create psychological safety among themselves

HOW TO READ THIS PART OF THE BOOK

Part III is devoted to connecting with your team and your organization. All the assignments, models and sources of inspiration included here are related to this domain. This part contains a total of 16 chapters. The first eight have been written primarily from the point of view of the leader as a person. The last eight chapters start with the leader as a role. As in the previous parts, all chapters start with a personal introduction.

In the first half of Part III, I deal with the tension that exists between intellect and emotion, the difference between groups and teams, and the quality of the team as a collective. I discuss frustrations in teamwork and the synergetic effects of collaboration.

In the last eight chapters of Part III, I talk about expressing your vision and the role of stories, what it means to be a High Performance Organization (HPO) and how, when you connect with a team or with the organization as a whole, you are able to engage with team development and leadership effectively.

It goes without saying that much of what you read in Part III will be familiar to you in your day-to-day practice as leader. It's up to you to further make the transition to the context of your own organization.

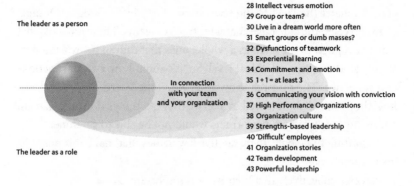

Figure 19: Overview of the chapters in Part III

I wish you much connection with your team and your organization!

CHAPTER 28

INTELLECT VERSUS EMOTION

PERSONAL INTRODUCTION

Thirty years ago, my life was predominantly ruled by what was happening in my head. Rationality determined what I could and could not do, and I acted accordingly. Even though as a child I was perfectly capable of accepting my feelings, dared to trust my intuition and act in line with it, I'd suppressed this ability during my adolescence.

As a result of my parents' painful divorce, I'd learned that as long as I refused to allow myself to really feel my emotions, I wouldn't get hurt. Of course, that wasn't true, because it was obvious I'd been hurt, while I did my best not to feel it.

This armour of rationality came at a price. For example, I found it difficult to enter into and maintain relationships with others. I was quite insecure, and I lived a rather reclusive life. To camouflage these disadvantages, I started overcompensating in my contacts with others. I lost count of the times I shouted myself down. I now know that many people weren't very pleased to meet me in that situation. This led me to feel more rejected more often, and I withdrew even more.

In the past 30 years, I have worked hard on myself. I discovered the power of accepting and truly embracing my feelings. The more in contact I am with myself, the more sincere my contact becomes with others. If I trust in myself, I can give true trust to others. If I truly respect myself, I can respect others with integrity, irrespective of whether I agree with their way of thinking or not.

In other words, the key to engaging in powerful relationships with others is to engage in the relationship with yourself. And, based on the sincere connection with yourself, you can engage in genuine connections with others at the team and organization levels, which helps in achieving the agreed-upon results (or even surpassing them).

ATTRIBUTES OF BEST TEAMS

What is the best team you were ever a member of and what are the attributes that made that team the best? The first thing you will probably think of is a business environment or a sports team. But try placing the concept of 'team' in a wider context. We can also talk of a team and teamwork within your family, within a group of friends, or in a club or society you've been a member of.

ONE-THIRD INTELLECT

I have asked countless people around the world the 'best team' question. Listening to the answers, a clear pattern emerges. A third of the specified attributes are related to the intellect.

Among other things, the best teams:
- Have an end goal in mind that has been commonly agreed on
- Are aware of the strategy needed to achieve it
- Have defined their priorities
- Have made clear agreements regarding tasks and roles
- Consist of team members with the relevant expertise
- Invest in personal and team development
- Have a clear and effective decision-making procedure in place
- Have an agreement regarding the resources required, and these have been allocated

These rational attributes are the firm conditions required for implementing the fundamental starting point of 'teams exist to achieve results.'

TWO-THIRDS EMOTION

By fulfilling only the rational attributes, a team will never be able to become the best team. Other qualities are required for this and these are concerned with emotion. This is only logical because teams and organizations consist of people. And, putting people together creates an emotional dynamic by definition, which contributes to creating a powerful connection and collaboration (or not).

The emotional attributes form two thirds of the answer to the question regarding the attributes of the best teams. For example, the best teams:

- Give and receive trust to articulate different thoughts
- Collectively share and celebrate successes of both the group and individuals
- Specify and articulate conflicts, because these are regarded as opportunities for new discoveries, growth and creativity
- Value with an open mind each other's differences in ideas, background, standpoints, personality, approach and way of living
- Give and receive feedback on a daily basis
- Create an atmosphere of mutual respect and genuine appreciation
- Have enthusiastic team members who look ahead and value each other

ATTRIBUTES OF POWERFUL LEADERS

If I ask people about the attributes of the best teams, consistently one-third of the answers will relate to rational attributes and two-thirds to emotional attributes. This ratio between intellect and emotion becomes even more skewed if I ask people about the attributes of powerful leaders.

In this empirical study, I have referred from the start to leaders in the broadest sense of the word. Besides leaders in a business or political context, you also have people you experience as a leader within your family, within your social environment, or within every other random connection that sounds logical to you.

The ratio between rational and emotional attributes in the answers to my question concerning powerful leaders is even more skewed than for the question concerning best teams: 10% are about rational attributes and as many as 90% of the answers concern emotional attributes.

Some of the attributes I constantly hear about leaders who are considered to be powerful are:

- He radiates pleasure, enthusiasm and passion
- He shows respect and trust
- He treats me as an equal
- He believes in me
- He challenges me
- He creates a safe environment in which I feel supported
- He takes the time to really listen to me and my viewpoints

The impact on the other person is that he feels heard and seen, he is stimulated to put in maximum effort, and he willingly follows the leader in achieving his vision and goals.

EQUAL

The consistency in the answers to the two questions leads me to observe that within the best teams, and regarding powerful leaders, conscious or unconscious attention is paid to the emotional side of engaging in connections and collaborations. Does this mean that in day-to-day situations more attention must be paid to the emotional aspects of collaborating instead of to the rational aspects?

In my opinion we have a paradox here. In a sense they are equal, and yet at the same time they're not.

When creating the best teams, the rational and emotional attributes are equal because paying less or no attention at all to one of the two elements will immediately create problems within the team or the organization. If, for example, you don't create enough clarity about rational attributes such as goals, tasks and procedures, questions about the direction and the functional side of the collaboration will arise. This has an impact on the effectiveness of the team.

If insufficient attention is paid to emotional attributes such as trust, respect and transparency, the collaboration will immediately become less sincere. This also has an impact on the collaboration and effectiveness of the team. In this context, both attributes are of equal value when creating best teams.

UNEQUAL

The starting point is that emotion and intellect are fundamentally of equal value in order for a team to be effective. Unfortunately, intellect still dominates, at least in the case of many leaders. Based on this focus, more attention is paid to optimally structuring the team.

For example, following the defined procedures becomes more important, and much emphasis is placed on accountability. When that happens, the process becomes laborious and there's less flexibility. The team works together in an increasingly mechanical way. The result is that the power of the connection and emotion is reduced to zero through over-organization.

In an extreme situation, employees are reduced to simply a means of production to achieve results.

Similarly, if the leader focuses primarily on the emotions and takes this too far, it will also have an impact on the effectiveness of the team. For example, if he insists on continually talking to everyone about the management side, instead of defining boundaries and determining the path to follow, at some point this will negatively affect the results. No choices are made, and the employees don't know what's expected of them (or they do what they think best).

In other words, the prime cause of imbalance between intellect and emotion is directly linked to the natural focus of you as a leader.

Additionally, I'm convinced that it is the emotional factor that contains the natural source of inspiration for powerful collaboration and achieving results. Think, for example, of the love for the patient, the attention for the pupil, the passion for numbers, the dream of a better world, etc. These motivations belong to the domain of the emotions and are an inexhaustible source of commitment.

If you can create the right circumstances to make use of this natural source in a sincere manner, results that were considered impossible before suddenly become realistic. For example, this can occur when teachers themselves start to connect more and are willing to make an extra effort in the classroom by making a connection between the source of inspiration of 'the growth of children' and the activities they carry out.

They work less for the money, more for their 'belief'. The same applies to all employees. The more they believe in the product or the service, and thus feel the connection, the more they are willing to work for it.

But there is a risk involved here. Based on loyalty and belief, employees may push their own needs to the background and accept too many changes and rules because they simply want to carry out their profession (focus on the customer). The belief or idealism then starts to work against them, which can lead to frustration, tension and burnout. In other words, the secondary cause of an imbalance between intellect and emotion is directly linked to how you motivate your employees (or unconsciously demotivate them). It pays to focus on the emotional factor as a leader.

A POINT TO REFLECT ON

What do you think would happen in society if you and your family members, neighbours, people with different cultural backgrounds or religious beliefs all worked on the emotional connection with themselves, and then engaged in an emotional connection with others? Would there still be so many wars, conflicts and arguments?

ASSIGNMENT: Accelerating excellence

In your next team meeting, ask this question: what is the best team you were ever a member of, and what are the three to five attributes that made that team the best?

Give them a couple of minutes to think about it and then invite everyone to share their thoughts with the others. Ask them to give a short description of the team they had in mind (just sharing these insights can lead to unexpected situations and fresh insights regarding the other person) followed by the three to five attributes.

Write the rational attributes on the left side of the flip chart, and the emotional attributes on the right. Once all the attributes have been written down, discuss with team members whether they can see any patterns. Discuss also the attention given to the rational and emotional sides of working within teams. Talk about what is needed to make this team the best team that has ever existed.

What insights do you discover and what agreements do you want to make about them? What kind of connection do you all want to have?

You can decide rationally to pay more attention to your emotions. Can you decide emotionally to pay less attention to your intellect?

CHAPTER 29

GROUP OR TEAM?

PERSONAL INTRODUCTION

During my training at the Royal Military Academy and in my career as an officer within the Dutch Royal Air Force, the management would continually emphasize how important the team was.

A team can only excel if you go for the same clearly defined goal; everyone is aware of their individual task and role, and takes responsibility for it; and everyone supports each other and collaborates based on camaraderie, trust and respect.

This intense connection, founded on rational and emotional factors, engendered a lot of personal satisfaction, pride and growth in me, as well as an enormous amount of loyalty to 'our' organization. And the results of that connection and collaboration were equally impressive. We and the organization were constantly amazed at what happened during drills. No matter how high the pressure became, we achieved the results that were demanded of us.

Yet, this 'we' thinking was not always present within the organization. At all levels within the Dutch Royal Air Force you had individuals who were more focused on personal politics, promising more than they could deliver. Some of my colleagues had massive egos, acting more out of self-interest than in the interests of the organization. Not surprisingly, this had a direct impact on our connection and in our mutual collaboration. My trust in them waned and I noticed that I wasn't prepared to do my best for them. Consequently, instead of emotionally connected teams, groups formed whose connections were based more on rational justifications.

This and later experiences in industry convinced me that there is a clear difference between a group and a team. Looking back, I realize that I had been a member of a number of groups in which we collaborated because we had to. But, luckily, I spent much of my time with my former colleagues in teams in which we were prepared to go the extra mile for each other, working together based on a genuine connection.

In this chapter I will cover seven important differences between groups and teams.

GROUP OR TEAM?

For years now, organizations have been under increasing pressure to improve performance while having fewer resources. Measures to cut costs and streamline processes have been implemented, people collaborate today independent of time and place, and every year the way we work together has to be more effective and efficient.

And so, now we have organizations with flatter structures, which are being run increasingly offsite and where employees work as members on multiple teams (virtual or otherwise). At least, most people typically assume they joined teams. However, what I observe is that people often refer to teams when they actually joined a group. Is there a difference? Yes!

Difference 1: Purpose

Within any group there is an overriding feeling that it has been created for administrative purposes. In other words, to keep the *span of control* manageable or to make it easier to remove a management layer. Within a team, on the other hand, the members deeply realize that the only way to achieve a goal that cannot be realized by one individual is to work together. It is this common purpose that binds and connects.

Difference 2: Role awareness

Within any group, each individual is preoccupied with his own task and little is known or understood about the tasks of the other group members. There is no overview of the contributions that each individual makes towards the end result, and this forms the basis for a lack of understanding, suspicion and the creation of 'little empires'. Within teams, the members are aware of the fact that everyone contributes to the end result, and that acquiring insight into each other's tasks and tuning into activities can lead to more streamlined processes.

Difference 3: Conflict resolution

Within any group, when conflicts arise, the members are often quick to point the finger at other members and expect the manager to resolve the situation. The manager is then the one who has to ensure that any problems are dealt with and resolved. Within teams, the members feel a bond with each other and take responsibility for the collaboration. Instead of talking about each other, they talk *with* each other, and the manager is only called in if conflicts escalate or threaten to do so.

Difference 4: Collaboration

Within any group, there is always some element of suspicion, causing members to be extra cautious about what they say. They make sure they don't say anything 'stupid.' This leads to their creativity being stifled, and their ability to resolve problems is weakened. The collaboration feels fragmented. Within a team, trust leads to open communication, resulting in everyone's contribution being valued. The members listen to each other's views and are aware of the benefit of different perspectives in finding solutions to the problems. Genuine connection is the result.

Difference 5: Governance

Within any group, command and control forms the basis on which a manager manages. The members are told what task they have to perform, when this has to be completed, and preferably how it has to be done. They are reduced to 'supplying hands.' Within teams, attention is focused on gaining commitment. Team members provide their opinions on the goals and how they think they can be achieved. In addition to their 'hands,' their 'minds' are also engaged. After all, two heads are better than one. And then, apparently impossible goals can be realized in a creative way.

Difference 6: Development

Also within any group, training is directed at developing and/or further intensifying skills that are required in the short term to execute the task that a member has been called on to perform. Within teams, members are encouraged to collaborate, to not be afraid of admitting to mistakes, and to be open to criticism. So next to standard vocationally oriented training, it's essential that the members receive training in the fields of personal development, team dynamics and so on.

Difference 7: Appreciation

Within any group, results are rarely celebrated. There is no culture of 'sticking out from the crowd.' Feedback is given primarily when things go wrong and if improvements have to be introduced. And, any successes are 'claimed' by the manager. Teams, by contrast, know how important it is to celebrate successes together. They are proud of what has been achieved. The manager realizes that he is responsible for creating the conditions in which team members can excel.

ASSIGNMENT: Team scan

Do you want to know if you're working together as a group or as a team? Then try doing the following exercise with your colleagues.

Take a big piece of paper and draw the following diagram on it. Then ask each colleague to write his initials on each scale according to how he perceives the mutual collaboration and connection. In general terms, collaboration connections that generally score higher on the **left side perceive less of a team feeling**, and collaboration connections that score predominantly to the **right have more of a team feeling**.

PURPOSE

Administrative   Common goal

ROLE AWARENESS

Focus on own task   Focus on process

CONFLICT RESOLUTION

Manager   Team members

COLLABORATION

Distrust   Trust

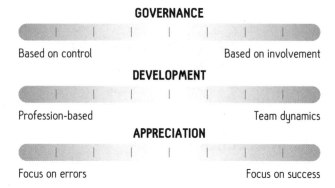

Then, start a discussion on your similarities and differences, and what you can learn from them. What agreements will you make at the end of the session? What tangible changes are you going to make in terms of connection and collaboration?

Be particularly aware of the atmosphere in which the discussion is conducted. Enter into the conversation with a feeling of curiosity about the insights of the other person, rather than wanting to defend your own viewpoints. If necessary, ask an objective colleague or an external facilitator to chair the discussion.

**How do you collaborate with team members
you wouldn't choose as a colleague yourself?**

CHAPTER 30

LIVE IN A DREAM WORLD MORE OFTEN

PERSONAL INTRODUCTION

Participating in a ten-day improvisation summer school program given by actor, playwright, theatre director and theatre teacher, Keith Johnstone was a major catalyst for me. At the end of the ten days, I was more than able to adopt a genuinely open and inquisitive attitude to thinking and working. Keith is one of the pioneers of contemporary improvisation theatre in general, and of theatre sport in particular.

During those ten days, I experienced and felt what it meant to say yes to every proposal that came my way. That's because one of the ground rules in improvisation theatre is saying yes unconditionally.

Everything the other person offers you in words and actions you take in, accept and build on. So, instead of 'no' or 'yes, but...' you say 'YES' and create something new from there. That's the moment you experience how creative the human mind is and what is possible if you dare to let go.

I was also challenged to use my body when engaging in connections, something else that was beyond my comfort zone. Imagine moving across the floor like a pride of lions for 90 minutes, fighting with each other, lying up against each other, etc.

And, I vividly recall the improvisation dance in which I was constantly in motion, 'glued' as it were to another man. I was forced to overcome some personal embarrassment, but it was a totally liberating experience.

I don't want to claim that in organizations we need to start moving more like animals or becoming physically more intimate with each other. What I'm curious about is seeing what would happen if we allowed a little more craziness onto the work floor and said 'YES' more often... and then built on the idea.

What effect would that have on the connection? What would this make possible in terms of results? That's what this chapter is all about.

PRINCE, PRINCESS AND KNIGHT

Children are constantly living in a dream world without inhibition and can become totally immersed in their role playing for hours. Sticks become swords, a towel becomes a cape and a paper crown takes on the role of a priceless treasure. It's so wonderful to watch – the uninhibitedness, the pleasure, how the children respond to each other, and the creativity.

What would it be like if within our teams we allowed the members to live in a fantasy world more often? What if we weren't constantly thinking about whether something was allowed or possible? Imagine if we started a process together without too much structure or without a sharply defined goal?

What if instead of saying 'no,' we said, 'What I like about that idea is ...' and started researching what we could learn from a proposal, and then built on it? If we could see differences as being complementary and we could let go of the feeling of being in competition? What would the impact be on the connection and the end result for your team?

Yet, too often people dismiss this with: 'That's not possible in the real world. We have goals to achieve and responsibilities to comply with.' This is true, of course. And I acknowledge that teams have to achieve results. That's why teams exist in the first place. It also means that teams that never achieve results have to be disbanded immediately. This is as far as I go in accepting the reasoning that living in a fantasy – in a dream world – is impossible in the 'real' world.

INTERACTION AND CREATIVITY

The learning for me here is the way in which creativity can be given the space to grow.

Look, for example, at the way children play together in a dream world. Based on a sense of wonder, the desire to do something together is born. New rules are invented as the game progresses. They are totally immersed in something together. There will, of course, be moments when children disagree with each other. These situations are voiced and resolved (usually quickly) so that the game can continue. The transparency of feelings, accepting different ideas and the desire to really play together are all elements that many teams can learn and grow from.

It's a shame we need to learn these kinds of skills again within a business context. Due to the focus on structure, results and having to do 'well,' we change from creative children to adult robots that run through their programmes.

Instead of brainstorming about the possibilities available to resolve problems or to analyse why or how a problem has been caused in the first place, we go for the first solution that appeals to us (or the one that is imposed upon us based on authority). And, we draw up an action plan to achieve this. We have been reduced from individuals with a wide view of the world and huge amounts of creativity to doers who have to achieve a goal, preferably with minimum effort and as quickly as possible. This leads to our creativity being suffocated.

THE BUSINESS-LIKE CHILD

Creativity is something we need to cherish, and you should give more space to the child in yourself within the business context. Move in that direction by doing and saying things whose added value you are not immediately aware of, or by deviating from the accepted standard, leaving options and solutions open for longer, generating wild ideas. What if you simply did something because you thought it would be fun?

It all starts with giving yourself permission. Do you allow the child within you some space?

Anyone who lives in a dream world now and then increases the chances of achieving better results. By giving yourself mental (and if you dare, also physical) temporary permission to live in another world, you create the opportunities to achieve better, newer or radically different solutions and results. In doing so, you are really taking responsibility for the basic starting point that teams exist to achieve results. From a business point of view, the dream world is thereby a powerful complement to the 'real' world.

The fun that is then engendered results in you and your colleagues collaborating with even more connection and pleasure.

ASSIGNMENT: Handbook for a brick

Take a pen and a piece of paper. For one whole minute write down everything you can think of that you can do with a brick. How many things have you come up with?

Now take one minute to become a hippie. Adopt a physical pose that is appropriate (sit on the floor), pretend you are smoking a joint, talk very slowly, give the peace sign, and whatever else comes into your head and body when you imagine a longhaired flower child. Yes, I admit this is going to look a bit weird. But give yourself permission to really do it, without thinking about it. Just for a little while, allow the child in you to live in a dream world.

After you have lived as this character for one minute, pick up your pen and paper again and write down what else you can do with a brick, that you didn't think of before. Remain in the same physical pose and make the same stoned hippie movements throughout this one minute.

What do you notice after this minute? Most people get a stream of new and original ideas through physically and mentally changing themselves. What lesson do you learn from this exercise that you can apply in the 'real' business world?

**You're the only one who can determine where
your dream stops and where reality begins.**

CHAPTER 31

SMART GROUPS OR DUMB MASSES?

PERSONAL INTRODUCTION

In the defence organization, in times of operational activity, decisions are made that can cost human lives. There's a very real chance that the casualties could include your your direct colleagues. This produces an emotional pressure and an intense feeling of responsibility when making decisions. You cannot and must not take this lightly.

This pressure – and the corresponding responsibility – undoubtedly contributes to creating intense connections at the level of team and organization.

Today, Dutch defence personnel are regularly sent on missions to unstable regions. People are actually getting killed while carrying out their tasks. I have an enormous amount of respect for the way they are able to function in challenging circumstances. It's the same kind of respect I have for police and firefighters. They also regularly find themselves in life-threatening situations and need to make difficult choices in a split-second.

For these organizations, once a decision has been made, it is assumed that everyone will comply with it unconditionally, even if they might not personally agree with it. On the one hand, you are expected to align yourself with the decision of your superior, the team or the organization, and on the other you have to act based on your connection with your personal norms, values and professional experience.

How do you cope with this paradox, in the heat of the moment, when you're in the middle of executing and have to act under pressure?

Although in many organizations the decisions taken do not directly result in human lives being lost, the conflict between loyalty to the decision versus taking personal responsibility must be reflected on. How do you and your colleagues view this paradox and what is its impact on your connection? In order to challenge you to discuss this topic within your team or organization, I have outlined a number of striking examples of collaboration.

Are you working with a dumb group or a smart mass?

SWITCHING RAPIDLY

As humans, we generally form our organizations using so much structure that the result is, hopefully, a well-oiled machine that's perfectly aligned to achieve the organization's goals. Everyone is aware of the goal and of his specific task in achieving that goal, processes and procedures are documented, and the products are supplied. Until, that is, the customer starts making other demands, the competition suddenly becomes a threat, someone with a big ego upsets the culture, and so on.

Then, especially in larger organizations, we have trouble switching rapidly and adapting the organization in the short term to the new situation.

Smart groups or dumb masses?

ANTS

Despite the fact that an ant can lift up to 50 times its body weight, on its own it doesn't get much done. A group of half a million ants is quite a different story. Together, they are able to collaborate in such a way that they can defend their territory and find the shortest path to food. If you place an obstacle in their path, it's not long before a newer shortest path has been found. Additionally, the tasks are allotted to the half a million ants via simple means of communication – using feel and smell. Their way of working is so effective that it has been comprehensively studied. The rules that have been discovered – referred to as swarm intelligence – are used in the logistics and use of the internet.

Smart groups or dumb masses?

SMOKE AND FIRE

How does a group of people react when smoke suddenly appears in a public space where they feel comfortable? Research shows that there's a great chance that they will ask themselves where the smoke is coming from, look around and, as long as the others also remain calm, nobody will actually take any action, even though there is a real risk of danger.

Another example is that if we look for a restaurant, we will generally walk past an empty one. And if we see a restaurant with a lot of cars parked outside, and we can see people inside, eating, we will usually go inside.

Our conclusion is that it must be good and the place to be. But how did those people get there in the first place?

Smart groups or dumb masses?

HONEY BEES

Because flying costs honey bees a tremendous amount of energy, it's very important for them to do this as efficiently as possible. Once the worker bees return to the hive, they communicate where the food can be found by means of their dance. Based on the quality of the food and the distance involved, a choice is made regarding which bees should fetch the food. To cover the many different fields full of flowers, while travelling the shortest possible distance, an optimal route is flown.

Determining such an optimal route between many objects is also referred to as the travelling salesman problem. It has taken a long time for us to develop computers capable of performing these calculations, and solve the problem mathematically. But bees have been able to do it for millions of years. What makes it even more extraordinary is that the workers don't travel at the head of the group when they return to the food source – they fly somewhere in the middle.

Smart groups or dumb masses?

THE CONNECTION QUOTIENT

In the animal kingdom, within a group, each animal knows what his role is and he can produce a superlative performance without being centrally managed. A crucial factor here is that not very many rules have been defined about how they have to collaborate. But the rules that *do* apply are sacred. Everyone keeps to them, without exception.

What would happen if we built our teams and organizations to be more aligned with this principle? What would it mean for the role of the managers? Managing would become a role that could be taken on across the whole network by anyone, depending on the situation. What would become possible if employees were willing to set aside their egos for the greater good? What would your work look like if you decided to put in 100% effort even on a bad day?

ASSIGNMENT: Complexity and the use of swarm intelligence

There's no simple answer to how people within teams or organizations should deal with the difficulty of being loyal to the decision *and* taking personal responsibility.

Instead of making a statement, in your role as manager, and managing with that goal in mind (at the risk of creating a dumb group), it is perhaps more useful to bring the issue out into the open. Discuss together the pros and cons of this issue and determine collectively how to approach this field of tension.

To initiate this discussion, try standing in one space with all your team members, or members of your organization. Get everyone to look around them and to pick out two people. You don't have to know them personally, as long as you can see them from where you are standing. Once everyone has done this, it's time for the follow-up instructions. These are as follows: walk to a place in the space so that all your three positions are in one straight line. The line is formed by:

- You on the one side
- One of the two people you have in your mind in the middle
  (decide which of the two you want to be in the middle)
- And the third person on the other side of the line, at a distance from the person in the middle that is equal to your distance from the person in the middle

equal distance

When everyone in the space has understood the instructions – if necessary, you can demonstrate by putting yourself in the right position with respect to the other two persons – the assignment can begin. It's up to you how you do this. And in view of the fact that everyone will start to perform the assignment simultaneously, at the beginning it will be chaos. But, gradually, you will observe that things automatically become calmer, until the assignment has been successfully completed. This could take a few minutes.

Give them the calm and space to achieve the final positions. When everyone is standing in their final position, ask how they experienced the assignment. Who thought it was impossible, how involved were you, did you consider giving up, how did you encourage each other, etc.

How long do you think it would take to reach the final position if you as a leader had to explain to every individual separately, via direct questions and instructions, the correct place to stand with respect to the two others? For this to succeed, you will need to know which two persons every individual had in mind. There would then be a complex – or virtually impossible – logistical puzzle that is difficult to solve on your own (where would everyone have to stand?). In the time it would take you as a manager to solve the puzzle, the other team members would be bored stiff.

In short, this is a perfect example to demonstrate the power of swarm intelligence in teams.

How can you open up and incorporate swarm intelligence into your team?

CHAPTER 32

DYSFUNCTIONS OF TEAMWORK

PERSONAL INTRODUCTION

I have six core values: personal growth, playfulness, family, trust, honesty and fierce courage.

I try every day to live and act as much as possible according to these tenets. Do I succeed in this, 100%, every day? No. But I *do* continue to reflect on why things don't go right sometimes, so that I can learn from it. I also continue to challenge myself to step outside my comfort zone and to live and work even more in line with these values.

Living and working based on these personal core values is part of my trademark. My clients and my colleagues experience the added value of this, directly and indirectly. In connection with the other, I voice what there is, remain curious, and challenge and support where necessary. People like this because it triggers a process of learning and change at the individual, team or organization level.

Living and working based on my core values encourages me to implement the five team strengths, as the business management author Patrick Lencioni refers to them. This prevents dysfunctions arising in collaborative efforts, which impacts the mutual connection and the results. And that's not what I want!

This chapter is about these dysfunctions.

PATRICK LENCIONI

In his book, *The Five Dysfunctions of Teamwork*, Lencioni (2002) describes five dysfunctions that act to obstruct real teamwork. These dysfunctions can reinforce each other, and the presence of one dysfunction increases the chance of the other dysfunctions also being present, thereby disrupting teamwork.

In other words, to be able to really work well and in connection as a team, it's important to learn to recognize these dysfunctions... and then to learn how to avoid them.

Dysfunction 1: Absence of trust

Trust is *the* basis for powerful teamwork and the building of genuine and honest connections. Conversely, the absence of trust makes optimal teamwork impossible. There is then a good chance that the team will revert to being a group. When it comes to trust, Lencioni suggests, team members have to dare to show their vulnerability in relation to each other, and their vulnerability concerning their own weaknesses, the skills they lack, the mistakes they make, or to openly ask for help.

Can they trust that if they do so, the vulnerability they have shown will not be used against them? If this atmosphere of safety does not exist, the team members will stop showing their vulnerability and will act increasingly in a competitive or political manner to protect their own reputation. This pattern forms the basis for the second dysfunction.

Dysfunction 2: Fear of conflict

No shine without friction. This Dutch expression encapsulates the notion that to achieve lasting connection and collaboration, it is important to have productive conflicts. When I say 'productive', I mean that the team members arrive at solutions for team issues in the short term by engaging in a dialogue about differences in insight. In effective teams, this dialogue can be carried out accompanied by emotions and passion without an adverse effect on the connection between the members.

In the case of teams where the members do not trust each other, an open dialogue isn't possible. Instead of constructive conflicts, an artificial harmony is created whereby team members keep their standpoints and concerns to themselves. And this lays the foundation for the third dysfunction.

Dysfunction 3: Lack of commitment

Well-functioning teams act based on genuine commitment, with members fully supporting the choice that has been made. During discussions, they will express their opinions wholeheartedly, and as soon as a decision has been taken they will execute it, even though they may find it difficult to support it personally.

This feeling of communal responsibility is of particular importance for members of management teams. They talk consistently with one voice because they are aware that their employees act in accordance with what they say and how they get their message across.

Minor differences of opinion between managers high in the organization will have increased enormously by the time they reach the employees at the bottom end of the organization. If fear of conflicts leads to opinions not being expressed, or consensus being sought, actions are likely to be taken that are not fully supported. Team members will cover their own backs and delay taking important decisions. A certain vagueness is created, and collaboration is merely paid lip service, which lays the foundation for the fourth dysfunction.

Dysfunction 4: Avoidance of accountability

Members of effective teams hold colleagues accountable for failure to honour agreements that have been made, or for actions taken against the common interest. Despite the fact that this can be awkward or tricky, and can lead to uncomfortable situations, they nonetheless feel a responsibility to do so. They take this risk not only because it results in the individual members growing in their role as human beings, but also because it achieves the results for the team.

In the end, this mindset leads to better mutual connection and mutual respect. In teams whose members do not feel committed to the agreements that have been made, or where a clear picture of the agreements is lacking, members will hardly be held accountable, if at all. It's extremely difficult to hold someone accountable for something that was never explicitly agreed on or made clear in the first place. And that's the perfect breeding ground for the final dysfunction.

Dysfunction 5: Inattention to results

Teams exist to achieve results. If a result is no longer required or relevant, the team loses its right to exist. It's as simple as that. Members of powerful teams are aware of this and are focused on achieving the results together. They fully realize what results they are working towards and they don't allow themselves to be distracted by less important issues. If the result is achieved, they enjoy the successes and celebrate them.

At the other extreme, there are teams that do not work towards a common goal and where the members do not hold each other accountable.

This allows room to focus on personal interests and matters such as ego, recognition or career planning. Or, the focus is placed on the importance of their own department, which occurs at the cost of collaboration on an organization-wide scale. The collaboration within the (management) team and the collaboration between the employees of the various departments then suffers. This is why this dysfunction has a deep impact on the whole organization.

If your interest has been aroused, and you want to know more about these themes and how to work on them in practise, I recommend reading Lencioni's book. Do you have the courage to acknowledge the dysfunctions that exist, to make them explicit and then to tackle them?

ASSIGNMENT: 'Inteamacy'

Lencioni asserts that mutual trust forms the basis for powerful connections and teamwork. If this is what you want, then making a start is easy – get to know the people you work with. And not just in the sense of their job title, but as individuals. This exercise will help you get started.

Spend an afternoon with your colleagues, take a photograph with you of when you were a child, play your favourite music and talk to each other about who you are. To give you some ideas about what you could talk about, I have listed a few questions you can share with each other. Feel free to add your own.

Which questions you choose, how vulnerable you dare to be and how much time you spend on this process is entirely up to you. The important thing is to enjoy the process. Each step in the direction of openness is welcome and contributes to your connection and mutual trust.

Questions could include:
- What is your family background? What values were you taught within that family? How important are they for you?
- What did you learn at school that you still make use of in your life today?
- What event in your life has had a major impact on you? What did you learn from it? And, how does this event influence your view on life?

- What work (or piece of work) do you look back on with the most pleasure? What work did you find the least satisfying? Why did you choose those specific experiences? What does this say about you?
- What are your hobbies? What do you find so attractive about them? How much time do you spend on them?
- What is your family situation? What challenges do you face? What are you most proud of regarding your family?

Don't focus on the dysfunction but look for the underlying problem.

CHAPTER 33

EXPERIENTIAL LEARNING

PERSONAL INTRODUCTION

Whenever I'm 100% convinced of an idea of mine, I find myself having problems listening to other people's opinions with genuine interest and being open to atypical ideas. If I'm not careful, I'll start trying to convince them that my way of thinking is right, and then attempt to sell them my idea.

Is this useful? Not at all! I know exactly what the added value is of staying curious and collectively exploring the pros and cons of the various trains of thought. I'm aware that a much better idea will often emerge if we engage in a joint exploration process. I'm convinced of the added value of collective brainstorming about problems and issues, and of incorporating all the ideas generated, however crazy or strange they may be, in the process of making choices. I'm aware that together we can come up with ideas that none of us would have thought of on our own.

But, I'm only human. I sometimes let my emotions get the better of me, and as a result I lose sight of my own impact.

So, despite the fact that I'm convinced about my idea, I try to remain open to other insights so that we can arrive at (better) choices together. What impact would this have on the connection and on the result of your team or your organization if this way of working were to be chosen as the standard?

Or, even more ambitiously, what if the process of resolving daily problems and issues together became part of an experiential learning culture?

Imagine a culture in which it's normal to learn from each other in daily practise, and to transfer knowledge, instead of following a one-day (or more) training course in order to acquire that knowledge? The advantage is that in such a culture you learn what you need at precisely the moment you need it. Not only does this create much more impact during the learning process (as I will discuss later in this chapter), it also contributes to more mutual trust and mutual connection. This is even more effective if you introduce a buddy system to accompany it.

PUT A STOP TO ALL THOSE TRAINING COURSES

Stop going to all those professional-development courses that don't produce any results.

Does the following situation sound familiar to you? You sit for the whole day at a U-shaped table, a trainer empties his knowledge and insights over you (supported by stunning images, and powerful one-liners) while you take notes. At the end of the day, you're told to put what you've learned into practise the next day.

Because the theory was explained so quickly, you hardly remember what was said that day. And then, because the next day you've got deadlines that need to be met, there's not much left of your intention to apply what you've just learned. After a couple of days, you've stopped thinking about it altogether. Once again, it's been a waste of precious time, money and effort.

A lot of training today rolls out this way. And, remarkably, there are still managers who opt for this scenario. Why, oh why? Don't do it!

THE 70:20:10 PRINCIPLE

I'm a huge fan of experiential learning, where the learning process is based on the 70:20:10 principle (Arets, et al., 2015).

The idea is that 70% of everything we learn comes to us in practise, through the experiences we have – just by doing it, and experimenting along the way, instead of talking about it. Another 20% we learn in discussions with others, through feedback given in an informal setting, with space that allows for backgrounds and knowledge to be shared, and mutual support. The last 10% is knowledge acquired in the traditional manner, through cognitive knowledge transfer, for example.

Managers need to actively facilitate the first two forms of learning – responsible for 90% of all learning – by giving people confidence, encouraging them to make mistakes, and assembling a group of people who can optimally carry out an assignment.

When offering traditional forms of knowledge transfer (the last 10%), it's important not to spend a whole day on this. Provide it in a compact form, where the essence of the issue is explained in an hour.

You can then challenge the participants to apply their newly acquired knowledge directly, in practise, and invite them to discuss the outcomes with colleagues (the above-mentioned 90% of the learning process). In other words, pursue a course of direct growth and development.

KOLB'S LEARNING CYCLE

The 70:20:10 principle, devised by strategic consultant Charles Jennings, is closely related to the theory developed in the 1970s by the American psychologist David Kolb. Although both models are regarded with some distrust for not being scientifically proven, they do provide a framework that is useful when reflecting on and discussing differences in people's learning styles. Both give you insights into your own learning style, which can be used to design effective learning interventions within the work environment.

Kolb (1983) states that it's necessary to follow a learning process cycle that always consists of four phases. The cycle, which Kolb calls *experiential learning*, consists of:

1. Having a concrete experience
2. Reflective observation
3. Abstract conceptualization
4. Active experimentation

The immediate experience, in the here and now, forms the basis for the observation and reflection (what went well, what went wrong?). These observations are collected and translated into a theory (laws, models, ideologies). From there, hypotheses or new plans and ideas are derived, which are then again tested in practise. This testing leads in turn to new experiences and skills.

Ideally, every individual should have access to four different capacities in order to undergo an optimal learning process.

He should be able to alternate between specific commitment (concrete experience) and analytical distance (abstract conceptualization), as well as between observer (reflective observation) and participant (active experimentation). However, Kolb's research reveals that people differ in their preferences and their capacities with respect to the different activities within this learning process:

- **The diverger** learns particularly via concrete experience and reflective observation. His primary capacity is to view concrete situations from different perspectives.

- **The assimilator** learns especially via reflective observation and abstract conceptualization. His greatest capacity lies in placing a wide range of observations within a single overarching explanation or conceptualization.
- **The converger** learns especially via abstract conceptualization and active experimentation. His predominant capacity lies in being able to quickly understand the core of an issue and the practical application of ideas.
- **The accommodator** learns largely via active experimentation and concrete experience. His prime capacity lies in trying out new behaviour and executing plans.

RUN THROUGH THE ENTIRE CYCLE

Each combination of preferences leads to what Kolb refers to as a learning style: your preferred approach to things. Implicitly, then, different people start their learning process at different phases in the cycle. Kolb does not, however, attach any value judgment to this. It's merely another entry point in the learning cycle.

The essential point remains that the whole cycle has to be run through. In other words: initiate the learning process in a way that appeals most to the person involved, and make sure that he runs through the other three phases after that.

When designing effective development programmes, it is important to take this learning cycle into account, in addition to the 70:20:10 principle. This way, there's a greater chance that the knowledge, insights and skills offered actually lead to powerful actions in practise.

ASSIGNMENT: Go forth and work as you learn!

How do you learn? And how do your colleagues learn? Review the past year using these questions as your starting point.

Which formal and informal instances of knowledge transfer took place? And how is learning designed around themes such as personal development and collaboration within the team? How satisfied are you and your colleagues with how the learning process within the organization is designed? What is the ratio between formal learning and informal learning, and between rational learning themes and emotional learning themes?

Organize a meeting with your team and your HR manager to talk about this. Express explicitly what you need, and agree on how to improve knowledge transfer in practise. By applying the 70:20:10 principle and taking into account Kolb's learning cycle, you will avoid sending people to training that will have absolutely no positive effect whatsoever.

Learning together on the work floor intensifies connections and collaborations.

CHAPTER 34

COMMITMENT AND EMOTION

PERSONAL INTRODUCTION

What is your favourite piece of music? Why? Perhaps it reminds you of an important event in your life, or a deeper desire you may have. Or, maybe you listened to this music intensively during a certain period in your life and there's now a connection between that period and the emotions you associate with it. There could be many other reasons that a piece of music has a special place in your heart.

Music creates emotion and connection. First and foremost, it does so in and with yourself. Music also creates emotion and connection between people. You can see this very clearly if you go to a concert or a festival. Large groups of people, who are strangers to each other, collectively enjoy the experience. Differences in background, faith, race, sexual orientation, etc., are generally forgotten in that moment.

Because music has such an impact on emotion and connection, my colleagues and I like to use it in our work.

For example, during team development trajectories, I will ask the team members to bring along their favourite pieces of music. Everyone gets to hear each other's favourite number and the reason that piece is so meaningful to them. This often leads to quite a few surprises, regarding the choice of music and the personal stories behind them. It provides insights into each other's personalities, creating more mutual understanding, and an emotional connection is created with each other.

COMMITMENT (HUMAN DOING)

There are two elements that are essential for powerful leadership. The first is concerned with 'human doing' – the commitment to achieving your personal goal or that of the organization. This means that as a manager, you are aware of what you want to achieve together, dare to express this, plan the required actions, and ask for help if necessary. Getting your environment mobilized is a prerequisite for this. After all, if the goal is clearly formulated, employees can gain clarity about the actions they are required to perform, and therefore also about their task/role in the organization. I use the word 'can' deliberately here. This is not something that occurs automatically; your contribution as manager is essential.

But be aware that you can be *too* committed. If you always hold on to the approach you've chosen, you will become rigid. So, in addition to your commitment, realize that when circumstances change, a new approach may be required (certainly in today's turbulent times). Or as Anthony Robbins says: "Stay committed to your decisions but stay flexible in your approach."

EMOTION (HUMAN BEING)

But you won't achieve powerful leadership through commitment alone. The second element that is essential here is concerned with 'human being', the ability to be 100% 'in the moment' and to show your emotions. To what degree are you prepared to do this? What I've noticed is that managers will often display their feelings of delight or anger, but that there seems to be a taboo on, for example, showing that you are feeling scared, sad or uncertain.

Once someone has taken on the role of manager, it seems that an unwritten rule comes into play that forbids him from displaying too many emotions. A manager has to be strong and always have the right answers.

This can partly be explained through evolution. If male primates, surrounded by their own sort, demonstrate weakness, they risk being taken advantage of, or worse. This is also why field workers dealing with male baboons will only shoot a tranquilizer into their behind if there are no other rivals in the vicinity. Otherwise, there's a risk that the other males will attack when they see the alpha ape fall to the ground. There's no such problem, however, with female baboons.

Being vulnerable and expressing this openly allows the people around you to be vulnerable and to express vulnerability. Here's a question to reflect on: do you dare to be the first to show your vulnerability?

I constantly observe that managers who express their emotions have a positive effect on the people around them. It facilitates connection.

In my opinion, expressing your emotions is not a weakness at all. Rather, it is more a sign that the manager is sure of himself and is a prerequisite for powerful leadership.

ASSIGNMENT: Dare to ask

To which team or organization goal have you committed but not yet achieved? Which emotions do you experience as a result? Are there colleagues who could help you take the next step towards achieving that goal? It may be that you don't yet know how they might be able to help you.

Approach the colleague you find most daunting, awkward, etc., and ask him for help. When you ask for help, specify the emotion you are experiencing at the time. Observe what happens.

**Commit yourself to expressing your true emotions;
they make you human and create connection.**

CHAPTER 35

1 + 1 = AT LEAST 3

PERSONAL INTRODUCTION

I'm constantly getting new business ideas. In my enthusiasm, I will start implementing an idea straight away. Thanks to the powerful and stimulating connection I have with my colleagues, these ideas often lead to productive outcomes. In reality, though, not all of them will generate good results. There are two important reasons for this.

The first has to do with time. Finding the balance between work and personal time (or rather, I should talk about integration) remains a challenge for me. That's because my work feels so important to me that once I start, I find it difficult to stop. Fortunately, I can rely on the support of others, like my wife Cindy, and my business partner Jaco, to help me reflect, slow down and focus.

The second reason an idea doesn't always lead to the envisioned result is that in the execution phase, I may suddenly come to the conclusion that perhaps my idea wasn't such a good one. It would have been more practical – and would certainly have saved me time and energy – if I'd thought about this before initiating any action.

Something that does help in deciding whether to actually implement an idea – which I'm beginning to do more frequently – is to talk about it with others. The result is a more clear-cut picture of whether my idea is only 'nice' or really 'important', and how important it is to implement it. This way I become aware of which ideas I want to invest my time in and which ones I don't.

This is a fine example of the power of diversity and collaboration based on connection. In this chapter, I will draw a parallel between this theme and the way geese collaborate. I'll be really curious to hear about the lessons you take with you from this for your own team.

SMART GEESE

In autumn, a lot of geese fly to the Netherlands, where they will spend the winter. Despite the fact that these birds are often associated with less positive attributes ('you stupid goose' or 'you fat goose'), they can work extremely well together.

Have you ever wondered, for example, why geese always fly in a V formation? The wing movement of each goose creates an upward thrust for the birds behind him, enabling the flock to fly 71% further than it could otherwise. Doesn't sound that dumb to me! If we translate this to the human work environment, the lesson we can draw is that people with a strong sense of community and mutual trust help each other to achieve their goals.

FIVE MORE LESSONS WE CAN LEARN FROM GEESE

But there are more lessons to be learned from geese. Incidentally, these lessons are not my own; they are often attributed to naturalist Milton Olsen, but further research reveals that the real author is the American academic Dr. Robert McNeish (1972).

Here are some of McNeish's fascinating observations, along with the lessons I've derived from them:

1. When a goose falls out of formation, it immediately feels the drag and resistance of flying alone. It quickly falls back into formation to take advantage of the lifting power of the birds in front of it. (Lesson: it is wise to stay connected with those who are going in the same direction as you are. You have to be willing to accept help and to help others.)

2. When the lead goose tires, it rotates back into the formation and another goose takes up the point position. (Lesson: it pays to take turns demonstrating leadership and doing the hard tasks. We have to respect and maintain each other's unique mix of knowledge, skills, backgrounds and talents.)

3. The geese flying in formation honk to encourage those up front to keep up their speed. They use ten types of calls to communicate, depending on the situation they are confronted with. (Lesson: we need to make sure our honking is encouraging rather than judgmental. In groups where encouragement is predominant, productivity is much higher.

An individual gains strength from the encouragement of his team members. Stand behind your self-worth and core values, and encourage the awareness of self and values in others.)

4. When a goose gets sick, two others drop out of formation and accompany it, helping and protecting it. They stay with it until it dies or is able to fly again. Then they join another group or re-join their own group. (Lesson: it is important to stand by each other in difficult times, as well as when we are strong.)

5. As soon as the geese have landed, each goes its own way to find food to and to produce the next generation. (Lesson: competition amongst each other may raise productivity, but as soon as the common goal can be achieved via better or simpler collaboration, the collective becomes more important.)

I'm convinced that if we behave more like geese, rather than acting so individualistically, we can work together more effectively and experience more pleasure at the same time. And that's the foundation for achieving powerful results.

ASSIGNMENT: Be geese-like

Sometimes, what a team leader does in a meeting is restricted to discussing only those actions that will lead to the agreed team result. In such situations, attention is paid purely to matching tasks and activities in order to achieve optimal results. This is a key element, but it's not the whole story. It's important because teams exist to achieve results, so rational elements such as vision, strategy, tasks and roles need to be discussed.

But, there's more involved here, because teams consist of people. As a result, a unique combination of dynamics, atmosphere, feeling of connection, etc., is constantly evolving. These emotional team factors lead to a team culture that indirectly also has a lot of impact on achieving results. That's why the emotional elements also form an important theme that needs to be discussed during a team meeting.

Place the subject of 'powerful collaboration based on diversity and connection' on the agenda of your next meeting. Give participants a copy of this chapter to read beforehand and discuss the lessons we can learn from geese flying in formation.

To what degree are you working like geese within your team? What would you gain if you all started to display a greater degree of goose-like behaviour? Close the meeting by asking whether everyone is prepared to act more like geese.

Synergy is a process in which connecting the parts produces more than the sum of all the individual parts.

COMMUNICATING YOUR VISION WITH CONVICTION

PERSONAL INTRODUCTION

For years I have been playing with the idea of writing a book describing my vision on the importance of connection. But where to start?

The answer came to me after meeting Stella, my Dutch publisher, at a wedding reception. I felt an instant connection with her through the way she approached her business life and her private life. After our initial meeting, which lasted just ten minutes, we made an appointment to talk about the essence of the book. The result was a resounding and mutual commitment to work together.

Writing this book is a first step in communicating my vision on the value of connection. My next step will be to speak about this important topic at conferences and seminars. This way, I can reach large groups of people even more directly, and inspire them to live a life based on genuine connection and contribute to a more connected world.

Convincingly communicating something you believe in, related to either business or personal issues, is the way forward to mobilizing people around you. I want to help you achieve this. How can you do this in such a way that people will be moved by your message and want to connect with you and your theme, and support you on this path? This is what this chapter is all about.

VISION

One characteristic of successful leaders is that they are able to get their vision across to others. They do this in such a convincing way that other people start believing in the vision and will want to help them realize it. The vision of a single person becomes a movement of many, who will want to transform the vision into action. The leader is no longer on his own, working by himself. Instead, many others will join him to do the work together. This illustrates perfectly the essence of the idea behind the African expression, 'If you want to go fast, go alone. If you want to go far, go together.'

How do you do that – convincingly communicate your vision to others? To find the answer to this question, you can read books, take courses, or go in search of inspiring leaders and study how they do it.

EIGHT TIPS TO COMMUNICATE YOUR VISION WITH CONVICTION

Dr. Martin Luther King, Jr., is an example of an inspirational leader who was able to express his great vision powerfully and mobilize people. His famous "I have a dream" speech still inspires me to this day.

I have analysed the way he delivered his speech and from it have derived the following eight tips for communicating a vision convincingly.

1. **Believe in your vision**. Great leaders believe in their own story. However big the vision is, have the courage to stand behind it. You don't have to know how you are going to achieve the vision; it all starts by expressing it and getting others to join you.

2. **Make it personal and concrete**. Use personal, real-world examples, integrate them into your story and link them to your core message. By revealing yourself and your vulnerable side, you create connection and trust.

3. **Visualize the end result**. People want to see what 'it' looks like when the vision has become reality. Based on their affinity with the new situation, they can connect with your story. In other words, paint a picture of the ideal end result instead of criticizing the current undesirable situation.

4. **Use metaphors**. Metaphors are ideal anchors to help remind people of the message. Look for metaphors that are easy to understand and familiar to the people your message is intended to reach.

5. **Vary the speed/intonation/silence**. Instead of delivering a torrent of words, it's important to build in some breathing space. Have the courage

to play with the speed of your delivery, your intonation (speaking more loudly and more softly), and plan in some pauses to allow the message to sink in and give people time to respond to them.

6. **Speak in the 'we' form**. Allow the vision to be bigger than your own ego. Bear in mind that you are merely the messenger in the service of a higher goal. The more you can tell your story and convey your vision with integrity, from a position of servitude, the more powerful it will all become.

7. **Repeat the core message and core sentence**. By mentioning the central elements of your vision several times, your message will become increasingly convincing. This power of repetition also applies when you are communicating your vision.

8. **Use your whole body**. Getting your vision across is more than simply a cognitive or verbal action. Engage with your whole body. Support the message with your body language, utilizing, for example, arm movements and clenched fists.

ASSIGNMENT: The speech as a mirror

Log onto YouTube for more examples of convincingly communicated visions and analyse how the speakers express them. What can you learn from them about having an impact on your audience?

Start experimenting with your acquired insights. What is your vision for the organization, or for society in general? Do you have the courage to stand up and express it? And, if you want to be even more adventurous, film your speech on your mobile phone and publish it on YouTube.

Enjoy communicating your vision with conviction and the impact you have within your organization.

CHAPTER 37

HIGH PERFORMANCE ORGANIZATIONS

PERSONAL INTRODUCTION

All colleagues in COURIUS believe that we must apply in practise what we advise our clients to do. This way, we experience personally what, for example, applying the theory of High Performance Organizations (HPOs) means.

What do you come up against in practise if you consistently use the five factors that contribute to a high performance culture (see later in this chapter) to assess your thoughts and actions? You also have to have the guts to make choices and implement changes that feel difficult or awkward for yourself or your colleagues.

One example of a choice that was personally difficult for me was changing the name of our company. I originally chose to maintain the name of my father's company, Buschman Consultancy. Later on, when I started collaborating with Jaco, we agreed that this name would continue to exist. In addition to the emotional charge involved, it was also a logical choice, considering that the name evoked positive associations for many of our existing clients.

The reason for ultimately changing the name to COURIUS was that I wanted the company to be seen by all the associates (both the existing ones and those that would join in the future) as more of a company owned by us all. In addition, the name would have to fit our vision of collaborating based on respect and complete equality. That's what we had been doing up to that point, and that's what we will continue to do.

And yet, the minute we walked into a client's office and introduced ourselves, I was always the one whose name was the same as the company's name. That influenced the way in which client relationships were formed, and I observed that it was also starting to play a role internally.

I wanted to put an end to this. When I proposed this to Jaco, he was astounded. He had never expected that I would be prepared to do this. I could understand his astonishment, because at the start of our collaboration, I certainly wasn't willing to take that step. Doing so strengthened the mutual connections and resulted in a next level of collaboration.

HPOs

Business consultant Dr. André de Waal has conducted extensive research in the characteristics of High Performance Organizations (HPOs). These are organizations that, by focusing in a disciplined manner on what really matters, have succeeded in achieving better financial and non-financial results over a period of five to ten years than their competitors or similar organizations.

He came to this conclusion after analysing more than 290 international studies conducted in the last 35 years in the field of high performance. In the mid-1990s, in a worldwide study, he tested the most common characteristics that emerged from this research among more than 3,200 organizations in the for-profit, non-profit and government sectors, using questionnaires. He amassed more than 35,000 respondents

De Waal discovered a total of 35 characteristics, which he subdivided into five factors.

It was no trivial study. It revealed that the turnover of HPOs grows 10% more than that of non-HPOs, the profit yield is some 29% higher, the return on investment and return on equity are roughly 20% higher, and shareholder value is 23% higher than that of non-HPOs.

Additionally, the non-financial performance of HPOs is significantly higher than that of non-HPOs: higher customer satisfaction, higher customer and employee loyalty and better quality of products and services (De Waal, 2008).

Here is a condensed rundown of the five factors:

Factor 1: Management quality

Are you a reliable and sincere person? Are you perceived as such by your colleagues? Are you considered a role model? How do you deal with difficult decisions? Are you capable of really deep listening? Do you ask more questions than you give answers? And, how do you deal with employees who don't function adequately?

These are just a few of the questions that are important in this context. So, when it comes to management quality, it's not about how smart the manager is, and whether he can formulate a good strategy, but more about how he deals with the human side of managing.

HPO managers are people who take responsibility for their results, who expect the same from their employees, who believe in something and communicate their vision appropriately. They act in line with their personal values and the values of the organization, and they don't make any concessions to them. These managers coach and facilitate their employees to enable them to perform better, and encourage them to get the best out of themselves. They communicate clearly with non-performers. Additionally, they are not afraid of making difficult decisions in this context.

Factor 2: Openness and action orientation

Within HPOs, conducting an open dialogue between management and employees, as well as between employees themselves, is something that occurs naturally. Instead of, for example, lecturing employees after they've made a mistake, they investigate what happened, identify what can be learned from it, and determine how these mistakes can be avoided in the future.

In fact, within HPOs, everyone is constantly experimenting, and making mistakes is all part of this process. This is an important aspect of the organization culture.

Another aspect of the HPO culture is the assumption that employees are more than just a pair of hands. They have good brains. They are able to carry responsibility and are even intrinsically motivated to do so. And within HPOs, they are given the room they require. The HPO leaders are confident that they will share their knowledge and experiences with each other. These leaders involve the employees when critical organizational processes need to be adapted. It's all about real collaboration for growth and results.

Factor 3: Long-term orientation

Managers within HPOs are aware that long-term results can only be achieved through good internal and external collaboration. The basis for internal collaboration is selecting high-caliber personnel.

Management positions are filled by people who have been trained within the organization. At the same time, the management team looks for external collaboration with suppliers, customers, and with society. Not only do they focus attention and energy on recruiting new customers, all relations are constantly being invested in. How do these new and existing customers view the organization, what possibilities for improvement do they see in the collaboration, and what opportunities do they envisage for achieving an even better organization result?

The key is to become structurally smarter together and to grow further. If the choice comes down to long-term profit or short-term turnover, the long-term option is the one to go for. This demands courage, certainly in the case of organizations that are shareholder-driven and where shareholder value is an important indicator of performance. HPO managers do not shirk difficult decision-making.

Factor 4: Continuous Improvement and Innovation

HPOs have developed a strategy that sets them clearly apart from their competitors. Management and employees are committed to the strategy and do their best to implement it.

At the same time, research is continually being conducted into how this can be done most effectively. Are the existing processes and procedures optimally designed, and are the tasks and responsibilities clearly defined? Are they still contributing to results in a smart and simple way? If the answer is no to any of these questions, improvements are suggested. If it turns out that certain processes have become outdated, they are discontinued. Additionally, product and service offerings are reviewed with a critical eye. Instead of waiting for clients to start complaining, and the market to become restless, everyone reflects proactively on what tomorrow's clients and markets will require.

Finally, these organizations fully realize what their core competence is. They excel in this and are viewed as innovators in their field. If complementary services or products are required, these are developed or acquired in the market.

Factor 5: Employee quality

The management team of an HPO realizes how crucial diversity is. This diversity is evident in both the management team and across the employee population. However diverse the employees are, the management team always looks for people with a high degree of flexibility, a drive to improve continuously, and the creative ability to come up with solutions.

The management team of an HPO also fully realizes that its employees don't come to work just to earn money. They work there because of the opportunity for personal growth. This is why investments are made in their work-related training, while attention, time and money are continually available for their personal development and team development. Employees are given ample room and trust to think about innovation and improvement of processes and products or services, and are encouraged to do so in conjunction with colleagues, suppliers or customers. As a result, employees get the chance to learn from others and to become inspired by them.

ASSIGNMENT: How do you rate on the HPO scale?

What is the HPO ambition of your organization? And, what about your own personal ambition in this area? To be able to provide a good answer to these questions, it's vital that you thoroughly understand the five factors involved. You can do this by taking a course or reading more theory on the internet.

In addition be sure to spend time in the field, to experience what works and what doesn't, talk with your colleagues about it, observe which questions remain unanswered, and then focus on finding the answers to these questions. This is directly aligned with learning according to the 70:20:10 principle, as explained in Chapter 33.

To provide some structure to this learning process, make a list of ten important themes that you on your own (or, if appropriate, with someone else) need to decide about in the coming period. Once you've compiled this list, discuss these ten themes with someone you trust and respect. As you do this, set each decision against the yardstick of the five factors of HPO. What insights does this reveal, and how are you going to take advantage of them?

Are you ready and willing to be a successful *and* valued leader?

CHAPTER 38

ORGANIZATION CULTURE

PERSONAL INTRODUCTION

In 2010 I went on holiday with my family to Norway and was over-whelmed with the natural beauty. As far as the eye could see, there were towering mountains, steep hills, crystal-blue glaciers, thunderous water-falls and wild-water rapids, not to mention the magnificent lakes and rugged, rocky highlands.

However, I observed that after a while I was becoming somewhat blasé. I no longer felt the urge to take it all in or to stop the car by the side of the road to take a photograph. And at some point, we made a conscious decision to take the shortest route to our next destination rather than the tourist route, where we would have been able to see lots of imposing sights. We had reached a kind of saturation point, and had even started feeling indifferent.

This same saturation mechanism is also present within organizations. Clients I have worked for, either individually or with their teams, start seeing the successes and the positive sides of their organization less clearly. The results achieved, the method of collaboration, the connection and the training opportunities all become 'normal' and are taken for granted.

Instead of talking about the good points, the focus switches to what's not good, or people even start complaining. When this happens, a down-ward emotional spiral has started, and it has to be broken. If this doesn't happen, the mutual connection suffers. And, this has a negative impact on the results achieved.

How do you reverse such a downward spiral? This chapter will give you an idea.

ORGANIZATION IMAGE

Companies spend money on branding to create an image that will be familiar for the target group *and* to communicate a brand promise.

If people are able to identify with those elements that the organization stands for, this will result in new customers, and especially ones that will become loyal customers.

However, if you only work on the outside, and not on the inside, this will ultimately be a waste of time and money. By this I am not referring to having the day-to-day operations in place so that you can fulfil your promises (the functional infrastructure). Of course, that's important, but at least as important is how your employees think and behave (the emotional infrastructure). To what degree do they identify with the product and image of the organization? And, to what degree do they act in line with the values of the organization?

Does this sound a bit vague? Then let me illustrate what I mean with some examples.

What happens to your image of an organization if you have a complaint and you are confronted with someone who shouts you down? Or, when you're at a party or having a night out and you get into a conversation with someone who talks in a negative way about the company he works for? What if you'd really like to help a customer but the colleague you're dependent on to enable you to do this has a nine-to-five mindset?

These are all examples relating to mentality and engagement. Entities can't be defined solely through processes and procedures. It doesn't matter if you've built up a wonderful image on the outside and the day-to-day running of the business is all taken care of. If this image is undermined by the ultimate execution, you've got a long way to go before you can restore that image. This negative effect will be accentuated even more because a bad experience is talked about on average seven times more frequently than a good one.

EMOTIONAL INFRASTRUCTURE

It is vital to focus attention on the atmosphere you want to have in the organization: the emotional infrastructure. Don't cease spending time and energy on creating an organization culture in which the employees are committed to the product and the goals. In the end, you want your people to be proud of the values your organization stands for, and to consider it an honour to be allowed to work there.

Creating this atmosphere is not a purely rational process. It's not sufficient for the CEO to point out why it's so important to work in a customer-friendly way, based purely on facts and figures. It's not sufficient if he displays the goals for the coming year merely in the form of a graph. Instead, it's about the leader expressing with passion and conviction what he stands for, what impact he will make in society and how that's reflected within the organization. Figures, however important, are just derivatives.

Examples of companies that have a culture of engagement and know what they want to contribute to society are Ben & Jerry's and Tony's Chocolonely. Author and motivational speaker Simon Sinek (2013) explains what they do differently compared with many other companies: "If you hire people just because they can do a job, they'll work for your money," he said. "But if you hire people who believe what you believe, they'll work for you with blood, sweat and tears."

WHY DO YOU WANT TO WORK FOR THE ORGANIZATION?

Creating a culture like the one described above starts by determining what impact the organization wants to make in society. When recruiting new staff, ask specifically why they want to work for your organization. Find out what they identify with, what appeals to them most, what their dream for the organization is.

Beyond recruiting, it's important that the HR policy is brought into line with this vision. To what extent are employee and management development programmes already based on these starting points? You need to create a culture based on a high Connection Quotient, whereby attention is paid to decisiveness, goals and results (functional infrastructure), as well as to emotional elements such as pride, engagement and trust (emotional infrastructure).

In the most extreme case, if employees or managers only think and act based on the functional elements, and not on emotional engagement, do you have the guts to ask them to leave the organization?

FIRST, GOOD PEOPLE

In his book, *Good to Great*, author and consultant Jim Collins looks at the points that have made a number of American companies more successful than others over several years.

He found that the leaders of these companies are modest, forceful, attentive, resolute, loving, confrontational, disciplined, full of trust, open and intrinsically motivated. Collins recommends: "First, good people; selecting the best – not the most expensive – people is much more important than vision or strategy."

ASSIGNMENT: Finding a story that moves

How well balanced is your organization in terms of attention paid to the functional and the emotional infrastructures? What is it that makes you want to work for the organization you're currently with?

The assignment is to consciously articulate in the coming weeks the organization story with respect to where your organization now stands emotionally (what is the culture?). Once you have created this story, start telling it and ask for feedback.

What moves people? What could be improved?

The true organization culture lives in the hearts of the employees.

CHAPTER 39

STRENGTHS-BASED LEADERSHIP

PERSONAL INTRODUCTION

I look back on my time with the Dutch Royal Air Force with great pleasure. But, my ambitions lay elsewhere. I much preferred to go from one department to another as an internal interim manager, implementing changes based on a personal vision and a clear-cut organizational goal.

Even then, early on, I was already trying to connect people in different places in the organization, putting into practise the 'integral management' that was so often being talked about at the time. For me, this concept means that you can lead a department regardless of the formal speciality that has been assigned to you.

It's about you daring to choose managers based on their qualities and ambitions, without focusing too much on the 'coding' or their background. Why, for example, could a business economist not become head of helicopter maintenance? Or, couldn't an air traffic controller become head of Management Information Systems?

My airbase commander at the time, who was aware of my attitude and ambitions, decided to have an open and honest chat with me about my career. Ultimately, he saw two options for me.

First, there was the option of staying with the air force and becoming an advocate for my vision. At the same time, he showed me how far ahead of the pack I was. It would mean, amongst other things, that I would meet a lot of resistance. I would have to take into account that the organization would move one step forward and then one, two or even three steps back. I would probably end up feeling fulfilled and being frustrated at the same time, yet it would support the organization moving forward.

The second option that he saw for me was to leave the air force and go into the consulting industry, where I would have more opportunities to make use of my ambition and drive. The first option would primarily be good for the organization, while the second would be mainly good for me. He left the choice down to me.

What I appreciate enormously to this day is that he went into our conversation with openness and sincerity. Like a good sparring partner, he looked with me at my qualities and my ambitions, and together we explored how I could use these in a way that suited me best. That was far preferable to starting to reason based on the question: how can I retain him for the air force?

For me, this is why the commander remains such a source of inspiration and an example of strengths-based leadership. To this day I am grateful for that talk, because it heralded an important turning point in my career.

DO WORK THAT IS SUITED TO YOU

The Gallup agency conducted a worldwide study in which 198,000 people were asked the question: 'Does your work take full advantage of your skills and training?' Combining the answers with data about the performance of the departments in which these people worked produced clear insights.

Where people answered 'definitely agree', there was:

- 50% more chance that they worked in a department with very little employee turnover
- 38% more chance that they worked in a more productive department
- 44% more chance that they worked in a department with a high degree of employee satisfaction

This relation persisted after follow-up research. Where departments were able to improve their scores for productivity and customer loyalty, and where there was less employee turnover, more employees answered the question with 'definitely agree.'

Based on these insights, it appears that it pays to allow employees to do work where they can make use of their strong points. The bad news, however, is that follow-up research by Gallup (2006) showed that only 17% of the employees during an average working day feel they're particularly able to make use of their strong points.

What would happen to the productivity and profitability of companies if they were able to increase this percentage to 30%, or even 60%? What would happen if managers were to actually make decisions and manage based on making use of their employees' strong points?

MOTIVATION ON THE WORK FLOOR

In 2008, Gallup again conducted research into the degree to which employees felt motivated at work. Here too, several clear-cut insights came to the fore.

In a work environment in which the manager first focused on the strong points of his employees, and secondly encouraged them to implement these strong points in their work (strengths-based leadership), 73% of the employees indicated that they were motivated. By contrast, in an environment where the manager focused on those areas where employee needed to improve (repair focused leadership), just 9% of the employees admitted to being motivated.

There are several more interesting insights to be distilled from the in-depth interviews Gallup has conducted over the past 30 years with more than 80,000 managers worldwide.

The results show that there are two assumptions that the world's 'best' managers make: first, that the talents of every employee are unique and permanent. There was a sense that employees cannot acquire competencies in everything. Additionally, these managers assume that the strong points (and therefore not the weak points) of an employee offer the most potential for growth. These managers spend a lot of energy in finding the right talent for each role. They focus on the result to be achieved (the what and the why) rather than prescribing the rules and activities that have to be executed (the how). They also spend most of their time with their employees, and everyone is managed and treated as individuals.

MAKING CONSCIOUS CHOICES

Are you making use of the strong points of your employees and colleagues? And are you making use of your strong points, in a way that is aligned with what you consider to be important in this world?

Someone who made a conscious decision to do this is Narayanan Krishnan. This talented and highly decorated professional chef saw an old man on the street one day eating his own faeces. He was so shocked that he resigned from his job within a week to care for and feed the homeless, elderly and mentally ill.

Of course we don't need to make such world-shattering decisions in our own lives. Yet, wouldn't it be wonderful if people did work that made optimal use of their strong points so that they had a maximum impact in the world?

A final insight from the Gallup studies: most people sign up for the organization, yet they leave it because of their manager!

ASSIGNMENT: Strengthening your development

What are your strong points and to what extent can you make use of them in your day-to-day work? Does your focus lie in developing your strong points, or are you trying to learn competencies that are less developed (and that are perhaps not appropriate for you)?

Take your time to formulate the answers to these questions. Do so first on your own, and then with people in your direct environment who you trust, and in whose company you can completely be yourself and can say what you really think.

Finally, go to your manager. Do you have the guts to stand for what genuinely motivates you and really suits you?

Focus on developing the strong points of your employees instead of the competencies they are only moderately good at.

'DIFFICULT' EMPLOYEES

PERSONAL INTRODUCTION

One of the things I enjoyed most about my role as manager was that I often got the opportunity to develop a common vision and then implement it in conjunction with others.

Working with employees gave me a positive energy boost, as I've always liked discussing their talents with them and helping them put those talents to good use. These conversations also helped me to reflect and grow. What are my talents, do I have the courage to make the best use of them, and how do I respond to the support I'm offered?

These are just a few of the questions that have kept me occupied for a long time now, and for which I have found answers.

I have also experienced moments that left me drained of energy. Those were the occasions where political games were being played. At the same time, I learned a lot from these trying encounters. I learned to think in terms of personal interests and organizational interests. I now know that the expression 'choose your battles' is an essential lifesaver. I acknowledge the importance of networks now, where you build up relationships with people before you actually need them. And, I also see that convincing and influencing are elements a manager has to have in his standard toolbox.

Dealing with difficult employees has been another energy drainer for me, for a very long time. My negative attitude towards these individuals made it difficult for me to establish a connection with them. I had to learn to accept 'difficult' behaviour, which came through working to understand why people react the way they do. Most of the time they have a good reason for doing so. What I've discovered is that the cause lies not so much in the individuals themselves but is more often the result of how the work is structured and organized.

WHAT EXACTLY ARE DIFFICULT EMPLOYEES?

I'm regularly asked what you have to do, as a manager or as a team, when required to deal with someone who doesn't want to collaborate. In other words, how to work with someone who constantly says: 'Yes, but...' (and is therefore really saying no). Or, those who *say* yes, but *do* no, so that you cannot rely on them. Even worse, there are those who are generally 'a difficult person' or who 'regularly behave in an anti-social manner' (whatever that may be). What approach do you take with such a person? Punish him, place him in isolation, give him specific tasks to perform, or simply ignore him?

THE BABEMBA TRIBE

When faced with difficult employees, we often look to quick fixes based on a negative approach.

The Babemba tribe from South Africa has a fundamentally different solution to this situation. If a person behaves unjustly or irresponsibly, he is taken to the centre of the village. Everyone stops working and all the men, women and children gather in a big circle around him.

Then, each member of the tribe speaks to the accused, one at a time. They recall all the good things this person has done throughout his lifetime – all his positive attributes, good deeds, strengths and kindnesses are recounted and applauded. This ritual can last for several days. To complete the ceremony, a song is sung that is appropriate for this person.

The circle is then broken, a joyous celebration takes place and the person is both symbolically and literally welcomed back into the tribe.

LOVING APPROACH

Although there are accounts on internet that dispute the validity of this story about the Babemba tribe, it contains an inspiring message. Rather than using punishment to correct unwelcome behaviour, a loving approach is more effective. By highlighting someone's positive sides, you help him 'reset' his own identity. If he recognizes himself in all the positive feedback, and accepts this unconditionally, he will no longer feel the need to rebel against the others.

The question is to what extent we can – or even want to – apply this method within organizations.

I'm convinced that it's always worth taking the trouble to view people through a positive lens. Everyone is born with a positive nature and is instinctively motivated to connect with others and work together. Of course, there may be circumstances that cause people to lose touch with these motivations. But, that doesn't necessarily mean that that person no longer wants to connect or collaborate. And instead of saying that this person is difficult, you have the choice to show a deeper interest in him. What drives him; what causes him to act the way he does?

If you're able to do that, it may well lead you to reassess your initial ideas about that person.

PERSON OR STRUCTURE?

In a number of cases, the so-called difficult behaviour of the other person has to do with unclear or badly formulated agreements within the work environment. If a lack of clarity exists within the organization or department with regard to the common goal, the tasks/roles, or the procedures/work agreements, this can easily result in a team that doesn't collaborate well... and 'difficult' employees.

For example, when two or more people make decisions based on differing goals (and they are not aware that their perception of those goals differs), sooner or later this will cause problems. They don't understand each other's choices, they have an opinion about them, and if it's not possible to talk about the reasoning behind these choices, bad interrelations can result.

The negative feelings that people then have with regard to each other are very real, but they are ultimately symptoms of bad coordination. And yet, in practise, the blame is so easily put on the employee: he doesn't want to cooperate, is always working against you, doesn't want to do anything, is disagreeable, etc.

THREE KEY QUESTIONS

If you need to deal with a team that isn't collaborating well, or with difficult employees, ask yourself the following three key questions. And also ask these questions to your team members, and discuss the answers with each other.

1. Are the common team goals unambiguous and totally accepted by you and your employees? The goals form the basis for engagement, provide direction and facilitate connection with the people involved. They form the foundation for all the activities that have to be executed.

2. Have clearly defined agreements been made with everyone with regard to task and role allocation? Is it clear to all team members what they can be held accountable for to achieve the desired results? And is it clear what everyone's core tasks are and what each individual contributes to the other team members' development and to the whole process?

3. Is it crystal clear for the team members how they jointly arrive at decisions and results? Are procedures and work agreements in place about how collaboration is to be accomplished? How are the natural fields of tension with regard to the collaboration as a whole and the individual's need to have room to maneuver dealt with.

You can also apply the key questions in your personal life, if you're having problems with difficult friends, family members, acquaintances, etc. But, you'll need to adapt your approach according to the person and the situation.

If, for example, the 'difficult' person is a friend, the questions could go like this: what is it that makes us friends? What do you expect from me and what do I expect from you? If we make decisions together, do you perceive that as equality?

ASSIGNMENT: The difficult thing about being difficult

Engage in a conversation with a colleague you perceive as being difficult. Use the three key questions outlined above to get a dialogue started about your collaboration. Try to discover whether there is a lack of clarity within the existing structure that might lead to difficult behaviour. This may result in new agreements concerning the themes of a common goal, task and role assignment, procedures and work agreements.

It's quite difficult to view someone as *not* being difficult if, in your eyes, he displays difficult behaviour.

CHAPTER 41

ORGANIZATION STORIES

PERSONAL INTRODUCTION

Standing in the spotlight, with all eyes upon you, is tense and stressful. Do you have a message that's worth telling? How should you stand and what do you do with your arms? What's the right speaking speed and the best way to truly connect with your audience?

These are all aspects that are important, which you can think about beforehand and work on through training and lots of practice. For instance, try standing in front of the mirror or asking someone to give you feedback.

If these questions are still racing through your head when you're standing in front of a group – usually whispered in your ear by your inner critic to make you feel insecure – they will have an adverse effect on your presentation. For example, you might notice that you suddenly start stuttering, that you're hopping from one topic to the next, or that you've forgotten part of your text.

How can you best cope in such a situation? Keep calm, take deep breaths, put a smile on your face and be transparent. If you're nervous or you've lost track of what you wanted to say, just admit it. It's not such a big a deal. It makes you vulnerable and sincere.

And just think about this: the audience consists of normal people who can easily imagine just what you're going through. And that serves to make a connection.

Is it really okay to be so transparent? Yes. The fact that I've given myself permission to be transparent relaxes me enormously. It helps me deliver the story and connect with my audience. Being transparent works not only in the work environment but also in my private life, where I value and apply honesty equally as well.

STORYTELLING

Telling stories and listening to them is something for all ages, all generations and all countries. Stories can be based on true experiences, things that may have taken place, or events that have simply been dreamt up. Whether they contain a message or are told just to entertain, the fact is that they always have some function.

By sharing events and experiences, whether true or fictional, we give meaning to life, a connection is born between the teller and the listener, and a collective memory is created. From stories we build the foundation of a culture.

STORIES ABOUT THE FOUNDER

In companies and organizations, stories serve to create and maintain an organizational culture. The story that's told by or about the founder also determines the culture, even years later.

For example, think about all the stories that have been spread about Steve Jobs. How, together with two others, he founded Apple in 1985 (the company he left after he was stripped of his management function). How he founded a new company that was ultimately bought by Apple. How this became his comeback, and how he ultimately took over the company again. How he, as CEO and brilliant marketer, grew Apple into one of the most successful and innovative companies in the world.

Jobs was renowned for his insights, his obsession with the smallest details, his clothing style, his persuasiveness – occasionally referred to by his employees as *a reality distortion field*. All the stories that have ever been told about him and his leadership style confirm the company culture that is summed up in Apple's old marketing slogan 'Think different.'

STORIES WITH GUTS

In addition to stories by or about the founder, it's about the stories that are told when new employees start working for the organization, when they leave, when an important event takes place, with the introduction of a new product, and so on. When laying out the vision and strategy with the corresponding necessary facts and figures, stories are ideally suited to bringing such an event to life.

In combination with a daring marketing campaign, this can lead to a unique statement and a story that will stick in people's minds for a long time. A striking example of this involves Sir Richard Branson, owner of, among other companies, Virgin Airways.

On the very day that the Millennium Wheel – the great ferris wheel in the centre of London, sponsored by British Airways – was to be erected, Branson got an early morning call telling him that, due to technical problems, the wheel wouldn't be up and running in time. He immediately arranged for a zeppelin to be hired, plastered with message, 'BA can't get it up.' That afternoon, the zeppelin flew over the spot where the world's press was waiting...

ORGANIZATION CULTURE

The sum total of all the stories that are told by or about the organization, in combination with personal experiences, form the organization culture. For you as a manager, it's important to be aware of this and promote it. That starts with having insight into how you deal with this yourself.

How do you talk about the organization where you work? Is that a business story with data, facts and figures? Or, is it a passionate story full of personal experiences and details? As far as I'm concerned, you don't need to choose between the two. Instead, it's important to connect them. After all, what you want to achieve is that your story inspires, stimulates, clarifies, connects, provides a context, gives direction and triggers actions.

You want to create an atmosphere for your employees and your customers, and evoke associations and emotions, so that the message is retained better and faster. To achieve this, you need a combination of rationality and emotion.

HOW TO CREATE POWERFUL ORGANIZATION STORIES

To help you tell powerful organization stories, I've come up with eight practical tips for you.

1. **Tell stories that are genuine**. Don't make them more attractive than they are; don't exaggerate. Here too, honesty will pay off in the end.

2. **Dare to show your vulnerability**. Indicate explicitly how the event you're talking about moved you, which personal questions it evokes, or how it helped to shape you.

3. **Let your passion and admiration shine through**. Go in search of what you're proud of in the story and highlight it strongly.

4. **Use upbeat words**. Dare to use words like 'wonderful', 'fantastic', etc. Let go of that paralyzing modesty.

5. **Give compliments**. Results are achieved through collaborating with others. In your story, give them the praise they deserve.

6. **Keep it short**. You must be able to tell your story in 90 seconds to two minutes. Longer stories will be forgotten, so stick to your core message.

7. **One core message, and one keyword**. What do you want to achieve by telling your story? Repeat the message and the keyword a number of times.

8. **Tell the story in the present tense**. Transport your audience into the here and now; tell the story as though it's happening in the moment.

METAPHORS

Besides stories with a narrative, as a manager you can also make excellent use of metaphoric stories to influence the organization culture. This way, you can get your clients or employees thinking about their own actions and their way of collaborating. Here's an example for your inspiration.

One evening, an old American Indian is telling his grandson a story about the turmoil within every individual. "My grandson, inside each of us there is a fight going on between two wolves. One wolf is afraid of change and of the unknown. This leads to apathy, a lack of direction, the inability to act, and missed opportunities. The other wolf embraces possibilities, makes plans for the future, enjoys what life has to offer, and achieving goals." The grandson reflects on these words for a minute and then asks his grandfather: "Which wolf wins?" The old Indian simply replies: "The one you feed."

ASSIGNMENT: Man with a mission

What story do you tell your clients and employees about the mission of your organization?

Is it a detailed, rational story filled with facts and figures? Or, is it a short, personal and passionate story that is at once inspiring, stimulating and connecting? Do you make use of metaphors? Ask others how they perceive your organization story, and how you could adapt it so it has even more of an impact.

After all, in the end it is in the minds of others that the story acquires meaning and does its work.

Everyone can tell good stories, but telling powerful stories is an art.

CHAPTER 42

TEAM DEVELOPMENT

PERSONAL INTRODUCTION

For many years now I have been assisting managers and teams, from middle management level to the Board of Directors, to collaborate in a results-driven and powerful manner based on a strong mutual connection.

Throughout these trajectories, I maintain an open attitude, am transparent and honest, and show respect for each team member. When I need to be, I am direct, confrontational and decisive. This approach works. The clients are satisfied, they achieve their goals and the atmosphere in the team improves. And, my clients regularly give me follow-up assignments.

The changes I have helped to bring about give me a lot of satisfaction, and I continue to explore how I can make my approach even more effective. That's part of my mental make-up (how can I be better tomorrow than I am today?) and I consider it important that every professional continues to look critically at his own style of working. Our clients deserve this!

In this context, I asked myself many years ago how I can tangibly render the effectiveness of my team development trajectories, in figures.

After a lengthy search, I discovered the assessments of the American agency Team Coaching International. Besides the fact that their assessments can be understood intuitively, and that their philosophy matches my way of thinking about the development of teams, they also work based on a clear system approach.

To cut a long story short, after having taken their course, I can now quickly and easily measure the impact of my approach and present it tangibly, in figures.

Additionally, the method and the assessment help my clients understand and resolve the issues they are working on. And, the method has resulted in me fine-tuning my thinking about the coaching of teams. Now, I pay more attention to the mutual connection between the team members, based on the six principles I'll review at the end of this chapter.

THE TRADITIONAL APPROACH

The traditional method of team development works at the individual level. For example, you make a team member aware of his dominant style of thinking, acting and communicating, and of the impact this has on collaboration within the team. There is a range of tools available to help achieve this, such as Belbin's Team Roles Profiling, DISC, MBTI, Insights Discovery and Management Drives.

The next step is to teach this person how he can make the best use of his talents and how he can communicate with colleagues more effectively. This results in a change in the mutual collaboration, and team results improve. In other words, changing the way an individual thinks and acts will cause the team to develop.

You can expand on this so that everyone within the team becomes aware of their dominant way of thinking, acting and communicating. If this information is then shared across the team, and they start to understand more about each other, they will be better able to make use of each other's strong points. From then on, they can make agreements about how to communicate with each other, leading to even better results for the team. This is fine of course, and it's still a traditional approach to team development.

Or, there's this variant: if two colleagues can't get along with each other, and this negatively influences the atmosphere in the whole team, then a consultant is called in to work on their relationship.

And, there's ultimate variant: if it turns out that someone 'doesn't fit' in the team, then he is replaced by someone who's 'a better fit.' Just as with an engine, if the defective part cannot be repaired, it will be replaced.

To summarize, within the traditional approach to team development, the assumption is that changing a part of the team will have an impact on the whole team. It's a perfectly legitimate way of influencing the team… yet there is also a modern and more powerful approach available.

SYSTEM APPROACH

The modern approach to team development is based on the system approach. This involves acknowledging that individuals have an influence on other team members. Additionally, it is assumed that the culture of the team has an even more powerful influence on the individual.

You've undoubtedly experienced this yourself when you were working in a team with low (or even hostile) morale, or a team that seemed to function effortlessly. Think back to what influenced the atmosphere of the team and what impact this had on business results and your way of thinking, acting and communicating.

The point of departure within this modern approach to team development is that the culture that the team creates has an enormous influence on the individual members, on their interaction, and therefore on the results achieved. And so, we can say, change the team culture and the results of the team will change correspondingly (both in a negative way and in a positive way).

Once the culture has changed so that there is sufficient mutual trust and respect, and that diversity is valued, in addition to further developing the culture, it is possible to 'zoom in' on the individual qualities. Only then is the time ripe for making use of techniques from the traditional approach.

SIX PRINCIPLES

When working on team development based on the system approach, six key principles can be distinguished (TCI, 2010). By consistently applying these, as a manager you make yourself and your team members aware of the way in which collaboration takes place, and you stimulate the desired team behaviour.

1. **Reveal the system to itself**. Holding a mirror presenting the prevailing culture to team members enables them to make their own choices about the direction they want to follow. What behaviour do you observe?

2. **Pay attention to the energy field in which the team is operating.** In other words, make explicit that which is not expressed in words but is present in the connection. What atmosphere do you perceive?

3. **Highlight and develop values diversity**. This is about appreciating and accepting everyone's opinion and way of thinking. Or, 'Everyone is right, but partially.' What is the strength of each team member?

4. **Listen for the undercurrents rising**. This is a special version of paying attention to the energy level. It is about naming the direction in which the team as a whole is developing. What can you see changing in the mutual connection?

5. **Reinforce co-responsibility**. All team members are responsible for the tasks allocated to them. And as team members, they have a collective responsibility to achieve the goals (and mission) of the team. This transcends the individual responsibility. How do team members support each other?

6. **Increase positivity, reduce negativity**. Instead of focusing on naming what has to be improved, a lot of attention is paid to things that are already going well and on how they can be expanded further. What is there to be celebrated?

These six principles are not overly complex. The real challenge lies in applying them consistently. Can you simultaneously put all six principles into action on a day-to-day basis? The goal here is for the team to continue achieving the agreed results based on a powerful connection. Perseverance is the key to success here.

ASSIGNMENT: May the force be with you

In the coming weeks, look at your own team or organization through the lens of the six principles described above. Which principle do you already practise automatically? Continue to do this consciously. Which principle would you like to apply more? Start putting more effort into this. You will notice that this demands focus and perseverance.

What impact do you expect this will have on the connection and on the results?

What is the difference between changing a team and developing a team?

CHAPTER 43

POWERFUL LEADERSHIP

PERSONAL INTRODUCTION

During our research into how we could make our collaboration work most effectively, my business partner Jaco and I talked extensively about our view of the world.

What is the importance of our work for society? What motivates us to dedicate ourselves to the human side of change? What are our common values, and where do we differ in our thoughts and actions? As part of this search, we spent a whole day with photo albums on our laps, sharing our life histories and personal stories with each other. It was a wonderful way of getting to know each other better and engaging in a genuine connection.

During this process, we decided that we would make it a condition for all future associates who joined COURIUS to dedicate time and knowledge to helping organizations and associations with a clear social goal to develop and increase their impact on society. And, it goes without saying, we expect the same from ourselves.

Additionally, every year we reserve a share of our profits to financially support these organizations and associations.

We have in fact set up a foundation, with a particular focus on these activities. Assuming that the company will continue to grow in terms of number of associates and turnover, this means that we will be contributing increasingly to achieving an inclusive society.

This too is a way of contributing to connection, not in our immediate environment, but in the lives of others. For me, this is what powerful leadership means.

RESEARCH BY KOUZES AND POSNER

According to the academics James Kouzes and Barry Posner, powerful leaders model the way, inspire through a shared vision, challenge the process, enable others to act and encourage the heart (2007).

They identified these five leadership practices after conducting thorough research into what powerful leaders do within an organization. The nice thing about these practices is that they are not specifically about the personal traits of the leaders, but their regular day-to-day activities. These are activities that can be learned by doing, reflecting, adapting, more doing, and so on.

Kouzes and Posner linked two activities to each practice. As you read about them, you will see that all the practices and activities are interconnected and reinforce each other during their execution. And, they are logical and easy to understand so that they can be applied directly in your daily practice (insofar as you aren't doing that already, of course).

Following these practices will have a powerful impact on the functioning of your employees, teams and the organization as a whole. And, as such, you will automatically have an impact on society.

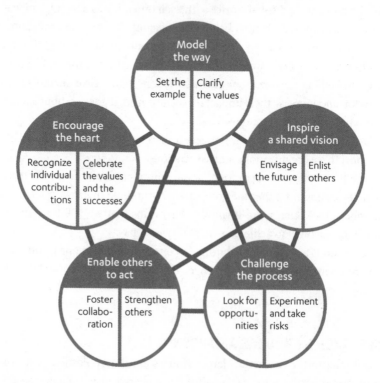

Figure 20: The five practices and ten activities according to Kouzes and Posner

Leadership practice 1: Model the way

Activity 1: Set the example. Children learn by observing and imitating. This principle continues to be valid when we become adults and we collaborate within organizations. What the leaders demonstrate in their day-to-day activities is imitated by the employees. So, instead of talking about the importance of trust and respect, for example, they set an example through execution. In other words, people first follow the person and then the plan.

Activity 2: Clarify the values. Powerful leaders act based on a deep belief in what is important to them. They are conscious of their personal values, make them explicit and act in accordance with them. They challenge their employees to act based on their own personal values. Additionally, they design the team and organization values that form the basis for the mutual connection and collaboration. If the leaders observe that the values are not being respected, they hold the employees to account, directly and visibly.

Leadership practice 2: Inspire a shared vision

Activity 3: Envisage the future. Powerful leaders dare to dream big about what is possible and have a deep-seated conviction that exceptional results can be achieved. Dreaming big involves organizational results (making a profit, maintaining continuity) and results for wider world (adding real value to society). Dreaming starts with letting go of limitation-based thinking (fixed mindset). Instead, the leaders continually ask themselves, "What if…" The dream (growth mindset) forms the organization's right to exist.

Activity 4: Enlist others. The dream – in organizational terms, ambition or vision – is transformed into a story that can be told and re-told in order to inspire others. Instead of forcing employees to realize your dream, it's about 'seducing' them to learn to see the potential of a vision and to internalize this vision. To achieve this, it's important that you are aligned with your employees' way of thinking. What do they consider important, what do they want to contribute to, what do they believe in? Then, the leader has to be able to link these insights to his own dream. Be careful not to be manipulative; try to exert this influence through inspiration and smart linking.

Leadership practice 3: Challenge the process

Activity 5: Look for opportunities. Powerful leaders are continually looking for how things can be improved. 'Things' refers here to both the rational side (results-based leadership) and the emotional side (connecting leadership) of organizations. Employees are encouraged to engage in contacts outside the organization. This forms the basis for new inspiration and new ideas.

Activity 6: Experiment and take risks. To be able to make this a continuously improving process, powerful leaders create a culture in which people encourage each other to innovate and take risks. Small changes are embraced, based on the notion that many small changes lead to big results. And, instead of penalizing employees for making a mistake, an attempt is made to identify what can be learned from it, both as an individual and as an organization.

Leadership practice 4: Enable others to act

Activity 7: Foster collaboration. Organizations consist of people whose actions lead to results that have been agreed upon. Powerful leaders realize all too well how important sincere collaboration based on a deep connection is. The basis for this is giving trust. The more trust that is given, the more trust is passed along through the organization. It's an infectious virus.

Activity 8: Strengthen others. Powerful leaders have a deep belief in the potential of their employees and the faith that they want to be responsible for the processes and results that have been agreed upon. This is why employees are allowed the space to act with a certain degree of autonomy and put energy into activities that they consider to be important. Of course, frameworks are defined, for example with respect to what has to be achieved and what each person's task is in realizing this. This basic attitude ensures that energy and pride on the part of the employees is released, leading to excellent results being achieved.

Leadership practice 5: Encourage the heart

Activity 9: Recognize individual contributions. Powerful leaders give abundant feedback to people they work with. This could be about what can be improved in terms of their actions, what is valued regarding their contribution to reaching the goal, or acknowledging their qualities as human beings. Even when an employee's contribution does not yield the desired result, the leaders see the positive intention and can appreciate this. The importance of this way of thinking is demonstrated in the work of author and science journalist Daniel Goleman (1996), which suggests that just 15% of the work of a manager is IQ-related, and 85% is tied to the EQ (Emotional Quotient).

Activity 10: Celebrate the values and the successes. An important question that powerful leaders have asked themselves is: does it matter to me as a leader who gets the credit? Think of the results that can be achieved if nobody worries about whose ego gets most attention. Powerful leaders have answered the question and act on it on a daily basis: they give others the spotlight and applause, and accept responsibility when something goes wrong. During public occasions, they express their thanks and show respect to teams and individual employees.

Finally, as something for you to ponder, here's a conclusion that Kouzes and Posner have drawn: if you don't believe in the messenger, then you won't believe in the message either.

ASSIGNMENT: Become COURIUS

The name of our company is COURIUS. It's a word that doesn't actually exist on its own, but is derived from a number of existing words. You can link these words to the five leadership practices of Kouzes and Posner.

First of all, we have 'courage': you need courage to show the way. Second, COUR is built up from 'co' (together) 'u' (you) 'r' (are), which results in 'You are together': the key philosophy to inspire based on a shared vision. Third, 'curious': in order to challenge the process, an attitude of curiosity is a prerequisite. Fourth, IUS is built up from 'I' and 'us': starting from the connection, you can enable others to act. And finally, the French word 'coeur' (heart): which can be logically linked to encourage the heart.

So, the name of our company is an appropriate expression of how we as specialists in the human side of change think and act in the connection with our clients. It captures how we focus on creating powerful connections with ourselves, the other, the team and the organization. And, it speaks to how we strive for a connected and inclusive world.

How do you apply the practices and activities identified by Kouzes and Posner in your work? Can you put them to use in an area that is beyond the boundaries of your organization to help improve the world? I would like to challenge you to reflect on this and to make a choice concerning what you intend to do more, less or differently from now on.

I also want to challenge you to make this intention known to people in your immediate environment. It has been proven that doing this will increase the chances of change actually happening. By expressing your intention, you increase your commitment.

Employees are not inspired by grand statements, but by sincere actions.

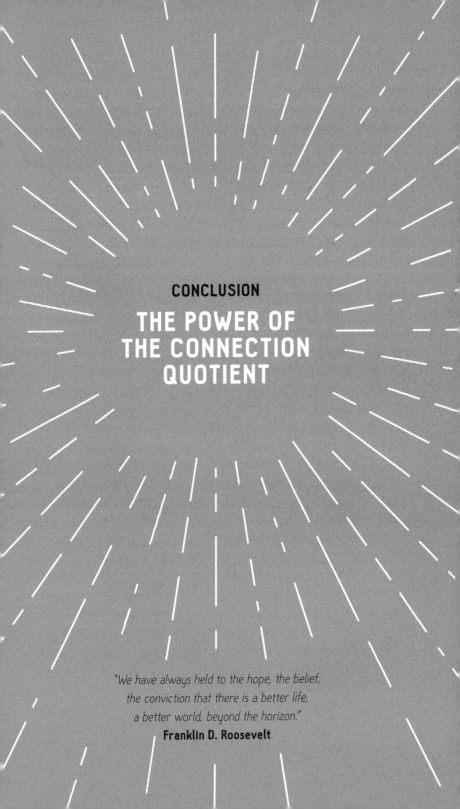

CONCLUSION

THE POWER OF THE CONNECTION QUOTIENT

*"We have always held to the hope, the belief,
the conviction that there is a better life,
a better world, beyond the horizon."*
Franklin D. Roosevelt

My purpose in writing this book is to show leaders how they can put into practise effective leadership based on their CQ. To help them achieve this, I have identified three domains: connection with yourself (Part I), connection with the other (Part II) and connection with the team and the organization (Part III). But, that doesn't mean you're there yet. There is a fourth domain: connection with the rest of the world.

However, before I explain this fourth domain of the Connection Quotient, I will discuss the emergence of the connection economy. I will also explain the three other domains, albeit briefly, in the context of the question: 'Who am I as a leader *and* as an individual human being?' These parts are the prerequisites for you if you want to – and choose to – operate within this fourth domain.

Also, in this final chapter I will revise the framework of the Connection Quotient that I introduced in the general introduction. You will see that a shift has taken place between the relation of the leader as a person and the leader as a role, based on the insights covered in this book.

Finally, I want to address you, my reader. Are you prepared to experiment with the Connection Quotient in your own life?

CONTEXT: THE CONNECTION QUOTIENT AND THE CONNECTION ECONOMY

The Connection Quotient is not superficial

Engaging in a connection could be interpreted as a superficial activity. You send out an invitation via LinkedIn or Facebook, seeking to be included in someone's network, and if your invitation is accepted, you think you're connected. Nothing could be further from the truth.

The Connection Quotient relates to a completely different core than that of linking people with each other and functionally building up a business network. It's a vision of leadership that determines – in every contact (including with yourself) and for every decision you make as a leader – what you do, how you do it and with what intention.

Embedded within the Connection Quotient is the fact that you're able to connect with your own sources, or secondary sources outside yourself. Key building blocks here are the connection with yourself, connection with the other, via connection with the team and the organization, to connection with the rest of the world. The Connection Quotient has its own value in each domain. At the macro level, it even turns out that we are building a totally new economy.

The connection economy

Modern-day thinkers such as entrepreneur and author Seth Godin (2012) and marketing strategist Clay Hebert (Altman, 2015) inform us that we are well on the way to building a connection economy. Core concepts within this economy are 'coordination' (making contact), 'trust' (determining who will join you) and 'permission' (who has the mandate to proclaim himself an expert?).

As a parallel to the notion of return on investment (ROI), the social marketing strategist Ted Rubin posited the importance of *return on relationship*™ (ROR). He views powerful relationships as the new currency that you need to cherish, in which you can invest, and which leads to measurable results.

At the same time, more and more platforms are emerging in which providers and customers worldwide – and also locally – are connected with each other. This is totally disrupting traditional revenue models. Take a look at these examples:

- Uber is the world's biggest taxi company – and yet, it doesn't own a single vehicle.
- AirBnB is the world's biggest provider of accommodations – and yet, it doesn't own any property.
- Facebook is the world's biggest media company – and yet, it doesn't create any content itself.
- Alibaba is the world's biggest retailer – and yet, it keeps nothing in stock.
- Crowdfunding platforms like Kickstart and IndiGoGo are expected to invest more money in new and existing organizations than the traditional venture capitalists – and yet, they don't possess any capital of their own.

New revenue models and organization structures

The Connection Quotient makes it possible to create new organization structures. By making use of its power, new revenue models can be created. The new revenue models and organization structures can be thought up and implemented by anyone, purely because the model is not something exotic – it's based on being a human being and wanting to connect with other humans. And, in essence, this is a quality every one of us has. In other words, connection and change, and the implementation of new revenue models and organization structures, are certainly not restricted to a small, elite group.

This is possible in the whole breadth of who we are: it connects us all! Good examples of this are the many online shops that are serious rivals to the small retailers and famous shopping chains.

THE THREE DOMAINS COVERED – WHO AM I AS A LEADER AND AS A HUMAN BEING?

If you resolve to be true to the three domains, and you make conscious choices regarding how you apply your CQ to this, this will result (increasingly) in more peace and space in your thinking and acting. And, almost automatically, this peace and space will allow you to ask yourself how you wish to connect with the rest of the world.

The core question in all this is: what footprint do I wish to leave behind in this world? To prepare you for this question, and for you to open up to it, I will briefly discuss the three domains from the perspective of the question: who am I as a leader *and* as a human being?

Domain I: In connection with yourself

Connection with yourself as the core of leadership

Connection with yourself means listening to yourself. It means being aware of your *gut feeling* and your intuition, and making use of them. Can you fully accept yourself, with both your positive and your dark sides?

It's not about becoming the best. Rather, the focus is on being the whole of who you are. It's not about wanting to be perfect, but being the best version of yourself that you can be at this moment. It's not about pretending to be bigger or smaller than you actually are, but about embracing everything that you encounter within yourself and being transparent about it.

Do this as much as possible without being judgmental. If you find you *are* being judgmental, then accept this and let it go as best you can.

Transforming inwards is transforming outwards

Change trajectories do not consist simply of rational insights or executing a new format without giving any thought to the process. In the introduction to Part I, I talked about the value of emotions. The value of working on the Connection Quotient is about integrating head, hands and heart, all at the same time.

To realize a transformation, it's necessary to first see and feel things. It's only when you commit to change at all levels that you'll get to where you want to be. Transforming outwards starts with transforming inwards. You will start asking yourself questions you've never asked before.

You will start demanding other things from your environment. You may even be cured of the *disease to please* and finally start standing up for yourself. Or, maybe you'll suddenly succeed in feeling deep down within you what that other person meant all the time when he said that you... (fill in whatever you think is appropriate). All at once, a mentor crosses your path to show you the way just when you were at a loss to know what to do. You no longer feel the need to fill silences, and you learn what it means to feel true compassion. This isn't because you've started doing more things, but because you have started to think, feel and see differently.

Being aware of what your energy drains are and what gives you energy

When it comes to the Connection Quotient, always having yourself as the starting point will help clarify where you stand and what you think. What is a vital issue for you and what is less important? The more you focus conscious attention on your inner self, the better and faster you will sense how true you're being to yourself, or whether you need to 're-source' yourself, and what you want to leave behind. This way, you retain – in contact with your source – enough energy and inspiration to do your work, appreciate the role others play in this, and continually improve.

Connecting with yourself works here like a compass. Connection with yourself gives you autonomy. Attention to connection with yourself reinforces what you find. It reinforces your unique place in the world.

5% inspiration and 95% perspiration

In general, people are willing to change, but they don't want to *be* changed. This means that you alone can truly initiate and execute your personal change.

Do you have the courage to remain loyal and to act based on your personal values, qualities and vision? This critical change is often accompanied by chaos and tension. Your inner critic will start working overtime and surface reasons why the change shouldn't take place. That's all good! It's a sign that something fundamental is about to happen.

To help you persevere, you can fall back on your intrinsic motivation. What is it that makes you want to achieve personal change? What is possible and what will happen if you become more of your true self? In this regard, remember that many changes don't fail through a lack of creativity or intent, but more due to lack of discipline and decisiveness. Change demands 5% inspiration and 95% perspiration.

Domain II: In connection with the other

With your orientation focused on the interests of the other or the team

Via David Maister's trust equation, I demonstrated the existence of a fraction, with a numerator (above the line) and a denominator (below the line). It's not so much the scores in the numerator – credibility, reliability and intimacy – that determine the result. It's more the denominator – self-orientation – that determines the outcome of the trust factor.

Figure 21: David Maister's trust equation

If someone acts primarily through self- interest and gives the other a feeling that he's of no real consequence, the denominator will have a high value.

As a result, the total value of the fraction will still end up on the low side. As long as your self-orientation is primarily focused on this self-interest, the relation trust you will build up will be minimal. If the denominator falls well below the value of 1, because you are continually and sincerely putting the interests of the team and of the other above anything else, this will have the effect of multiplying the trust you will encounter in the world.

Connected listening

I have outlined several perspectives on listening in this book. By offering you different takes on the art of listening, I want to make you aware of just how important this theme is and the impact it has on the connection with others. Why? Because awareness is a prerequisite for making conscious choices regarding a different attitude, and displaying new behaviour in the relationship with the other (and the behaviour of the other in relation to you). This increases the impact on the connection that is experienced within the relation.

In terms of listening, we can distinguish:

- How do I listen to him? (three steps; see chapter 22)
- How does he listen to me? (five styles; see chapter 26)
- How do *we* listen to each other? (four levels; see chapter 15)

I have arranged these categories in relation to each other in **Figure 22**.

Three steps How do *I* listen to him?	Five styles How does *he* listen to me?	Four levels How do *we* listen to each other?	
Internal	Not listening	Downloading	
Internal	Pretending to listen	Downloading	
Internal	Listening selectively	Debate	
Focused	Listening attentively	Dialogue/Presencing	} Connected
Intuitive	Listening with empathy	Dialogue/Presencing	Listening

Figure 22: Integration of the various categories of listening

The three categories ensure a dynamic dance between the *me, he* and *we* positions. On the one occasion you are the sender, and on another you are the receiver, and at the same time we are engaged in a conversation together. The more aware you are of this dance, the better you can play around with it in terms of connection.

If you also consciously make the choice to focus on the other from the me position, and you make use of your intuition, are prepared to listen attentively and with empathy from the he position, and you both go for the dialogue or presencing within the relation (we position), then you are in a situation of connected listening (see **Figure 22**). In the conversation, you are listening at a deep rational *and* emotional level to the question and the answer.

To achieve a state of connected listening, it is vital that you both:

- Have the intention to engage in connected listening
- Are prepared to consciously play with the different positions
- Invite each other to switch positions
- Make it known to the other if the conversation is not flowing well

Domain III: In connection with the team and the organization

Character traits of effective leaders

Research conducted within Google (Garvin, 2013) shows that leadership style does not completely explain the success of effective teams compared with less effective teams. The influence of the leader's style on the success of the team is more limited than one would intuitively expect, and less than is suggested during many leadership training courses. Nonetheless, research shows that eight character traits are present in leaders of all successful teams.

According to Google, effective leaders:

1. Are good coaches
2. Communicate trust and do not micromanage
3. Express interest in and pay attention to the success and wellbeing of their employees
4. Are results-driven
5. Are good listeners and sharers of information
6. Are supportive regarding the career development of their employees
7. Have a clearly-defined vision and strategy
8. Possess crucial technical skills

Intellect and emotion

If you reflect on these eight character traits of effective leaders, you will notice that five of these (almost two-thirds) concern the informal and relational side of leadership, and one-third have to do with the formal and rational side of leadership. This is in line with the proportions presented in Chapter 28 ('Intellect versus emotion'). Intellect and emotions are both important, and it seems that the key to powerful results lies in engaging in an emotional and supportive connection with the people within the organization.

Leadership as a relational concept

The discourse on what good leadership is typically focuses on the formal position of the leader. A leader is someone who is appointed, he holds this formal position, and therefore can claim rights and obligations.

By contrast, if you consider leadership to be separate from authority and the formal position, then it is more a relational concept. Leadership is then linked to 'followership'. You are a leader with regard to someone else. This way, it's possible to be a leader without necessarily holding the position of a manager, or without formal positional power. Leadership is then derived from a subtle and (inter-) personal process, where common power is the key, based on the leader *and* the followers.

From this perspective, both the environment and the team around the leader result in a leader being formed (Bolman & Deal, 2008). This means that skills such as listening with the intent to understand, making real contact and being in connection with your employees precede the formal side of leadership. The connection from person to person then also precedes the visionary side of leaders, as they march ahead of the troops, or make difficult decisions.

The metaphor of the stones and the cement

In terms of the Connection Quotient, you might say that a team without a high Connection Quotient is a pile of loose stones. Big stones, small stones, jagged stones, stones with protrusions and indentations. It's not until you lay cement between the stones that you can build a wall that stands firm. Thanks to the cement – the Connection Quotient – stones of various sizes and shapes, with or without protrusions (in other words, teams of various sizes and a wide range of individuals), can be transformed into a solid structure. The Connection Quotient makes allowances for the uniqueness of each individual and enables an organization of people to collaborate seamlessly.

No stones, no wall. No people, no organization. Without cement, all you have is a heap of loose, precariously piled-up stones. Similarly, without a high Connection Quotient, all you have is small groups of people who are incapable of pushing each other to new and permanent heights. In other words, you're left with a group of people you can't build on. The wall becomes a solid structure thanks to stones and cement. The organization becomes solid thanks to people *and* the Connection Quotient.

Collaborations that transcend organizations?

To be able to flourish (or even survive) as an organization in the connection economy, and in a connected society, more and more organizations are engaged in both formal and informal external collaborations. This form of collaboration can be typified as engaging in partnerships between people and organizations for mutual benefit.

I define a partnership here in the broadest sense of the word: as the ability to engage in a lasting connection with another entity, to support each other in realizing each other's ambitions. This definition shows that engaging in partnerships goes further than looking for and finding suitable investors or a fellow entrepreneur to be able to bear the business risks.

Many organizations are increasingly engaged in collaborations outside their own organizations – including (and especially) with unconventional partners – to stay ahead of the pack in the field of innovation, and to bridge so-called *skill gaps* (Stuart, 2016).

Domain IV: In connection with the rest of the world
Introduction to the fourth domain

The fourth domain is about being in connection with the rest of the world. I have made a conscious choice not to devote separate chapters to this last domain of the Connection Quotient. Why? Because I expect that if you are in connection with yourself (Part I), you will also realize who you are, what you want to achieve in life, and what you wish to contribute to the world.

If you are then in connection with the other (Part II), you will experience what the impact is on the other in the personal contact, if you choose to connect completely rationally and emotionally with him. And this has a positive impact on yourself. A self-reinforcing circle has been set in motion and you experience at a deeper level what being a human means for you.

Finally, your 'being' and your work acquire more and more meaning based on the deep connection with the team and the organization (Part III). Your personal and business ambitions merge: this creates balance, space and energy.

By experiencing the three domains from a personal perspective, and basing your thinking and acting on this, a space is created, along with the desire to reflect on the footprint you wish to leave in the world. This occurs automatically, which is why it does not need any further introduction.

And so, the fourth domain is at the same time such an essential element of the Connection Quotient that I have chosen to devote an extensive section to it in this final chapter.

ASSIGNMENT: Connecting with the world from a functional perspective

From your position of the leader as a role, you make connection with the rest of the world on a daily basis. How do you model your day-to-day activities, whether or not you have a formal leadership position? What is for you personally the added value of being connected to the world around you? And, are you encouraged and invited to do so by others, or is it the result of an intrinsic motivation?

Connection with the rest of the world based on the leader as a role
Consciously or unconsciously, a leader always makes use of the power of the Connection Quotient. His role and his responsibility do not stop at the borders of the organization. The connection doesn't stop when it's not about achieving the company goals or the full-year plan. After all, with the Connection Quotient as the basis, you are always connecting. Period!

The core of connection is that it is an energy that is constantly seeking to build bridges. And, it doesn't matter which worlds need to be bridged. No distinction is made between 'inside the organization' and 'outside the organization.' The connecting just carries on regardless.

Below, I will provide a few insights to give you something to reflect on regarding the need to leverage your CQ in connection with the rest of the world, based on your position of the leader as a role.

Connecting with the world as a sales market
From your traditional position of the leader as a role, you view the rest of the world primarily as a potential sales market, as a source of workers or as a possibility to engage in partnerships (in the broadest sense of the word). This form of connection with the rest of the world is largely familiar and is often applied. This is where the focus lies primarily on the interests of your own organization.

A common example of engaging in functional connections is setting up national and international collaborations so that the organization can position better or create new sales markets. Or, for example, it could be about engaging in collaborations with other organizations to create new services and products.

Connecting control and innovation
Research conducted by author Richard Foster (2012) shows that the average lifespan of American organizations is rapidly declining. In 1958, the lifespan of organizations in the Standard & Poors 500 Index was on average 61 years. In 1980, it was a mere 25 years. And at the end of 2011, it had fallen to just 18 years. Today it's even less.

The key reasons for this are that organizations are not able to respond flexibly to changes in market demand, have failed to integrate new technologies, or have been unable to re-invent themselves. The organization's product, service and level of innovation conflicts with the urge to control and optimize business processes. The only constant today is change.

The challenge is then to connect with the market and technological developments (and to look ahead), and to then adapt accordingly. This demands an organization structure and culture within which control and innovation are interrelated.

Connecting start-ups and grown-ups

Within the functional connection with the rest of the world, new trends are emerging. As a result of the introduction of open standards and platforms, and the speed with which innovations are taking place, for many organizations the option of doing everything themselves is no longer a long-term solution. That's why more and more partnerships are being created between new and innovative organizations (startups) and existing large organizations (grown ups).

The grown ups help startups – with capital, knowledge and networks – to acquire a position in the market and to upscale. In turn, the startups help the grown ups access new developments in the market and provide a culture with a strong focus on innovation. Thanks to the connection with startups, the grown ups are able to update their products and services without needing to invest huge amounts in R&D.

Connecting technologies

By connecting existing and new technologies, products and services are created that were not previously available. There are apps that perform medical checkups via your smartphone, self-driving cars, computers that give legal advice regardless of time and location, 3D printers for products or spare parts, drones that deliver the products you ordered online, personalised meals that have been cooked by a robot (or 3D printer), and so on.

The consequence of all these developments is that the work previously done by humans is now increasingly being replaced by technology. What impact does this have on the labour market and on society?

Connecting with 'talenteds'

Talented Millennials choose consciously to make a connection with, and to work for, an organization with which they can identify and where they're given the opportunity to develop at a personal level.

Additionally, it has been my experience, through my work as a personal coach and leadership trainer, that this group generally considers existing large organizations to be inflexible and hardly inspiring. Many prefer to start a company themselves, to join a startup, or to look for an organization that represents and upholds values they personally consider important.

In other words, the war for talent is still being waged in the labour market and this will only increase in intensity in the years to come. The grown ups will continue to find it difficult to recruit and retain the talented Millennials.

Connecting with the world is (still) a human activity

Positioning your company, responding quickly to market developments, creating powerful partnerships, connecting control and innovation, connecting various technologies, recruiting and retaining talents, and forging many other connections with the world is ultimately (still) a human activity. It demands an open and inquisitive mind on the part of the leader, as well as the genuine intention to want to connect within the company and the rest of the world.

As the global executive search firm Spencer Stuart (2016) has noted, being prepared for the future, from your position of leader as a role, demands an open and connection-oriented attitude: 'Alliances and partnerships have never been more necessary, requiring leaders to be strong relationship builders (…) companies will need leaders with open, collaborative, partner-focused mindsets who can think holistically across today's interconnected ecosystem.'

ASSIGNMENT: Connecting with the world from a humanity perspective

Make a list of social injustices that sadden you as a human being.

Do they include famine in the Third World, the unequal treatment of certain groups, and knowing that child labour still exists? Or, are you more concerned about causes closer to home? Do you feel for the lonely neighbour around the corner, or the impact of poverty on children in your own town?

Once you've completed the list, ask yourself which injustice you feel most affinity with, and which of your qualities you want to make use of to help alleviate the problem. Or, are you aware of the injustice but consciously deciding not to take any action yourself? What's stopping you?

Connecting with the rest of the world based on the leader as a human being

How does the leader as a human being deal with connecting with the rest of the world? This leader is first and foremost emotionally involved with the world around him. Business issues then acquire an extra dimension.

Questions that arise include: how can I run my business without exhausting the Earth's natural resources? How do I deal with the impact of our activities on the environment? What does sustainable entrepreneurship mean for us? What is our company doing to encourage diversity and inclusivity? Do we offer positions for the disabled? How important is our work for society? Or even, more precisely, what impact does our organization *want to have* in society?

In addition to this business-oriented view of how the leader as a human connects with the rest of the world, other questions touch on broader social involvement. How, for example, do I view the issue of refugees? What can I do for people who are suffering due to drought or natural disasters? What contribution can I make to help achieve equal rights for girls and women? How can poverty be combated in a sustainable manner, and do I want to help? What impact is climate change having on the world, and what can I do about it?

The business and social questions within this fourth domain can be reduced to a single core question: what footprint do I want to leave in the world? To get you to reflect on this question, and to make choices, I will elaborate on a few topics.

Connecting with the world as a marketing ploy

Organizations and their leaders sometimes make charitable gestures because of the impact they hope they'll have on their positioning vis-à-vis competitors. It becomes an image issue.

It becomes all about doing something that shows them taking Corporate Social Responsibility (CSR) seriously, but it's purely for the benefit of their image. The hope of these leaders is that the gifts will influence clients who recognize themselves in the attention that is being paid to social themes and, based on this, will want to connect with the organization and purchase its products.

However, if the leader (and the organization) lacks true connection with the themes, then CSR becomes a hollow marketing ploy. It is simply 'greenwashing' that will be unmasked in the long term. This rational reasoning has a negative impact on the connection with the world.

The challenge is to search for what you as a human being want to emotionally connect with in this world.

What kind of world do I want to pass on to my children?

Our children are both the ideal point of departure for reflection and a powerful mirror. What I notice is that they're not just interested in making money and/or a career. This generation is increasingly driven by connection, meaning, purpose – they're making conscious choices about the life they want to live, and where they want to work.

And, in that way, they are also the comparative mirror, reflecting ourselves. What drives me? How important is it for me to earn money and/or build a career? What sacrifices am I making while pursuing these – for myself, my family, my friends and the world? How much time and space am I putting aside so that I can reflect on these kinds of questions?

The new generation

Together with the Millennials, our children are part of the new generation. It's a generation that symbolizes a conscious attitude towards life and the creation of a sustainable society. They think and act consciously with the aim of achieving a better world, whatever that may mean to them.

They pursue this, among other ways, through social media and crowdfunding, to acquire the necessary marketing and startup budgets.

Consider Peerby, an initiative intended to encourage the sharing of used household materials. Within a few days of announcing this initiative, the Dutch company had raised one million euros through crowdfunding (*Nu.nl*, 2016). By July 2016 – just a few months later, when they closed the crowdfunding initiative – they'd raised more than two million euros. This was remarkable, given that original target amount was just €300,000 (OnePlanetCrowd, 2016).

Increasingly broader basis for contributions to a better world

Working to achieve a better world is no longer the lofty realm of idealists. In the past, 'doing good for the world' was typically linked to the image of *tree huggers*. In the last few decades, however, environmentally aware thinking and acting has become more widely embraced, and even encouraged by national governments.

A steadily growing group of people are beginning to realize that, when buying a car, house, food or clothing, they always have a choice. For example, should I go for a hybrid or an electric car? Or, why buy a car at all if a car-sharing service like the Dutch operation Greenwheels – or public transportation – can do the job just as well and contribute to a healthy world at the same time?

And am I willing to pay a little extra for organic meat or vegetables in order to contribute to the quality of life on this planet?

Personal involvement and engagement

It's becoming increasingly important to ask, 'What kind of world do I want to leave for my children?' and 'How do I connect as a human being to the rest of the world?' When looking for and implementing solutions, concepts such as ethics, integrity and being socially responsible are increasingly the first things that come to mind.

The question becomes to what extent we then intervene. For example, can income disparity, the wealth gap and the greed-driven lifestyle of bankers be addressed through the introduction of a code of conduct that includes a banker's oath? That surely won't produce another mentality. It will take something else – an intervention at a level other than the intellect.

This has to happen at a level where there is at least intrinsic motivation, authentic involvement with the world, heightened consciousness and the acceptance of responsibility. If, as a human being, you make a connection with the world from this deeper level, you can still decide to donate to a good cause.

Based on your CQ, you ask yourself: am I giving money to a charitable cause in order to establish a profile, or because I'm truly and honestly making a connection with the social problem it is trying to resolve? In other words, is there engagement on my part?

In the light of engagement, everyone can stand up as a leader. Everyone can be triggered.

Consider an initiative undertaken by Boyan Slat, a Dutch student of aviation and aerospace engineering at Delft University. At the age of 17, at the TEDx Delft event in 2012, he presented a simple method for cleaning up the plastic soup that is clogging the oceans. He felt an intrinsic commitment to this problem, and a year later dropped out of university to kickstart The Ocean Cleanup. As of August 2019, his idea/talk had turned into a non-profit organization with global reach, and the first results from deploying 'Wilson' (the passive drifting system) in the Great Pacific Garbage Patch are visible.

Leadership and personal action increasingly intertwined

When engaging in connection at a societal level, leadership and personal action are becoming increasingly intertwined. We see the leader as a human *and* the human as a leader. Often there is no longer the notion that functional leadership can be separated from the personal call that someone feels, bears and carries out.

If you set the actions of such a leader against traditional leadership, then the leader is the one who looks further than these traditional/functional sides of leadership. The leader and the stake become one. He himself – as a human who makes a connection with a bigger whole – has become the stake. However large and complete, or small and specific, however abstract or concrete, a leader views this bigger whole.

When looking at the Connection Quotient in relation to the rest of the world, we are concerned with all those affairs that fall outside the formal boundaries of an organization and your role. We embrace those affairs in which authentic personal commitment to society is felt.

What footprint will you leave behind in this world?

As soon as you make connections outside the boundaries of your role and your organization, and at the same time focus on improving society, as a leader *and* as a human being you are leveraging your CQ for the benefit of the rest of the world. And, that is completely independent of how big or small this rest of the world is, or how big or small your impact is on solving the major problems out there.

At its core, it's about asking yourself what footprint you'll leave behind in this world.

ASSIGNMENT: What footprint will I leave behind in this world?

Business book author Daniel Pink (2010) assumes that intrinsic factors have a massive influence on people's behaviour. These factors are determined by autonomy (the perceived extent of self-determination and control over the environment), mastery (the compulsion to improve something or someone) and meaning (belonging to a community). If you look at yourself with respect to these three factors, ask how powerful are they are in your my life.

Do I have, demand or claim my autonomy? What is so important to me that I want to contribute to improving it? And, with whom do I feel connected?

Making conscious choices results in behaviour, in action, and in impact on others in the world around you. Again, what footprint will you leave behind when you have passed away?

Revising the framework of the Connection Quotient

Functional knowledge is a 'hygiene' factor

In this book, I am assuming that the leader has a high level of professional expertise. The basic assumption is that he's adequately equipped to read reports, set the appropriate priorities in his business operations, filter management information according to relevance and make decisions based on all this. The focus is not explicitly on perfecting systems, structures and reports, or on learning skills such as scenario thinking, change management, negotiating, running meetings, persuading, and so on.

Countless other books have been written about these rational activities. I would go so far as to say that this type of book is probably over-represented in the literature of leadership.

The Connection Quotient is a human activity

The more you work with the Connection Quotient, the more you will come to realize that importance of the humanity aspect. Above all, leadership is ultimately a human activity.

The Connection Quotient is also a human activity. If your approach to leadership is too technical, you will lose sight of the core of leadership. After all, you always bring 'yourself' along, and therefore your values, visions, feelings, wishes, thoughts and desires. Your followers are also people who work and act based on these fundamentals. And thus, leadership becomes increasingly the art of finding mutual agreement based on these foundations.

It's no coincidence that within universities and MBA programmes there is a clear tendency towards more attention being paid to the human aspects. These insights influence the framework I presented in the general introduction. You see that the dividing line in the previously presented framework gradually sinks deeper.

Being human is crucial

The lowering of the dividing line in this graphic (more person than role) represents the fact that the crucial element within leadership is the human factor. The Connection Quotient plays a role largely in the upper part of the framework.

This is where the individual gets his voice; it's where connections and contact moments from human to human, from heart to heart, take place. It's where the human dimension is determined, where trust reigns, where the leader is given space to operate and where he uses his intuition (sometimes irrationally, and never unknowingly).

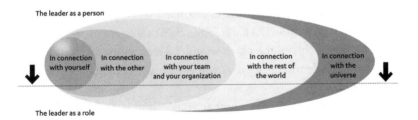

Figure 23: The Connection Quotient with a shifted dividing line: more attention to the human aspects

Figure 23 on the previous page therefore shows a more accurate representation of the state of affairs than I suggested in the general introduction. The importance of the human factor is increasing; the factor of the leader as a role needs to be well organized, and is increasingly becoming a 'hygiene' factor rather than a goal to be focused on in your development. And… as a leader you need them both!

Domain V: In connection with the universe?

In **Figure 23**, I have introduced another modification: the domain 'In connection with the universe' has been added.

Is this a fifth domain within the Connection Quotient? Is it in fact a domain in which the distinction between the leader as a role and the leader as a person is no longer relevant?

Whereas in the first domain the emphasis was on you as an inward-oriented individual ('Who am I in my core?'), in this fifth domain, the accent could be on you as an outward-oriented individual ('What is my role in the bigger whole?'). It is where the focus lies on being a complete person, in mental connection with each other and a higher power.

For me, the domain 'In connection with the universe' is about spirituality (what name do you give it?). It's about a deeper being and knowing, without there being a rational explanation for it. It's about being destined to do something on this earth and acting intuitively based on this realization. And, it's about coincidences that at first don't seem to be related to each other, but as time goes on turn out to be interconnected.

Perhaps it's the domain that opens itself when people meditate – what New Age author Eckhart Tolle (2005) talks about in his book, *A New Earth*. This is the place where Tibetan monks, shamans and high priests take you on a journey to worlds and experiences you have never known.

I leave to you to decide whether you believe in this fifth domain, and what its impact is on the Connection Quotient within the other four domains. I am just asking the question; I don't claim to know the answer.

AND NOW... YOU!

It's your turn

All the chapters in this book are intended to help you, the reader, gain insight into your CQ and to further develop it. The intent is to stimulate you and challenge you to engage with the connection with yourself, the other, your team and your organization – further, more often and deeper.

You can use and apply your CQ as an extra and non-competing perspective on all the other leadership styles and leadership lessons you've already made acquaintance with and will continue to encounter in the future. In that regard, I stated the following in the introduction and above:

> Leadership doesn't start with the connection with the others; the true starting point is the connection with yourself.

> Leadership doesn't stop with the connection with the organiza-tion; it goes further in the connection with the rest of the world (and perhaps even outside that).

Start experimenting!

My invitation to you is to start experimenting with the Connection Quotient. This means trying new things. Some activities will pleasantly surprise you and others will not. I hope that you will allow yourself to make mistakes in this process. If you start experimenting too much based on fear, your creativity will disappear, and you will only try things out that are safe and already familiar to you.

Central to the notion of experimenting is trying something new and being allowed to fail. Have the pleasure, courage and perseverance to start working on your CQ in all its many facets, and to make mistakes along the way. Give yourself the explicit permission to try something new. If you succeed, celebrate your success with others. But if it turns out a mess, be willing to remedy the situation (and retain the trust in yourself that you can do this). If you keep this in mind, you can also claim the space for *the daring experiment*, whatever that may mean for you.

A perspective that can help you engage with the experiment is this: if you fail quickly, you also learn quickly. When you're afraid to fail, you delay failure, and therefore you also delay the learning. Or, in the words of entrepreneur and marketing lecturer Bernie Schroeder: "It's not a question of 'fail fast *or* win big,' but rather a question of 'fail fast *and* win big.'"

Whether you are a leader, manager or employee, you deserve a high Connection Quotient as a key to your own leadership or other type of development. You deserve conscious growth in yourself, in your contact with others, in teams and organizations... and in connection with the rest of the world. Not because you have to, but because you have the courage to do so.

Enjoy your journey!

AFTERWORD AND ACKNOWLEDGEMENTS

It's 25 November 2008. I've just published my blog, entitled 'Design the relation,' and decided that this will be the first in a series of postings that focus on themes such as coaching, leadership and team development.

In addition to my work as coach, trainer and consultant, I also want to communicate my experiences and insights to others in this way that assists them in their personal development, the development of their team and that of their organization.

My inner critic is working overtime, making me insecure and draining me of energy. Can I write? Is my style attractive and unique enough? Are the topic and my perspective interesting enough? Are there actually people out there waiting to read my blogs? And can I keep on writing regularly?

Today, 11 years later, I know the answers to these questions. As of 1 August 2019, I have written 85 blog posts; the newsletter I send out via COURIUS has more than 10,000 subscribers; the website is visited regularly; and I am the co-author of the book *Het leiderschapsalfabet (The Leadership Alphabet)*. The Dutch version of *The Connection Quotient* (released in 2016) became the best-selling management book in just two weeks after its release, was on the long list for Management Book of the Year 2017, and is now in its 5th edition.

During this whole journey, I have acquired new insights, knowledge and skills, both functionally and in terms of content, as well as personally. I have learned more about myself as a person.

I would never have been able to go on this journey, which actually started around 2003, on my own. The requested (and unsolicited) help from others has been indispensable. Others have helped me move forward, through their roles as sparring partner, thorn in my side, inspiration and motivator. With their help, I have developed into the person I am today, and I have been able to write this book.

I want to thank them from the bottom of my heart, using the insights from Joseph Campbell's *The Hero's Journey* as my guiding principles.

Phase 1: The call to adventure

It can overcome you at any moment – the feeling that you 'have something to do' in this life that is bigger than yourself. You can't quite express it in words or imagine the possible consequences. At the same time, you know it's there, that you have to go on a journey.

That feeling may have its origin in an event that caused a huge impact (an illness, dismissal, divorce or an accident) or as a result of an unexpected situation (you read something, watch a film or meet someone). You're given a wake-up call and you know one thing for certain: you have something to do. At this instant, you can see and feel it very clearly, but describing it is far more difficult.

I can't recall exactly when I got my call to adventure. What I do remember is that in the period 2003-2005, a few situations occurred that were linked with the feeling of wanting to contribute to a connected world: my divorce, letting go of my management role, taking Co-Active Coaching Fundamentals training, and reading the book *Nonviolent Communication: A Language of Life*, by Marshall Rosenberg (1998).

My thanks in this phase go especially to my father, Simon. Despite the difficult period we shared together, you have always been there for me, never judging me or putting me under pressure, but encouraging me with your questions and points for reflection. I know that you will continue to support me unconditionally in other phases, and in the new journey that lies ahead of me. Thank you, from the bottom of my heart!

Phase 2: The refusal of the call

You've had a wake-up call and are totally ecstatic for a while. But then, that warm feeling is transformed into one of doubt and fear. Will you be able to do it? Do you dare to do it? Are you allowed to do it? What are the consequences of embarking on the journey? And are you willing to accept them?

Multiple sub-personalities engage in short-lived or lengthy internal dialogues about desire and fear. The adventurer, the believer and the hero are eager to go on the journey. The critic, the security seeker and the doubter prefer to maintain the status quo. Which internal voice do you listen to? Will you embark on your journey or not? And what influence do the people in your environment have on your decision? It's a phase in which looking doubt straight in the eye will lead to commitment and perseverance.

My divorce left a deep impression on me, and for many years afterwards I continued to ask myself if it had been the right choice, considering the impact on my children. Letting go of my management role was also a huge change and a risky move. I felt that I wanted to work as a coach, but at the same time, I thought: well, there are so many coaches in the Netherlands already. Can I make a living from it? Many ex-colleagues couldn't understand my choice, yet others admired me for my courage.

My gratitude in this phase goes especially to my very dear friends Anton, Erwin and Gerhard. Over the years, we have spoken so many times about our fears, dreams and desires. I want to thank you for your unconditional trust in me, your sincere opinions, your confrontations and the kicks up my backside that were (occasionally) absolutely necessary. You too were important in every phase, and this will always be the case. I love you all!

Phase 3: The mentors

The mentors will cross your path. They will support you in the different phases by offering you new insights and knowledge, providing you with new perspectives, introducing you to the appropriate people, and so on. It's as though they always appear at just the right moment.

But, it may also be the case that you've known them for years and that they suddenly come up with that new insight. Coincidence or fate? Apparently, you're ready to meet them.

Mentors aren't necessarily people, by the way. They can also be a book that gives you just the nudge you need. Or, perhaps a film. Two kinds of mentors that often appear are the *liberator* and the *unlocker*. The liberator gets you to take the next step, make a decision or choose a path. The unlocker is more direct, and forces you to make choices through confrontation.

During the Co-Active Coaching Fundamentals training, and follow-up courses afterwards, my trainers were constantly forcing me to rethink my ideas. Their eternally positive approach and their trust in me reinforced my belief in myself. During his improvisation training sessions, Keith Johnstone was a wonderful example to me, with his passion and professional expertise. Many mentors have crossed my path in recent years – too many to mention.

My thanks in this phase go especially to Ad Lugten, my manager at Capgemini. You welcomed me into your management team, acknowledged how people-oriented I was and encouraged me to do more with this quality. You gave me the space to make mistakes, supported me in a turbulent phase of my life, and made it possible for me to follow the training necessary to become a coach. You were therefore a key link for the fundamental career switch I set in motion. I don't know if you're aware of how important you were to me, and I don't think I ever explicitly told you. I'm doing that now, Ad. Thanks! You totally deserve the credit.

Phase 4: Crossing the threshold

The moment has finally arrived when your desire has grown to such proportions that you say yes to the adventure. To get this far, you've taken some enormous steps. You're ready to step into the unknown.

This moment when you say yes feels frightening, but at the same time it's so liberating. From your comfortable and familiar world, you cross the threshold to the new world. The journey has now really begun, and you don't yet know what's in store for you. Whether the crossing was smooth or rough, one thing is certain: there's no going back.

I can remember vividly that I had already started working for myself while I was still working at Capgemini. It was only one day a week, because I didn't dare to spend more time on it than that. But my desire grew every day, driven by the fact that I wanted to be a freelance trainer for the Coaches Training Institute. The time was ripe for me to say yes.

My gratitude in this phase goes especially to Cindy, my wife. During one of our holidays, you made it clear to me that you supported me unconditionally and that it was time to make the leap. "If it doesn't work out," you said, "we can always find some cabin in the middle of nowhere to live." Shortly afterwards, I got an assignment as a self-employed entrepreneur, via my network, and handed in my letter of resignation. You've continued to support me all this time, even now when my career is putting so much pressure on our family, and therefore also on you. Thank you, my darling!

Phase 5: The trials

When you're on a journey in the new world, you will have strokes of good luck and strokes of bad luck. Your perseverance will be put to the test and you will start developing new skills. And, although it sometimes seems as if the whole world is conspiring to stop you from succeeding, the most important battle you can win is the one against yourself.

How do you deal with setbacks, with people who reject you or give up on you, and with your fears? Do you persist, or do you give up? Do you follow your desire, or go along with what others want? Do you blame others, or ask yourself what your part was? Do you wallow in excuses to convince yourself that something isn't possible, or do you start exploring the options? Do you remain in reflection mode or do you take action?

After all, you only learn by doing, even if you fail. And because trials always appear when you least expect them, you can only partially prepare for them. The most important thing is therefore to be in the here and now and experience what there is, what is expected of you, what is required.

A significant element of entrepreneurship is putting yourself on the market and getting loyal clients. And, it's my personal mission to inspire people to engage in connection with others, based on a connection with themselves. I very quickly came up with the idea that I could achieve both goals at the same time through blogging.

The idea was one thing, but taking action and setting things in motion was quite another. In the beginning, it took me hours to complete one blog post. I spent a lot of time looking for and finding the right topic, and then more time finding the right words (or even just a single word). Added to that, being an entrepreneur was something new for me. All at once, I had to do everything myself. I was now the one who had to give myself a kick up the backside.

My gratitude in this phase goes to Jaco. Our collaboration started out as a client relationship, we evolved into sparring partners, and finally he became my business partner on 1 April 2014. You were always encouraging me and being positive, your inexhaustible energy helping me to reach that dot on the horizon. Your unique way of thinking and acting produced atypical and practical solutions for seemingly complex issues. You were, and still are, unquestioningly always there for me, including during the realization of this book and everything related to it. It never ceases to amaze me how strong you are and how you are able to complement me so well. I thank you for being 'you,' for your trust and your support. It's a joy working with you, and I'm sure that won't change in the future! I look forward to many more years of joy and pleasure together.

Phase 6: The treasure

Seizing the treasure is what the journey is all about. Beforehand you had all kinds of ideas about what it could be and what it might look like. During the journey, you may realize that the treasure is different to what you imagined.

It can be something tangible (for example, a new house), an experience (such as personal values you live up to) or a change in your personal situation (a new relationship or job). However huge and compelling, or perhaps small and mundane, the impact of the treasure doesn't matter at all. Every change counts, for you and the world around you. But I know one thing for sure – you will have changed permanently, and in doing so you will change others too.

During a leadership trajectory in 2008, we were continually talking about the *stake* (the contribution). What is your contribution to the world, and who do you need to be in order to make that contribution? And do you dare to think big, without letting yourself be limited by who you are now, what you know now and the knowledge and skills you have?

This stake is expressed in a mantra with the following structure: '*I am <metaphor> that will <impact>*'. At the time, I formulated a stake that has evolved over the years. It still forms a key theme for the way I act and think: '*I am the Casanova that will seduce you to be your best self.*' Based on my stake, I then looked for what my business specialities were. They turned out to be executive coaching, team development, High Performance Teams, and so on.

These are the forms in which I continually carry out my work. In 2015, I discovered my true basis: the Connection Quotient.

In this phase, my thanks go especially to Stella (my publisher) and Guido (my editor).

Stella, it was your innovative way of looking at the world of publishing, combined with your smile and energy, that caused me to decide within ten minutes of meeting you that I wanted to collaborate with you in writing and publishing this book. You challenged me to become personal, and above all, you came up with the title *The Connection Quotient*. These words turned out to be crucial, both for the book and for the path my thoughts and actions subsequently took. What a present! I can't thank you enough for that.

Guido, you have the talent of listening to what is being said and being able to distil the essence from it. You helped me link the book to developments in the field of leadership. You made a huge contribution to the structure of the book, and with your expertise and insights, you also helped improve the quality of the content. Thank you for all your inspiring discussions and your honest feedback.

Phase 7: The return

You have the treasure in your possession and are embarking on your return journey to your old world. One element of this journey is the internalization of the treasure so that it becomes a part of who you are, what you think and what you do. Additionally, the return journey can be tense, with a final trial waiting to test you. Perhaps you've made some new friends and you realize that it's time to say farewell to old friends. Or, maybe your new skills and knowledge have made you arrogant or a know-it-all in the eyes of others. Perhaps an enemy will try to steal your treasure to use as his own, to change the world.

Whatever the reason, on your return, the old world will look different because you are seeing it with new eyes. Enjoy your new life and be grateful. Allow yourself the time to accept the new you... and to be surprised by a new call for the next journey that will present itself.

As I write this afterword, I realize that this is exactly the phase I find myself in today. I'm discovering more and more what the Connection Quotient means for me, and how it determines my thoughts and actions in this world. During this process, I also feel that a new journey is just around the corner: the desire to speak at national and international events seems to be growing every day. It's the next step in realizing my contribution: inspiring people.

How exciting! I am confident that this dream will become a reality. I believe in myself. I know that I can do it. And, I have taken the first steps.

My thanks in this phase go especially to my colleagues in COURIUS. Jaco, Monique and Nynke, your constant encouragement and unwavering trust in my ability are a special source of inspiration. It feels so good to observe how all of us are driven by the same dream: to contribute to a better society. I thank you for your support throughout my personal journey, as well as our common one. I am really curious to know how we will develop as a team and an organization, and what impact we will have within society!

Finally

My final word of thanks is for my clients. I thank you all for the faith and the space you gave me to act as I have. Thanks for occasionally knowing beforehand what I was intending to do with a sort of standard approach, but more often working through things in total ignorance when using an experimental approach. Many of these interventions proved to be powerful and effective, while some did not produce the results you and I had hoped for. You have developed as individuals, as teams and organizations. And as a result, I have also been able to develop further and grow. I thank you for this wonderful interaction! And, I very much look forward to many more fantastic encounters and inspiring collaborations.

Marco Buschman,
Oss, April 2020

INSPIRATION AND RESOURCES

Altman, Ian. "Top 10 business trends that will drive success in 2016." *Forbes*, December 1, 2015. http://www.forbes.com/sites/ianaltman/2015/12/01/top-10-business-trends-that-will-drive-success-in-2016/#2aa6baf05571.

The Arbinger Institute. *Leadership and Self-Deception: Getting out of the Box.* San Francisco: Berrett-Koehler Publishers, 2009.

The Arbinger Institute, Duane Boyce. *The Anatomy of Peace: How to Resolve the Heart of Conflict.* San Francisco: Berrett-Koehler Publishers, 2016.

Arets, Jos, Jennings, Charles and Heijnen, Vivian. *702010 naar 100% performance.* Maastricht: Sutler Media, 2015.

Artgym. "Discover the leader within you." Last modified 2019. http://artgym.com/wp-content/uploads/2017/10/Artgym-Archetypes-01-final.pdf.

Baas, Ed J. *Luisteren naar binnen. Zelfanalyse met de film 'As it is in Heaven' als inspiratiebron.*(Inspired by the movie 'As it is in Heaven' (Kay Pollak 2004)). Houten: Zwerk Uitgevers, 2009.

Baumeister, Roy F. "The need to belong: Desire for Interpersonal Attachments as a Fundamental Human Motivation." *Psychological Bulletin*, Vol. 117, No. 3 (Fall 1995): 497-529. https://roybaumeister.com/1995/10/15/the-need-to-belong-desire-for-interpersonal-attachments-as-a-fundamental-human-motivation/.

Bennis, Warren. *On becoming a leader: The Leadership classis (revised and updated).* New York: Basic Books, 2009.

Bolman, Lee G. and Deal, Terrence E. *Reframing Organizations: Artistry, Choice, and Leadership.* San Francisco: Jossey-Bass, 2008.

Brugman, Karin, Budde, Judith and Collewijn, Berry. *Ik ken mijn ikken: Ontdek andere kanten van jezelf met Voice Dialogue.* Zaltbommel: Uitgeverij Thema, 2010.

Buckingham, Marcus and Clifton, Donald O. *Now, Discover your strengths: The revolutionary program that shows you how to develop your unique talents and strenths – and those of the people you manage.* New York: The Free Press, 2001.

Campbell, Joseph. *Hero with a Thousand Faces.* Novato: New World Library, 2015.

Cao, Jing and Cortez, Michelle. "IBM Extends Health Care Bet With Under Armour, Medtronic." *Bloomberg*, January 7, 2016. http://www.bloomberg.com/news/articles/2016-01-07/ibm-extends-reach-into-health-care-with-under-armour-medtronic.

Coelho, Paulo. *The Alchemist: a Fable About Following Your Dream.* New York City: HarperCollins Publishers, 1994.

Collins, Jim. *Good to great: Why Some Companies Make the Leap... and Others Don't.* New York City: Harper Collins US, 2004.

Covey, Stephan R. *The seven habits of highly effective people: Powerful lessons in personal change.* New York: Simon & Schuster, 2004.

Covey, Stephan M.R. and Merrill, Rebecca. *The speed of trust: The one thing that changes everything.* The Free Press, 2008.

Crasborn, Joost en Buis, Ellis. *Hoe boek voor de coach. Tips, modellen en vragen voor werkgerelateerde individuele coaching.* Zaltbommel: Thema, 2008.

Cross, Rob, Rebele, Reb and Grant, Adam. "Collaborative Overload." *Harvard Business Review*, January/February Issue, 2016: pages 74-79. https://hbr.org/2016/01/collaborative-overload.

Damasio, Antonio. T*he feeling of what happens: Body and emotion in the making of consciousness*. Boston: Mariner Books, 2000.

Deci, Edward L., Koestner, Richard and Ryan, Richard M. "A meta-analytic review of experiments examining the effects of extrinsic rewards on intrinsic motivation." *Psychological bulletin*, Vol. 125, No. 6 (December 1999): 627–668. https://www. researchgate.net/publication/12712628_A_Meta-Analytic_Review_of_Experiments_ Examining_the_Effect_of_Extrinsic_Rewards_on_Intrinsic_Motivation.

Derks, Lucas en Hollander, Jaap. *Essenties van NLP: Sleutels tot persoonlijke verandering*. Utrecht: Servire, 1996.

Dijksterhuis, Ap. *Het slimme onbewuste: Denken met gevoel*. Amsterdam: Bert Bakker, 2007.

Duhigg, Charles. "What Google learned from its quest to build the perfect team." *New York Times*, February 25, 2016. http://www.nytimes.com/2016/02/28/ magazine/what-google-learned-from-its-quest-to-build-the-perfect-team.html.

Dychtwald, Ken, Erickson, Tamara J. and Morison, Robert. *Workforce Crisis: How to beat the coming shortage of skills and talent*. Boston: Harvard Business Review Press, 2006.

Fisher, Len. *The Perfect Swarm: The Science of Complexity in Everyday Life*. New York City: Basic Books, 2010.

Foster, Richard N. (2012). "Creative destruction whips through corporate America. To survive and thrive business leaders must 'create, operate, and trade' without losing control." *Innosights*, Winter 2012. http://www.innosight.com/innovation-resources/strategy-innovation/upload/ creative-destruction-whips-through-corporate-america_final2015.pdf.

Gagné, Marylene and Deci, Edward L. "Self determination theory and work motivation." *Journal of Organizational behavior*, Vol. 26 (January 2005): 331-362. https:// selfdeterminationtheory.org/SDT/documents/2005_GagneDeci_JOB_SDTtheory.pdf.

Gallup, Research and Royal, Kent. "What engaged employees do differently." 14 September, 2019. https://www.gallup.com/workplace/266822/engaged-employees-differently.aspx.

Garvin, David A. "How Google sold its engineers on management." *Harvard Business Review*, December 2013. https://hbr.org/2013/12/ how-google-sold-its-engineers-on-management?referral=00134.

Giles, Lynne C., Glonek, Gary F.V., Luszcz, Mary A. and Andrews, Gary R. "Effect of social networks on 10 year survival in very old Australians: the Australian longitudinal study of aging." *Epidemial Community Health*, Vol. 59 (2005):574–579. https://www.ncbi.nlm.nih.gov/pmc/articles/PMC1757078/pdf/v059p00574.pdf.

Gladwell, Malcolm. *Blink: The power of thinking without thinking*. New York: Back Bay Books, 2005.

Gladwell, Malcolm. (2008). *Outliers: The story of success*. New York: Little, Brown and Company, 2008. https://banco.az/sites/default/files/books/outliers-the_story_ of_success.pdf.

Gladwell, Malcolm. *The Tipping Point: How Little Things Can Make A Big Difference*. New York: Little, Brown and Company, 2009.

Godin, Seth. *The Icarus deception: How high will you fly?*
London: Penguin Books Ltd., 2012.

Goleman, Daniel. *Emotional Intelligence: Why it can matter more than IQ.*
London: Bloomsbury Publishing PLC., 1996.

Goleman, Daniel. *Vital lies, simple truths.* London: Bloomsbury Publishing PLC., 1998.

Goleman, Daniel. "Emotional intelligence, Social intelligence."
Last modified June 12, 2007. http://www.danielgoleman.info/
three-kinds-of-empathy-cognitive-emotional-compassionate/.

Gottman, John. *Why marriages succeed or fail: And how you can make yours last.*
New York: Simon & Schuster Paperbacks, 1994.

Jaworski, Joseph. *Synchronicity. The Inner Path of Leadership.*
Oakland: Berrett-Koehler, 2000.

Johnstone, Keith. *IMPRO: Improvisation and the Theatre.* Abingdon: Routledge, 1987.

Johnstone, Keith. *Impro for storytellers.* London: Faber and Faber Limited, 1999.

Kahneman, Daniel. *Thinking fast and slow.* New York: Farrar, Straus and Giroux, 2011.

Katzenbach, Jon R. and Smith, Douglas K. *The wisdom of teams creating the high-performance organization.* Brighton: Harvard Business Review Press, 1992.

Knoope, Marinus. *De creatiespiraal: Natuurlijke weg van wens naar werkelijkheid.*
Nijmegen: KIC Nijmegen, 1998.

Kodden, Sebastiaan. *Be a HERO: How To Bring Out Leadership In Everyone.*
Utrecht: BigBusinessPublishers, 2017.

Kolb, David A. *Experiential Learning: Experience as the Source of Learning and Development.* New Jersey: Pearson Education Inc., 2015. http://ptgmedia.
pearsoncmg.com/images/9780133892406/samplepages/9780133892406.pdf.

Kotter, John and Rathgeber, Holger. *Our iceberg is melting!* London: Picador UK, 2006.

Kouzes, James M. and Posner, Barry Z. Encouraging the heart. *A leader's guide to rewarding and recognizing others.* San Francisco: Jossey-Bass, 2003.

Kouzes, James M. and Posner, Barry Z. *The Leadership Challenge: How to make extraordinary things happen in organizations (fifth edition).*
San Francisco: Jossey-Bass, 2012.

Kuipers, Ben en Groeneveld, Sandra. *De kracht van high perfomance teams: Zes ingedienten voor excellent presteren in de publieke sector.* Amsterdam: Mediawerf, 2014.

Landy, David and Sigall, Harold. (1974). "Beauty is talent: Task evaluation as a function of the performer's physical attractiveness." *Journal of Personality and Social Psychology,* Vol. 29, No.3 (1974): 299-304. https://www.researchgate.net/
publication/232466827_Beauty_is_talent_Task_evaluation_as_a_function_of_
the_performer's_physical_attractiveness.

Lammers, Marc. *Coachen doe je samen: Winnaars hebben een plan, verliezers een excuus.* Baarn: Tirion Uitgevers, 2007.

Lee, Richard van der, Taffijn, Pieter, Besseling, Miriam, Kwakman, Hans en Buschman, Marco M. *Het leiderschapsalfabet: De uitdagingen van het moderne leiderschap.* Assen: Koninklijke van Gorcum, 2014.

Lencioni, Patrick M. *The Five Dysfunctions of a Team: A Leadership Fable.*
New Jersey: John Wiley & Sons Inc., 2002.

Lingsma, Marijke en Hoedt ten, Francine. *Conflictcoaching: Een nieuwe energiebron voor managers, een verruimende visie op conflicten.* Amsterdam: Boom/Nelissen, 2009.

Lommel, Pim van. *Consciousness beyond life: The science of the near-death experience.* San Francisco: HarperOne, 2011.

Lyubomirsky, Sonja. *How of happiness: A New Approach to Getting the Life You Want.* London: Penguin Putnam Inc., 2008.

Maister, David H., Green, Charles H. and Galford, Robert M. *The trusted advisor.* New York: Simon & Schuster, 2001.

Masselink, Robbert. (2016). "Goed besturen vraagt om verbinding." LinkedIn. Last modified June 21, 2016. https://www.linkedin.com/pulse/goed-besturen-vraagt-om-verbinding-robbert-masselink.

McNeish, Robert. "*Lessons from Geese.*" Suewidemark. Last accessed March 25, 2020. http://suewidemark.com/lessonsgeese.htm.

Mehrabian, Albert. *Silent messages: Implicit communication of emotions and attitudes.* Belmont: Wadsworth Publishing Company Inc., 1971.

Meurs HRM, Duurzame Inzetbaarheid: Vrijheid en verantwoordelijkheid. https://www.eelloo.nl/wp-content/uploads/2014/12/Vrijheid-verantwoordelijkheid-Meurs-HRM-in-de-Gids.pdf.

Miller, Anna. (2014). "Friends Wanted. New research by psychologists uncovers the health risks of loneliness and the benefits of strong social connections." *American Psychological Association*, Vol. 45, No. 1. January (2014): 54. https://www.apa.org/monitor/2014/01/cover-friends.

Nu.nl. "Uitleendienst Peerby haalt binnen paar dagen miljoen euro crowdfunding op." Last modified March 20, 2016. https://www.nu.nl/internet/4233505/uitleendienst-peerby-haalt-binnen-paar-dagen-miljoen-euro-crowdfunding.html.

OnePlanetCrowd. "Peerby | AanDEELhouder in spullen delen." Last modified May 17, 2016. https://www.oneplanetcrowd.com/nl/project/138624/description%20/.

Pink, Daniel H. *Drive: The Surprising Truth About What Motivates Us.* Edinburgh: Canongate Books Ltd., 2010.

Pollard, Dave. *Finding the Sweet Spot: The Natural Entrepreneur's Guide to Responsible, Sustainable, Joyful Work.* Vermont: Chelsea Green Publishing, 2008.

PWC (2012). "Millennials at work. Reshaping the workplace." Last modified 2012. https://www.pwc.com/gx/en/financial-services/publications/assets/pwc-millenials-at-work.pdf.

Rosenberg, Marshall B. *Nonviolent Communication: A Language of Life.* Encinitas: Puddledancer Press, 2003.

Scharmer, Otto C. *The Essentials of Theory U: Core Principles and Applications.* Oakland: Berrett-Koehler Publishers, 2018.

Schoor, Jaco van der en Wiel, Guido van de. *Teams van de toekomst: Leidinggeven aan het nieuwe samenwerken.* Amsterdam: Boomuitgevers, 2013.

Schouten, Jan, Baak, Anke and Kamminga, Wiebe. *Improving teams: On Working As A Team.* Zaltbommel: Thema, 2010.

Senge, Peter, Scharmer, C. Otto, Jaworski, Joseph and Flowers, Betty S. Presence. *Exploring profound change in people, organizations and society.* London: Nicolas Brealey Publishing, 2005.

Sinek, Simon. *Start with Why: How Great Leaders Inspire Everyone to Take Action.* London: Portfolio; 2011.

Sitskoorn, Margriet. *Train Your CEO Brain: And Become Your Best Self.* Alphen aan de Rijn: Vakmedianet Management, 2017.

Spencerstuart. "CES 2016: Five key trends and what they mean for leaders." Last modified January, 2016. https://www.spencerstuart.com/ research-and-insight/ces-2016-five-key-trends-and-what-they-mean-for-leaders.

Swaab, Dick. *We Are Our Brains: From the Womb to Alzheimer's.* London: Penguin UK, 2015.

Szollose, Brad. *Liquid leadership: From Woodstock to Wikipedia – Multigenerational management ideas that are changing the way we run things.* Austin Texas: Greenleaf Book Group Press, 2010.

Taylor, Jill B.T. *My Stroke of Insight.* London: Hodder & Stoughton General Division, 2009.

Team Coaching International (TCI). "The TCI Team Diagnostic™. A Powerful Assessment Tool That Transforms Teams." Last modified 2020. https://teamcoachinginternational.com/programs/program-team-diagnostic/.

Thorndike, Edward L. "A constant error in psychological rating." *Journal of Applied Psychology.* 4, Issue 1, January 1 (1920): 25. https://scinapse.io/papers/2008535554.

Tiggelaar, Ben. *Dream Dare Do: Managing the most difficult person on Earth – yourself.* Soest: Tyler Roland Press, 2009.

Tolle, Eckhart. *A New Earth: Awakening to Your Life's Purpose.* New York City: Penguin UK, 2005.

Tuckman, Bruce W. "Developmental sequence in small groups." *Psychological Bulletin,* Vol. 63, No. 6 (1965): 384- 399. https://www.scribd.com/document/349275228/ Tuckman-1965-Developmental-sequence-in-small-groups-pdf.

Tuckman, Bruce W. and Jensen, Mary A.C. "Stages of small group development revisited." *Group and Organization Studies,* 2, Issue: 4 (December 1, 1977): 419-427.

Waal, Andre de. *What Makes a High Performance Organization: Five Factors of Competitive Advantage Than Span the World.* London: Global Professional Publishing, 2012.

Whitworth, Laura, Kimsey-House, Henry and Sandahl, Phil. *Co-Active Coaching: The proven framework for transformative conversations at work and in life – (fourth edition).* London: John Murray Press, 2018.

Williamson, Marianne. *A return to love: Reflections on the principles of a course in miracles.* London: HarperCollins Publishers, 1992.

Wiseman, Richard. *Did you spot the gorilla? How to recognize the hidden opportunities in your life.* London: Arrow Ltd, 2004.

Woolley, Anita W., Chabris, Christopher F., Pentland, Alex, Hashmi, Nada and Malone, Thomas W. "Evidence for a collective intelligence factor in the performance of human groups." *Science,* 330, October 29, 2010: 686-688. http://www.chabris.com/Woolley2010a.pdf.

Yip, Jeffrey, Ernst Chris and Campbell Michael. "Organizational Leadership White Paper Series 'Boundary Spanning Leadership'." *Center for Creative Leadership (CCL),* 2016. https://www.ccl.org/wp-content/uploads/2015/04/ BoundarySpanningLeadership.pdf.

INDEX

ABOUT COURIUS

SPECIALISTS IN THE HUMAN SIDE OF CHANGE

Getting started with the Connection Quotient
Reading this book will get you thinking about what the Connection Quotient means for you. You will become aware of your connecting qualities, acquire new insights and start (or continue) to develop them. This way you will be contributing to building a lasting collaboration within the teams and organizations you work for. This in turn will lead to powerful results. This development – of yourself, your team and your organization – is an ongoing process of being curious, inspiring, reflecting, experimenting, failing, recovering, achieving goals and celebrating successes. COURIUS will support you throughout this journey.

Motivated team
We are specialists in the human side of change. Our team consists of enthusiastic and motivated individuals with a passion for their profession. We have many years of experience in the field as managers, advisers, trainers, executive coaches and team coaches. We have the knowledge and expertise required to optimally support you, your team and your organization.

Achieving impact through an experiential approach
Practice makes perfect. When designing and executing our programmes, we implement them in practice by making your challenges our priorities. Experiential learning is therefore our standard, but everyone has their own learning style, which is why we make use of different forms of teaching and ways of working. This means that we work in the here and now, allowing you to experience the learning principle. We do this based on the notion that when the focus is on the effectiveness of behaviour, it is important not to think in terms of 'good' or 'bad,' but of the impact it has on the other person. That's why we provide confrontational yet respectful feedback, enabling you and your team and organization to change… and grow.

What can we do for you?

COURIUS offers a broad selection of leadership programmes, master classes, training courses, business coaching, team development and consultancy. We also provide interactive lectures at customer sites and during congresses. Call us on **+31 412 752633**, or mail us at **Info@courius.com**. We hope to meet you soon!